BEYOND DEATH

BEYOND DEATH

THE CHINCHORRO MUMMIES OF ANCIENT CHILE

BERNARDO T. ARRIAZA

FOREWORD BY JOHN W. VERANO

SMITHSONIAN INSTITUTION PRESS

WASHINGTON
LONDON

This book is edited by Nancy Dutro. Book and jacket design is by
Kathleen Sims.

The images shown on the back are of an artificially mummified child
and of the Atacama coastline (plates 3 and 4, *infra*). The image on
the front is of a red mummy head (plate 20). Photos are by
B. Arriaza.

Library of Congress Cataloging-in-Publication Data
Arriaza, Bernardo T.
    Beyond death : the Chinchorro mummies of ancient Chile /
Bernardo T. Arriaza.
        p. cm.
    Includes bibliographical references and index.
    ISBN 1–56098–512–7
    1. Indians of South America—Chile—Arica (Dept.)—
Funeral customs and rites.   2. Indians of South America—
Chile—Arica (Dept.)—Anthropometry.   3. Indians of South
America—Chile—Arica (Dept.)—Material culture.   4.
Mummies—Chile—Arica (Dept.)   5. Embalming—Chile—
Arica (Dept.)   6. Arica (Chile : Dept.)—Antiquities.   I.
Title.
F3069.1.A74A76 1995
393′.3′0983123—dc20   94-39295
                                                      CIP

British Library Cataloguing-in-Publication Data is available.
Manufactured in the United States of America.
99 98 97 96 95   5 4 3 2 1

⊗The paper used in this publication meets the minimum
requirements of the American National Standard for Performance of
Paper for Printed Library Materials Z39.48–1984.

For permission to reproduce illustrations appearing in this book,
please correspond directly with the author, or the owners of the
works as listed in the individual captions. The Smithsonian
Institution Press does not retain reproduction rights for these
illustrations individually or maintain a file of addresses for
photo sources.

**DEDICATED TO
THE PEOPLE OF
ARICA**

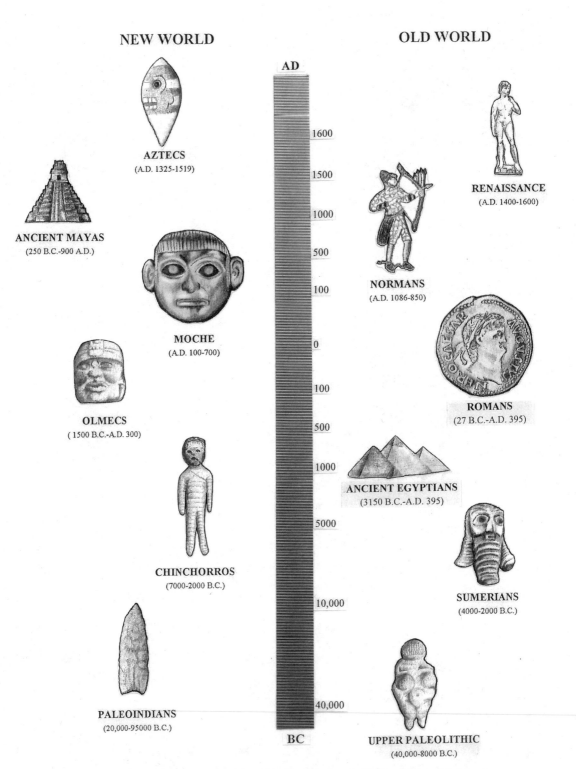

Time line showing relative position of the Chinchorros to main Old and New World cultures (drawing: D. Kendrick-Murdock).

CONTENTS

LIST OF ILLUSTRATIONS AND TABLES

Frontispiece: Time line showing relative position of the Chinchorros to main Old and New World cultures (drawing: D. Kendrick-Murdock)

Text figures

Tables

FOREWORD

For those of us who work on the physical anthropology and archaeology of prehistoric Andean societies, the Chinchorro stand out as one of the more intriguing of early South American cultures. Why are the Chinchorro unusual? In many respects, they differ little from other early fishing societies that developed along the Pacific coast of South America between the fifth and first millennia B.C. True, the Chinchorro people show some early technological advances in their fishing and marine mammal hunting gear—but in other respects, their material culture, settlement pattern, and level of social complexity was very similar to other contemporary semisedentary and sedentary coastal peoples of western South America.

Where the Chinchorro stand out most prominently is in their practice of artificial mummification of the dead. Naturally mummified bodies are known from various arid regions of the Americas, but unequivocal examples of *intentionally* mummified remains have been found in only two New World archaeological contexts: the Aleutian Islands and the arid desert of northern coastal Chile occupied by the Chinchorro people. The Chinchorro are exceptional, moreover, for the sheer number of mummies known and the variety and complexity of their mummification techniques. Very early radiocarbon dates for some Chinchorro sites, which may date as far back as 8,000 B.C., as well as the unusually long duration of Chinchorro as a cultural tradition, have also drawn the attention of archaeologists and, more recently, physical anthropologists.

Archaeological investigation of the Chinchorro culture dates back to the turn of this century, with Max Uhle's pioneering work. The last fifteen years, however, have witnessed an impressive array of multidisciplinary studies that focus on the physical remains of the Chinchorro people themselves. This interest in Chinchorro mummies coincided with a particularly active period in the development and refinement of laboratory techniques for studying human skeletal amd mummified remains, and in methodological approaches to diagnosing ancient disease. New analytical techniques that were applied to Chinchorro mummies include the determination of trace-element and stable-isotope content of bone and soft tissue as indicators of ancient diet, and the analysis of coprolites (dessicated feces) as indicators of both dietary content and parasite load. In the last few years, additional techniques, such as the extraction of cocaine metabolites from hair samples (to identify coca leaf chewing) and the recovery of DNA from bone and soft tissue, have opened new pathways for researchers to explore. Bernardo Arriaza has been directly involved in many of these innovative studies, both as a field excavator and as a laboratory specialist in paleopathology.

Currently, the available literature on the Chinchorro consists almost exclusively of technical articles scattered through Chilean and North American archaeology and physical anthropology journals. Arriaza has felt for some time that a synthesis of Chinchorro mummy research was needed, both for colleagues in the field of paleopathology and for the nonspecialist reader as well.

Constructing such a synthesis is a challenging task, as not all workers agree on details of Chinchorro classification and chronology. As is the case in many regional archaeological sequences, over the years various scholars have developed their own classificatory schemes, terminology, and interpretations of Chinchorro society. Naturally, this complicates any attempt at a synthesis of previous work. Nevertheless, Arriaza attempts to clarify problems of chronology and nomenclature by proposing a five-phase scheme, based on a synthesis of previous classificatory frameworks and incorporating more recent radiocarbon dates and archaeological field data.

Arriaza provides a fascinating overview of physical anthropological studies of the Chinchorro, reviewing findings from the study of their skeletal morphology, indicators of activity patterns and disease in bone, teeth, and soft tissue, and the physical evidence of intentional modification of soft tissue and bone performed as part of the mummification process. He also attempts to reconstruct the social context and meaning of Chinchorro funerary practices. Two of the more intriguing questions about Chinchorro mummification are Why? and What did it mean? These questions, in some ways, are the most challenging to approach. The Chinchorro left no written record describing their concept of death or their reasons for confronting it through artificial mummification, and any remnants of Chinchorro oral traditions have long since faded into the collective memory of native peoples of the coastal desert. Nevertheless, Arriaza attempts to draw out the symbolic meaning and social significance that mummification and curation of the dead might have had to the Chinchorro people. In reading this book, one is impressed by Arriaza's respect and genuine fondness for the ancient Chinchorro people. Perhaps it is his empathy with them, and his dedication to their study, that brings the Chinchorro to life so vividly in this volume.

John W. Verano
Department of Anthropology
Tulane University

PREFACE

An excavation at the Morro 1 site in Arica, northern Chile, in 1983 provided nearly one hundred well-preserved Chinchorro mummies. Initially, the data from Morro 1 was synthesized in the form of a laboratory report focusing on Chinchorro mummification techniques (Arriaza, Allison, and Standen, 1984a). This report formed the framework for the original article published in the journal *Chungará* (Allison et al., 1984) and the development of this book, which attempts to go beyond interpretations already made by the aforementioned scholars. In this book I explore the social life of the ancient Chinchorros. The hope is to rescue the Chinchorro people who were lost in our previous studies, which focused primarily on the artificial mummification techniques.

This book represents ten years of data collection, and attempts to synthesize the knowledge gained to date by many scholars during the last seventy years. It also aspires to provide possible meanings behind Chinchorro mortuary practices. It is an effort to unravel the Chinchorros' unwritten history—to present a reconstruction of their daily lives.

Studying the Chinchorro mummies gave me a feeling of continuity with the past, a connection that arose from the realization that all human beings, past and present, share the suffering caused by the loss of a loved one. It made me wonder what other emotions the Chinchorros experienced when someone in their group died. Were the elaborate treatments for the dead and the mystic beauty of the mummies materializations of love and devotion rather than demonstrations of social status?

The Chinchorro fishers who inhabited the Atacama coast for millennia were obviously deeply concerned with the afterlife and caring for the dead. Caring for deceased relatives is an ancient custom, but why the Chinchorros went beyond the expected and developed artificial mummification is intriguing, especially when one considers how long ago it began (ca. 5,050 B.C), and why it lasted for so many millennia.

Although some of my hypotheses here cannot be tested, I believe they are worth speculating about since the various aspects of the mortuary practices of the Chinchorros make them unique in Andean and world prehistory. As new mortuary evidence is found and more creative ways of studying and interpreting the past are developed, concrete answers will emerge about the Chinchorros' daily life and the reasons for their behavior.

Perhaps some discussion here may seem conjectural. But it is nevertheless important because ancient cultures like the Chinchorro were not merely artifacts; they were people with bone, flesh, and, more importantly, emotions and deep concern for the souls of the dead, as many people still are today. Empathy for them leads me to envision the Chinchorro fishing people going from a mourning stage of grief and despair, full of social uncertainties, to a state of joy as the morticians finalized and displayed the artificially mummified body. The morticians performed rituals calling upon deities to restore harmony to life. The final ritual of presentation of the mummies to the deities reintegrated the mourners to their daily activities. They went on about their lives, believing that the spirit of the deceased could return to its own body to perpetuate its existence among the living. Mummies were likely kept, cared for, and located directly within the Chinchorro communities until burial was deemed appropriate. Perhaps after a number of mummies had accumulated, some could have been laid to rest. I believe the mummies were considered living entities by the Chinchorros, just as later Andean societies treated mummies as deities that needed to be cared for.

The Chinchorros did not vanish with time; on the contrary, their culture gave rise to subsequent populations that flourished along the Andean coast, forming a prolonged maritime tradition that still exists today. However, thousands of years would pass before the descendants of the Chinchorro would be touched by the complex civilizations of the Tiwanaku, the Inca, and the Spanish. The Chinchorros were far from achieving the status of a civilization, but this does not detract from the richness of their ideology and the uniqueness of their mortuary practices.

The Chinchorros' legacy consists of the mummies and cultural materials housed at the Archaeology Museum of San Miguel de Azapa at the University of Tarapacá and other institutions. Today, the Chinchorro mummies are very fragile and are deteriorating rapidly. Efforts are being made by the University of Tarapacá and collaborators to assure their preservation for future generations. The preservation of the past is the preservation of humanity's ancestral memories. Thus, the responsibility for the conservation of ancient cultural materials, including the Chinchorro mummies, should be felt not only by the scientific community, but by all of us.

ACKNOWLEDGMENTS

I wish to express my gratitude to those who contributed their time and expertise to make this book possible. Leta Franklin reviewed the original draft of the first chapters. Thanks to Karl Reinhard, Arthur Aufderheide, and Karen Wise for providing me with insight into their current research on Chinchorro topics. I am grateful to Leticia Latorre for her laboratory assistance and to Vivien Standen for sending me her master's thesis. I offer my gratitude to Debra Kendrick-Murdock, Tom Cantrell, Raúl Rocha, Beth Szuhay, and Juan Chacama for their cooperation and talent in rendering the drawings for this book. Special thanks go to the reviewers, Arthur Aufderheide, Ethne Barnes, Arthur Rohn, Betty Meggers, and John Verano. I am indebted to all my friends and colleagues of the University of Tarapacá for their support, especially to Iván Muñoz, who was most encouraging. Many thanks are owed to Paola Schiappacasse for her bibliographic assistance and to Pamela Lawrence for her invaluable help reviewing my drafts. Special thanks must go to Vicki Cassman, with whom I discussed the many ideas for this book, for her enormous editorial assistance, and to Suzan DiBella, who added the magic touch to the final manuscript. Many thanks are owed to my editors at the Smithsonian Institution Press for their promotion and to the anonymous reviewers whose suggestions greatly improved the original manuscript. I am grateful to the National Geographic Society and to David McNelis from the Office of Research at the University of Nevada, Las Vegas (UNLV), for financial support. Last, but not least, I am appreciative of Dean James Malek and my colleagues in the Anthropology Department at UNLV who have been supportive of my research.

Bernardo T. Arriaza

CHAPTER 1

INTRODUCTION

October 20, 1983, unfolded like any other day of archaeological research at the Archaeology Museum of San Miguel de Azapa, University of Tarapacá, in Arica, northern Chile. A phone call disrupted the daily research activities, bringing news that human mummies had been discovered while the local water company was digging trenches for improving the water system. The digging took place near the city center, on the slopes of a bluff called *Morro de Arica*. But the call itself was nothing out of the ordinary; at the museum, we were accustomed to phone calls reporting the discovery of ancient human remains—the entire modern city is built over the ruins and cemeteries of ancient cultures. This is necessarily so because the Atacama Desert with its sterile mountains of sand and extensive dry flat expanses forms a natural barrier that constrains the city boundaries. Consequently, every time construction workers dig within city limits, the chances of coming across archaeological remains are extremely high.

An archaeological team was quickly dispatched to the field to take control of the situation. However, this experience turned out to be unique and the day remembered because the ancient mummies we saw this time proved to be completely different from those we were accustomed to seeing. They were thousands of years older. These bodies had received extremely complex treatments of artificial mummification and were not naturally desiccated as are most mummies from Arica. Only a few people in the world knew anything about these artificially prepared mummies, called Chinchorros. We knew we were in the midst of a rare find. Suddenly, the whole Archaeology Museum of San Miguel de Azapa was buzzing with the news of the discovery. The workers had cut through an ancient cemetery, partially exposing many bodies. Fortunately, the workers, shocked by the discovery of the mummies, immediately stopped their digging, avoiding further damage. As we arrived, the scene was mesmerizing: a profile of the trench revealed several mummies lying on their backs, lined up in a row, as if they were traveling together through eternity, when their trip was unexpectedly interrupted (pl. 1). The mummies' black shiny faces glistened against the brown sandy soil of the bluff. Their peaceful expressions contrasted with the astonished faces of the gathering crowd. With the construction project postponed, Vivien Standen and Guillermo Focacci, archaeologists from the University of Tarapacá, began several months of work rescuing

1

Fig. 1. Three red mummies during excavation at the Morro 1 site (photo: R. Rocha).

the artificially prepared mummies (pl. 1, fig. 1) with the assistance of several other colleagues. At the laboratory, paleopathologist Marvin Allison and I took on the task of analyzing the mummies.

Although we knew about the Chinchorros, only a handful of articles had been written about them since their discovery by Max Uhle in 1917. The discovery of more Chinchorro mummies presented a fantastic opportunity to address some of the greatest mysteries of our local prehistory. Who were these people? Why did they prepare their dead in such a complex way? What was the meaning of their mortuary rituals? And to what extent did the mortuary practices reflect the social organization of this ancient society?

To address these questions, a clarification about the word "mummy" is necessary. Technically, a mummy is a dead body in which the process of putrefaction was slowed by natural or artificial means. *Natural mummification* often produces a desiccated cadaver as the result of unusual conditions, such as those of a hot desert climate. In addition, high salt concentrations in the soils, such as the nitrates present in the Atacama Desert, act as natural preservatives by absorbing body fluids and discouraging microbial attack. In the Atacama Desert most of the soft tissue of the natural mummies, such as internal organs, genitals, and even facial features are remarkably well preserved (pl. 2). These types of natural mummies or desiccated bodies are common in many countries with dry environments, such as Chile, Egypt, Mexico, southwestern United States, and Peru. Other examples of naturally preserved bodies, not necessarily desiccated, include the bog people of northern Europe, who were preserved by the tanning action of "sphagnan," an anionic polysaccharide substance found in peat (Painter, 1991). Bodies also have been preserved by extreme cold, in Alaska, Greenland, the Andes, and the Alps (see Brothwell, 1987; Hansen, Meldgaard, and Nordqvist, 1991). The Ice Man, recently found in the Italian-Austrian Alps, is a good example of a frozen naturally mummified body (Höpfel, Platzer, and Spindler, 1992).

Artificial mummification, on the other hand, does not leave preservation to chance (pl. 3). The mourners actively attempt to preserve the deceased's body, including its physiognomy. They halt decay of the corpse by removing the internal organs and by stuffing the skull, thoracic, and abdominal cavities with various materials to regain volume. Artificially preserved bodies are found worldwide, in Chile, China, Europe, Egypt, and North America (Alaska) (see Cockburn and Cockburn, 1980; David and Tapp, 1984).

Artificial mummification sometimes is loosely used as a synonym for embalming. The word "mummy" is derived from an ancient Persian term meaning bitumen. This black, tarlike substance was used to paint corpses in Persia. Bodies desiccated owing to natural conditions often have a brown-black color, and it was thought they had been covered with bitumen, thus the word "mummy" was applied to these bodies. The word "embalming," in contrast, is derived from the word balsam, or aromatic ointments, which were used to perfume and preserve the corpse (Cockburn and Cockburn, 1980; Comas, 1974).

From an anthropological point of view, what is interesting to us is that artificially preparing a body is a far more demanding funerary task than a normal burial practice leading to natural mummification. Artificial mummification requires skilled labor and high-energy input. Thus, mortuary practices are important because the treatment of the body, its grave, quality and types of grave goods, and the rituals performed during and after burial are not random phenomena; they are shaped by ideology, metaphysical belief in the hereafter, and social position of the deceased, among other variables (Arriaza, 1988; Bloch and Parry, 1982; Chapman, Kinnes, and Randsborg, 1981). Death lies at the heart of each society. The search for eternal existence, spiritual or physical, appears to be a universal human endeavor. Consequently, the study of death and differential mortuary treatments can provide clues for understanding ancient cultures.

In archaeology, cultural artifacts traditionally have been used to make inferences about ancient social intercourse and beliefs. But the study of human mummies provides a new way to catch a glimpse of the collective feeling and the social life of yesterday's people. Mummies are archaeological treasures holding prehistoric information about ourselves and our past. Mummies and skeletons provide insight into diseases, clothing, food, art, metaphysical beliefs concerning life and death, and ancient social systems. They provide a window to view the achievements of humanity, now trapped in desiccated flesh.

A mummy is often seen as a symbol of death. But it is also a symbol of victory because the process of natural decay has been slowed. The individual is dead, yet he or she is still with us physically as a mummy, defying the advance of time and projecting a sense of immortality.

Our fascination with mummies is testimony to our fear of the unknown and of death itself, which we have not yet been able to conquer. Mortuary analyses, specifically the study of mummies and their grave goods, open the door to exploring the emotions and beliefs ancient people had about death. Mummies are like time travelers, holding secrets to our past. They tell us of our ancestors—their biological, social, and spiritual worlds. Let us now turn to the mummies and learn from their clues about the daily lives of the Chinchorro people.

CHAPTER 2

THE CHINCHORRO CULTURE

The Chinchorros were groups of fishers who settled along the dry Atacama coast. They adapted to life in the harsh desert by learning the secrets of how to extract food from the ocean and swampy coastal environments where plants, birds, and animal life could be found in abundance. Their technology was simple, yet remarkably efficient, and it changed little for thousands of years. Fishhooks were made of shells, and the fish were attracted by the glitter of mother-of-pearl. Fishing lines were made of plant fibers and reinforced with animal or human hair. Stones, rubbed into small cigar shapes, were used as sinkers. Reeds extracted from the swamps were woven into baskets to collect food or twined into mats for sleeping or covering their small huts. Although the Chinchorros never developed ceramics, smelting to make metal tools, or loom-woven textiles—all technological achievements associated with more developed cultures—they created a cult to the dead that rivals those of complex societies.

Past Discoveries

The labor of many scholars shoveling sand in the Atacama Desert over the course of more than seventy years has blazed the trail for present Chinchorro studies (table 1). Max Uhle (1917), a German scholar, was the pioneer. He discovered twelve bodies buried in an extended position at the Morro 1 site (the rest of this site was rediscovered in 1983) and several other mummies two kilometers away on a beach called Chinchorro. Uhle (1922:54) also mentioned that he had observed similar extended mummies, up to twelve kilometers inland in the Azapa and Lluta valleys. This scholar provided the first written description of the cultural vestiges of the Chinchorros and published a series of papers describing this culture, which he called the "Aborígenes de Arica" (Arica Aborigines, Uhle, 1917, 1919, 1922). Today, the name Chinchorro, which literally means "raft" or "fishing net" in Spanish, has been given to this culture after the beach site where Uhle first found the mummies.

On the basis of simplicity of the grave goods and the lack of ceramics (radiocarbon dating was not developed until 1949), Uhle proposed that the Arica Aborigines lived

Table 1. Chinchorro mummies found to date

Site	No. of Mummies	Types of Mummies[1]	Associated Museum[2]	References
Acha 2	1	Natural	Arica	Aufderheide, Muñoz, and Arriaza (1993)
Acha 3	2	Natural	Arica	Muñoz and Chacama (1993:42)
Camarones 17	2	Black	Arica	Aufderheide, Muñoz, and Arriaza (1993)
Chinchorro 1	3	Black	Arica	Aufderheide, Muñoz, and Arriaza (1993)
Camarones 8	1	Red	Arica	Aufderheide, Muñoz, and Arriaza (1993)
Morro 1-5	17	Red (1n)	Arica	Guillen (1992); Focacci and Chacón (1989)
Maderas Enco	3	Black	Arica	Universidad de Tarapacá, rescue (1991)
Morro 1-6	69	Natural	Arica	Focacci and Chacón (1989); Aufderheide and Allison (1994)
Hipodromo, Arica	1	Black	Arica	Universidad de Tarapacá, rescue (1990)
Camarones 14	23	Natural (4b)	Santiago	Schiappacasse and Niemeyer (1984)
Morro 1	96	All types (8b, 27r, 25m, 36n)	Arica	Allison et al. (1984)
Arica	4	Black (1r)	Valparaíso	Vera (1981)
Pisagua Viejo	4?	Complex (black?)	?	Núñez (1976)
Camarones 15	1	Natural	Arica	Rivera (1975)
PLM 8	9	Red (and black?)	Arica	Alvarez (1969:182)
Chinchorro	9?	Complex (black?)	?	Alvarez (1961) (In Bittmann, 1982)
Bajo Molle	5	Red	?	Schaedel (1957:71–72)
Quiani	4	Natural (1r)	?	Bird (1943:245–246)
Punta Pichalo	1	Red?	?	Bird (1943:246)
Arica	?	Complex?	?	Latcham (1928)
Arica	2	Complex	?	Skottsberg (1924)
Morro	12	All types (9r, 2m, 1n)	Santiago	Uhle (1922)[3]

Table 1. (*continued*)

Site	No. of Mummies	Types of Mummies[1]	Associated Museum[2]	References
Chinchorro	?	Complex	?	Uhle (1922)
Patillos	13	Red	Iquique	Nielsen Collection (Museo Iquique)
TOTAL	282			

1. b = black; r = red; m = mud-coated; n = natural (see chapter on mummification techniques). Skeletonized isolated evidence was not included.

2. Arica: Museo Arqueológico, San Miguel de Azapa; Santiago: Museo Nacional de Historia Natural; Valparaíso: Museo de Historia Natural; Iquique: Museo Regional de Iquique.

3. In these complex mummies, incisions are clearly visible in at least one illustration provided. Uhle also said that the mummies were painted red, although the face coat paint varies among red, yellow, white, and black. Thus these complex mummies were put in the red category.

about the time of Christ. What impressed this scholar, and still impresses us today, was the elaborate treatments given the bodies.

Uhle recorded three basic types of mummification techniques:

1. *Simple treatment:* naturally desiccated bodies, produced by the aridity of the Atacama Desert.
2. *Complex treatment:* bodies artificially preserved by removing all of the internal organs, filling the cavities with human or animal hair and grass, and stitching the incisions. The deceased was painted with earth colors, usually red, a human hair wig was added, and the body was then buried in an extended position. Uhle (1922:65) pointed out that most of the mummies he studied, including men, women, and children, displayed this complex treatment.
3. *Mud-coated mummies:* cadavers covered with a thin layer of a cementlike substance. According to Uhle, these mummies were buried slightly tilted to one side, as if they were sleeping.

Uhle thought that Type 1, or simple mummies, were the most ancient, the second type developed from the first, and the third was a degeneration of the second. Today, with radiocarbon dating techniques and the new finds from Morro 1 and other sites, we know that naturally mummified bodies, Type 1, are found at the beginning and end of the Chinchorro culture (7,020 B.C. and 1,110 B.C., respectively). Complex artificially mummified bodies, Type 2, are found between these dates. Simpler artificially mummified bodies, Type 3, or mud-coated mummies, are found after the complex mummies, marking the end or decline of the Chinchorro mummification practices. Uhle was basically correct in his ordering of the mummy types, but erred in determining the antiquity of the Chinchorro mummies.

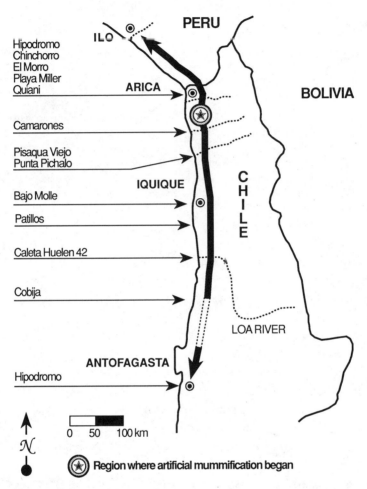

Fig. 2. Map of reported Chinchorro sites along the Pacific coast of
Peru and Chile. Solid arrows represent the spread of artificial mummification practices, and the dashed arrow indicates areas of probable spread (drawing: T. Cantrell).

Anker Nielsen, a Danish researcher, continued Uhle's work. In the 1940s he excavated artificially prepared mummies in the city of Iquique (see fig. 2, Bajo Molle
and Patillos area). Unfortunately, Nielsen never published a report of his discoveries,
but one of his key finds was the recovery of a small doll-like mummy (Bittmann,
1982). Little mummies like this later became known as "statuette mummies." These
statuettes often contained human fetal bones and were prepared in the same way as
adults (fig. 3).

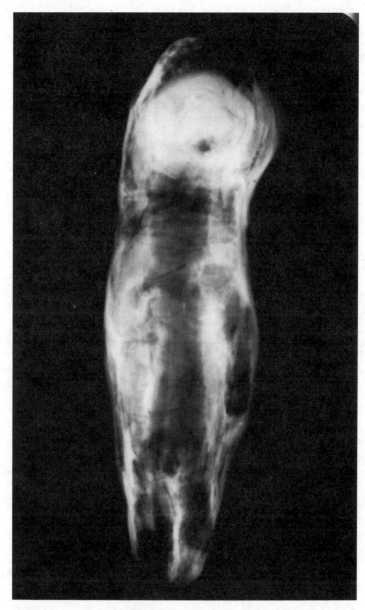

Fig. 3. Radiograph of a statuette mummy from Arica (photo: R. Rocha).

In Uhle's time anthropologists perceived culture as a process of material progressive evolution; that is, artifacts and societies became more complex with time, thus reflecting a more intellectually advanced society. Consequently, they focused their attention on the artifacts of complex cultures such as the Tiwanaku and the Inca, but disregarded the social interactions of more simply organized societies that were lacking ceramics. Archaeological excavations were guided toward discovering artifacts, and mummies received only sporadic attention.

In 1924, Swedish researcher Carl Skottsberg published a description of a number of mummies excavated in Arica, three of which were Chinchorro. Two were mummified human twins belonging to Uhle's Type 2; they were about 45 cm in length and two to three months old. The third Chinchorro mummy was an adult male covered with mud (Uhle's Type 3). All were buried in an extended position (Skottsberg, 1924:32–39). Four years after Skottsberg's publication, anthropologist Ricardo Latcham (1928, 1938), who studied extensively in the Atacama area, confirmed the widespread distribution of artificially prepared mummies. He noted that the Chinchorros not only inhabited Lisera Beach in Arica and the Azapa Valley on the outskirts, but also cities south of Arica, including Pisagua (Punta Pichalo) and Cobija (fig. 2). His findings were fascinating because they expanded the recorded geographic range of the Chinchorros to about 600 kilometers along the coast. Latcham also described the coast as full of ancient mounds of cultural debris, seen as shell middens, which were to provide important clues for understanding what the aborigines ate and how the marine fauna have changed through time.

During the 1940s, North American archaeologist Junius Bird followed Latcham's lead and became interested in the coastal shell middens. He began systematically studying these middens to understand the socioeconomic maritime adaptation of the Atacama people. His research revealed that, indeed, the ancient Atacama people had rich usage of coastal resources and a heavy maritime dependence. During his diggings of shell middens, Bird found a Chinchorro child with complex mummification. His studies in Arica (Quiani Beach) and in Pisagua confirmed the existence of Chinchorro mummies south of Arica. Bird also called attention to the fact that the masks of some mummies were repainted (Bird, 1943:246). He suggested that the mummies were not buried immediately, but were maintained in the camp for display and redecorated from time to time.

On the basis of evidence of fishing technology, Bird (1943:307; 1946:587–589) divided the early peopling of the coast into two periods: the First Pre-Pottery Period, characterized by the presence of shell fishhooks, and the Second Pre-Pottery Period, which had cactus fishhooks (table 2). Later, archaeologist Grete Mostny (1964) revisited the area where Bird had worked and dated two hearths from a midden at Quiani Beach, finding that the Arica fishers were living there as early as 4,220 B.C.

In the 1960s, as the modern city of Arica was expanding, local archaeology gained momentum as new cemeteries were uncovered. Historian Luis Alvarez (1961, 1969), for example, described eighteen Chinchorro mummies he excavated from the Chinchorro and Playa Miller beaches. Impressed by the fact that the mummies were defleshed and the

Table 2. Names for Chinchorro mummies

Cultural Name	Reference
Arica Aborigines (Aborígenes de Arica)	Uhle (1917, 1919)
First and Second Pre-Pottery Periods (Primer y Segundo Períodos Precerámicos)	Bird (1946:587–589)
Patillo Complex (Complejo el Patillo)	Schaedel (1957:25)
Chinchorro (Chinchorro)	Dauelsberg (1963:201) (In True and Núñez, 1971:66)
Chinchorro Complex (Complejo Chinchorro)	Núñez (1965:46)
Chinchorro Tradition (Tradición Chinchorro)	Rivera (1975:28)
Chinchorro Cultural Complex (Complejo Cultural Chinchorro)	Bittmann and Munizaga (1976:64)
Chinchorro Culture (Cultura Chinchorro)	Alvarez (1961) (In Bittmann and Munizaga, 1977:120)
Camarones Complex (Complejo Camarones)	Llagostera (1992:92–93)
Quiani Complex (Complejo Quiani)	Llagostera (1992:94–95)

skin replaced by clay, Alvarez suggested that the Chinchorros probably practiced anthropophagy or cannibalism. Alvarez also found eight "statuette mummies" at Playa Miller Beach (PLM 8 site) which were about seventeen to thirty centimeters in height. The radiocarbon date associated with the Playa Miller 8 site is 2,140 B.C. (Núñez, 1976:122)

In 1965, archaeologist Lautaro Núñez shed light on the Chinchorro chronology with the first radiocarbon date derived directly from sampling a Chinchorro mummy from the site of Pisagua Viejo. The derived date of 3,270 B.C. was much older than Uhle ever dreamed. Núñez (1969) concentrated his efforts on understanding who the Chinchorros were by attempting to characterize them through their cultural materials. Núñez believed the Chinchorros were groups of hunters and gatherers who came from the southern Peruvian highlands and moved along the unpopulated Chilean coast, exploiting different coastal econiches. They hunted camelids, such as alpaca and llama, and collected wild plants. In 1975, archaeologists Lautaro Núñez, Vjera Zlatar, and Patricio Núñez showed through their discoveries that the coastal populations were indeed spreading along the shoreline. At the site called Caleta Huelén 42, south of the modern city of Iquique, in the drainage of the Loa River, they found a fishing camp with skeletons buried under the hut floors. The bodies were buried in an extended position and had mud-filled orbital cavities consistent with a Chinchorro burial treatment. Núñez and co-workers radiocarbon dated the site to 2,830 B.C. and the skeletons to 1,830 B.C. Caleta Huelén 42 provided conclusive evidence for placing the Chinchorro as far south as 600 kilometers from Arica and reinforced the findings by Latcham and Nielsen.

In the 1970s, anthropologists Bente Bittmann and Juan Munizaga (1976), exploring the complexity of Chinchorro mortuary practices and their social meanings, showed that the Chinchorros had knowledge of anatomy, dissection, and body desiccation. These scholars suggested that the Chinchorro mummies could represent the oldest known examples of artificial mummification practice in the world. They noted (1976, 1977) that the Chinchorros used throwing sticks, darts, harpoons, weights for fishhooks, lithic knives, and basketry as part of their tool kit. However, they felt it was the artificial mummification practice that characterized the Chinchorro culture and distinguished it from other contemporary cultures in the Andes.

Ironically, the mummification practice that brought the Chinchorro culture to the attention of the public also led to the destruction and loss of mummies and artifacts. Merchant marines visiting the port of Arica, early this century, took mummies and other archaeological artifacts as souvenirs and distributed them around the world. Very few of the mummies excavated before 1970 are available for study, and it is not clear what has become of most of them or where they are located. Some ended up in Chilean museum collections. Archaeologist Jaime Vera (1981), for example, published a detailed description of four complex Chinchorro mummies, remarkably well preserved (fig. 4), housed at the Museum of Natural History of Valparaiso (about 2,000 kilometers from Arica). These Chinchorro mummies, he noted, were donated to the Valparaiso Museum about 1915 and had come from Arica; thus, they probably represent some of the specimens excavated by Uhle. Vera's published descriptions also provided radiocarbon dates for two of the mummies (3,290 B.C. and 3,060 B.C.). Other Chinchorro mummies have been found at various Chilean museums and at the American Museum of Natural History in New York. The Chinchorro collection in the latter museum corresponds to Bird's finds.

By the 1980s the Chinchorros had gained a solid place in Chilean and Andean prehistory, but not in world prehistory. In 1984 the excavations of archaeologists Virgilio Schiappacasse and Hans Niemeyer at the Camarones gorge, about 100 kilometers south of Arica, added a new twist to Chinchorro studies. Of four radiocarbon dates obtained, one of a Chinchorro mummy pushed the Chinchorro chronology back to 5,050 B.C., nearly two millennia older than the first date obtained by Núñez (1965). Moreover, at Camarones 14, of the twenty-three bodies found, only the children, five in total, were artificially mummified (Schiappacasse and Niemeyer, 1984:87–94); thus, artificial mummification could have started with children. Others, such as Vera (1981), had previously described artificially prepared mummies of both adults and children, but they were not as ancient as those from Camarones 14 site.

It was during the 1980s, with the finding at the Morro 1 site, that Chinchorro mummies gained popularity among professionals, as well as the public. The local Arica newspapers

Fig. 4. Artificially mummified Chinchorro child described by Vera, 1981 (red style). Museum of Natural History, Valparaiso, Chile (photo: B. Arriaza).

described the fortuitous discovery of the Chinchorro mummies as a "spectacular finding," and the news of ancient mummies in northern Chile suddenly spread like a breeze across the world. What made the Arica mummies interesting to the public was not only their antiquity, but also the amazing preservation of their bodies and their mystic beauty. Even their facial features and genitals were still intact after thousands of years.

A total of ninety-six Chinchorro mummies were exhumed from the Morro 1 site, about 38% of which were naturally mummified and 62% of which were artificially prepared. The findings at the Morro 1 site revealed incredibly sophisticated mummification techniques, but the three basic types described by Uhle still held true. Nine mummies were radiocarbon dated, providing a range of dates from 5,860 B.C. to 1,720 B.C. (Allison et al., 1984:163–165). Thus, some Chinchorro mummies from Arica were nearly contemporaneous with those found with early dates at Camarones 14 by Schiappacasse and Niemeyer (1984). The Morro 1 mummies demonstrated that Chinchorro burial practices show great variation in mummification styles.

The mortuary variation observed in Chinchorro funerary practices has led to some confusion about the mummies themselves. A crucial archaeological issue is how the term "Chinchorro" should be defined (table 2). Also, what sites can be considered Chinchorro? Several sites along the Chilean coast, south of the Loa River, have been associated with the Chinchorro culture on the basis of evidence of similar fishing technology and mortuary practices, but the evidence is not, always conclusive. Bittmann (1982) commented on possible Chinchorro sites, such as in Cobija, where three bodies associated with shellfish hooks were found buried lying on their sides and covered with red ocher. This site has a date of about 3,110 B.C., contemporaneous with dates of Arican Chinchorros. Bittmann's view of Cobija Chinchorros is supported by Ricardo Latcham (1928, 1938), who found evidence of Chinchorro in Cobija. Bittmann also mentioned that south of Cobija, in the local hippodrome in the city of Antofagasta, three skeletons buried in an extended position were covered with red ocher. Grave goods included bone harpoons and reed mats. Therefore, the city of Antofagasta could represent the extreme southern frontier of the Chinchorro culture (fig. 2).

North of Arica, in the Peruvian city of Ilo, archaeologist Karen Wise (1991) reported evidence of several extended burials, skeletons, that appear to be Chinchorro-related. Wise also found evidence of an occupational site, and radiocarbon dates for the hearths were from 5,850 B.C. to 4,250 B.C. Thus, the range of Chinchorro occupation could extend from Ilo (Peru) in the north to Antofagasta (Chile) in the south, a distance of about 900 kilometers (558 miles).

Definition of Chinchorro Culture

The study of the Chinchorro is often muddled by semantics. Several terms are found in the literature which in some references are only vaguely defined. They are: Chinchorroid, Chinchorro complex, Chinchorro culture, Chinchorro tradition, Arica Aborigines, Camarones complex, and Quiani complex (Alvarez, 1969; Bittmann and Munizaga, 1977; Llagostera, 1989; Núñez, 1969, 1976; Olmos and Sanhueza, 1984; Rivera, 1975, among others; table 2).

Most Chinchorro studies have made contributions by giving detailed descriptions of how the mummies were made and providing radiocarbon dates for selected specimens, but few have addressed the issue of what is Chinchorro. Núñez (1969) was one of the first to attempt to define the Chinchorro complex versus other local Arica cultural phases. However, Bittmann and Munizaga (1977) and Bittmann (1982) emphasized for the first time anthropological theory, the meaning behind the mortuary practices, and the need for creating a Chinchorro bioarchaeological research strategy. They presented a thorough review of Chinchorro findings through the early 1980s, and put forth six main tasks to be resolved in future work: (1) define Chinchorro terminology, (2) establish the origin of the Chinchorro people, (3) develop a Chinchorro chronology, (4) determine which mummification techniques were used through time, (5) study the role and social implications of mummification, and (6) investigate what happened to the Chinchorro people. More than ten years have passed since these scholars outlined these points, but few efforts have been made to address these issues. In the following chapters these topics will be systematically addressed, as well as the following additional questions: How long did the practice of artificial mummification last? Did the intense handling and manipulation of cadavers affect the health of those who performed the rituals? What was daily life like among the Chinchorro?

In order to proceed it is essential to answer the first of the six points brought up by Bittmann and Munizaga—what is Chinchorro and how is this term used? The other points will be discussed in chapters that follow.

In this book the terms "Chinchorro," "Chinchorros," or "Chinchorro people" will be used as synonyms for the Chinchorro culture. To avoid ambiguities, *Chinchorro culture* (or *Chinchorros*) is defined here as preceramic and premetallurgic (presmelting) fishing societies who inhabited the Atacama coast of southern Peru and northern Chile from at least 7,020 B.C. to 1,500 B.C., who buried their dead in an extended position, and practiced *both* natural and artificial mummification. These dates, however, may vary a century or two depending on the region. The nearly 6,000-year range presented here is much greater than any previously reported dates for Chinchorro. However, it is the complex artificial mummification practices, their antiquity, and duration for thousands of years that make the Chinchorro culture intriguing and exceptional. Their complex mummification techniques are indeed the oldest known in the world. This is remarkable inasmuch as the Chinchorros were a technologically simple society.

This characterization of Chinchorro by their tradition of burying the dead in an extended position with natural or artificial mummification (Arriaza, 1993a) needs to be differentiated from Rivera's term of *Chinchorro tradition* (Rivera, 1975, 1991; Rivera et al., 1974), which is based on a long legacy of maritime subsistence. Rivera's Chinchorro tradition included later preceramic and ceramic cultural phases from the city of Arica, such as Quiani, Faldas del Morro, and El Laucho (1,500 B.C. to 500 B.C.). However, Quiani, Faldas del Morro, and El Laucho phases did not have artificial mummification and the dead were buried lying flexed on their sides. They also had complex forms of head gear, textiles, and metal ornaments. In more recent work, Rivera (1991) placed the Faldas del Morro phase together with the later Alto Ramirez highland tradition. According to Rivera (1991), copper, gold, and silver metallurgy and experimental pottery are found at the end of the Chinchorro tradition. It must be emphasized that Chinchorro culture as used in this book does not persist into the metallurgic or ceramic periods, as neither technology has been found in recent Chinchorro studies from the Arica and Camarones area.

Despite the differences, both terms, Rivera's "Chinchorro tradition" based on technology and Arriaza's "Chinchorro culture" based on mummification practices, are valid depending on the problem being addressed. However, Chinchorro tradition should not be used as a synonym for Chinchorro culture as used here. The latter considers Chinchorro as being composed of different stages of cultural development—as defined by different mummification practices and bodies buried in an extended position—rather than a continuous maritime tradition that lasted into the early ceramic period.

Because the term Chinchorro is rarely defined by other Andean scholars, many times "Chinchorro" seems to be used vaguely to imply complex artificial mummification; thus, Chinchorro and complex artificial mummification become synonymous. In other cases it is not clear whether scholars refer to artificially prepared mummies, natural mummies, or to the Chinchorros as a cultural group. In simple words, the use of Chinchorro or Chinchorro culture to denote only complex artificial mummification, as used by Bittmann and Munizaga (1977:121) and other scholars, is highly problematic. Limiting Chinchorro to mean bodies with only complex artificial mummification suggests either the coexistence of various cultures who practiced natural and artificial mummification or asynchronic cultures. Neither view is fully supported by the archaeological evidence. Instead, the evidence indicates that Chinchorro was a single culture with biological and cultural continuity which had three basic stages of cultural development: a gradual increase in the complexity of mummification practices, a decline, and eventual disappearance of artificial mummification. A maritime subsistence strategy was maintained throughout. In other words, Chinchorro mortuary variation was not the product of mummification reserved for elite groups or the consequence of various coexisting cultures, but a feature of only one culture evolving through time. Finally, if complex artificial mummification started with children, as seen in the Camarones 14 site studied by Schiappacasse and Niemeyer (1984), then the use of the term "Chinchorro" or "Chinchorro mummy" for artificially mummified people would be misleading. In all probability, it would require the separation of naturally mummified parents and artificially mummified children as parts of two distinct cultures—one with artificial mummification and one without.

Artificial mummification in the Chinchorro culture and the definition of Chinchorro has not received much attention because previous researchers were concerned with understanding subsistence strategies. Thus, the unique Chinchorro cultural practice of artificially mummifying their dead became buried under technological analyses. Munizaga (1980:131) gave a similar critique, commenting that perhaps the lack of focus on the mummies reflected different research interests between archaeologists and physical anthropologists.

Definition of a Chinchorro Mummy

As defined in the previous section, the term "Chinchorro mummy" could be a body naturally or artificially mummified. A Chinchorro mummy should be described using a combination of the following evidence: position of the corpse, body treatment, associated technology, geographic area of burial, and radiocarbon dates. A Chinchorro mummy was either wrapped in a reed mat or camelid skin shroud or covered with mud, and buried in an extended position, laid on its back with legs extended or semiflexed. The body could have been buried naked or with a genital cover. Thus, a Chinchorro body was transformed into a mummy either by natural or artificial means, and various mummification techniques and styles, such as black, red, bandage, mud-coated, and natural, existed through time (Allison et al., 1984; Arriaza, 1993a; Standen, 1991).

The Chinchorro mummies were often aligned and buried in groups in shallow pits in the sand. Few grave goods were placed with the Chinchorro mummies; most were associated with the Pacific littoral tradition of the Atacama Desert, such as harpoons, shell and cactus fishhooks, composite fishhooks, weights for fishhooks, lithic knives, lanceolate lithic points, throwing sticks, darts, and basketry materials. Absence of ceramics, woven textiles, and metal artifacts is also typical. Chronologically, all these Chinchorro preceramic Atacama coastal burials cluster within the dates of 7,020 to 1,500 B.C. It is important that future studies are as explicit as possible in the explanation of the term "Chinchorro" and specifically the kind of mummies being considered.

The Quiani Problem

Great confusion also surrounds the term Quiani and its relation to Chinchorro. Quiani has been used to indicate three main ideas: (1) the sites studied by Junius Bird, Quiani 1 and 2; (2) a preceramic cultural phase called either Quiani phase or Quiani Complex which includes the preceramic periods of Bird (1943, 1946), the sites excavated and dated by Grete Mostny (1964), and the Arica Aborigines of Uhle (1919) (see Llagostera, 1989:63; Schaedel, 1957:74); and (3) a later horticultural phase, Quiani 7, described by archaeologist Percy Dauelsberg (1974). In North America, scholars refer to Quiani as the preceramic sites studied by Bird, but in Arica, Quiani is the term given to the cultural phase immediately following the Chinchorro, or that described by Dauelsberg (see Santoro and Ulloa, 1985).

Bird (1943, 1946:588–589) was the first to study the Quiani site and, on the basis of two different and asynchronic fishing technologies he found at this site, he chronologically divided the preceramic of Arica into an early First Pre-Pottery Period (Quiani 1) and a later Second Pre-Pottery Period (Quiani 2). Although Bird (1943) found one artificially prepared Chinchorro mummy at the Quiani site, it was not dated. Years later, Mostny (1964) obtained dates of 4,220 B.C. and 3,680 B.C. from Bird's Quiani middens and these dates were associated with Quiani 1 and Quiani 2, respectively.

In contrast to Bird's findings, cactus and shell fishhooks today are considered contemporaneous, coexisting as early as 4,000 B.C., rather than sequential; however, studies regarding this issue are few. At the Acha 2 site (Arica) cactus hooks were found dating to 7,020 B.C., much earlier than at Quiani 2 (Muñoz and Chacama, 1982:73–78; Muñoz and Chacama, 1993:39). Also at Camarones 17 and Quiani 9 sites, both types of hooks clearly coexisted about 4,980 B.C. and 4,420 B.C., respectively (Aufderheide, Muñoz, and Arriaza 1993:191; Muñoz and Chacama, 1982:73–78; Muñoz and Chacama, 1993:39; Muñoz, Arriaza, and Aufderheide, 1993:120–122). At Camarones 14 both types of hooks were found to coexist also (Schiappacasse and Niemeyer, 1984:34). Apparently, cactus hooks are found even in late periods (ca. 500 B.C.) while shell fishhooks disappear about 3,000 B.C. (Muñoz and Chacama, 1982:82).

Using Bird's fishhook chronology, archaeologist Agustín Llagostera renamed Quiani 1 and Quiani 2 as Camarones Complex and Quiani Complex, respectively (fig. 5) (Llagostera 1989:63–64, 1992). Llagostera (1989, 1992) stated that it was during Quiani 2, or Quiani Complex as he called it, when Chinchorro artificial mummification practices peaked. Both of the terms "Quiani Complex" and "Camarones Complex" are here considered part of the Chinchorro culture because the fishhook evidence from Acha 2 and Camarones 17 invalidates the theories of Bird (1943, 1946) and Llagostera (1992). In simple terms it is no longer believed that shell fishhooks predated cactus fishhooks and that Quiani 2 (ca. 3,680 B.C.) marks the first appearance of cactus hooks.

Instead of depending on Chinchorro tool technology for setting up a chronology, it is suggested here that Chinchorro mummy styles, which can be radiocarbon dated and seriated, represent a better chronological instrument. Moreover, fishing tool kits may vary according to local subsistence strategies, but mortuary treatment based on common beliefs is independent of particularities of subsistence. In Chinchorro studies, mortuary treatment represents a more powerful expression of group identity and ideology than artifacts do.

Quiani 9 is another preceramic site which needs to be mentioned. Quiani 9 was a base camp and is geographically close to the middens excavated by Bird. Archaeologists Iván Muñoz and Juan Chacama (1982), who studied Quiani 9, considered it further evidence of early people adapting to the coast. The description of the site, fortunately, does not add to the confusion regarding the term "Quiani."

In Arica, Quiani is also used as a synonym of the phase epitomized by the findings at the Quiani 7 site reported by Dauelsberg (1974). At Quiani 7 (ca. 1,500–1,300 B.C.), artificial mummification was no longer practiced. Instead, the bodies were buried separately and lying on one side with flexed legs. Elaborate turbans, the first evidence of hair braiding, and incipient horticulture were found associated with Quiani 7 people (Arriaza, 1988; Dauelsberg, 1974).

All these Quiani-related terms represent various excavations of middens and cemeteries from the same general area at the coast of the city of Arica. Today, the preferred definition of Quiani as used by Arican scholars indicates the cultural phase following the Chinchorro culture or the Quiani of Dauelsberg (1974), not the Quiani of Schaedel

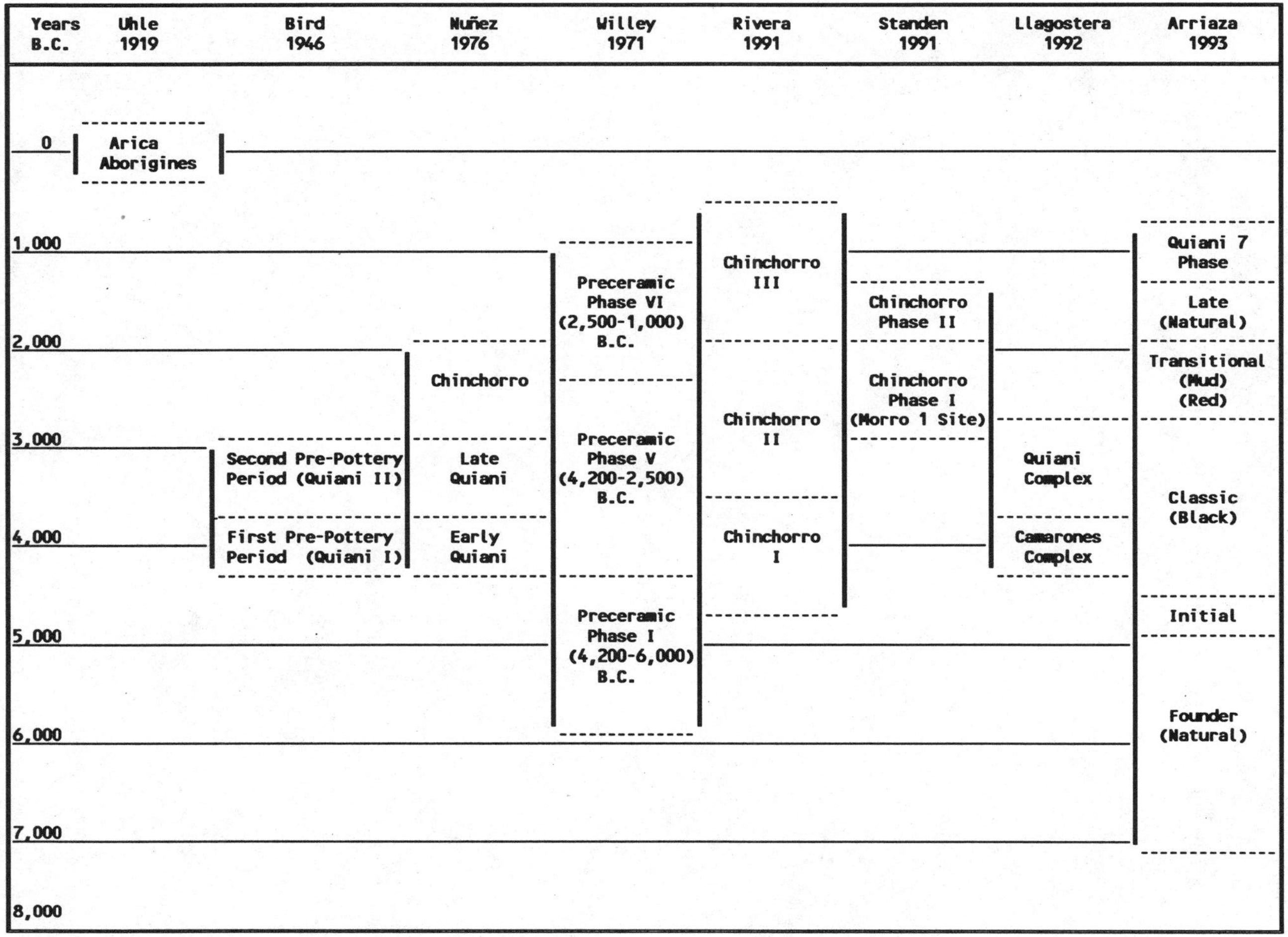

Fig. 5. Various Chinchorro chronologies (graph: B. Arriaza).

(1957), Bird (1943), or Llagostera (1989) (see Santoro and Ulloa, 1985). Because both Quiani phases of Bird and Llagostera's complexes are associated with Chinchorro, it is best not to use the terms Quiani and Camarones Complex.

In summary, Quiani 1 and 2 of Bird (1943, 1946), Quiani 9 of Muñoz and Chacama (1982), and Quiani and Camarones complexes of Llagostera (1989, 1992) are all considered to be part of the Chinchorro culture. Quiani 7 of Dauelsberg (1974), however, is a post-Chinchorro site.

CHAPTER 3

THEORY BEHIND DEATH RITUALS

Nature of Death Rituals

Attempting to understand the rituals surrounding death thousands of years ago is no easy undertaking. To keep the evidence in perspective and limit speculation, it is necessary to explore anthropological theories behind mortuary rites.

In most Western philosophies, when people die, their contribution to society suddenly comes to an end. This is not the case in many other societies in which the living continue to interact with the dead. The Laymi people of Bolivia are a good example. They believe the dead live in the same place as the living and even use the same fields to harvest chile peppers (Harris, 1982; 1983:146). For the Runa people of Peru the spirits of the dead cultivate potatoes (Allen, 1988:56). According to anthropologist Catherine Allen (1988:56), in the Runa world view, spiritual entities (*Machukuna*) live in a parallel world, like a mirror. With dreams, wind, and moonlight the two worlds communicate. And even though the fields of the living and those of the spirits are in the same physical place, the fields are not the same. The continued interaction of the living and the dead may explain why some societies have the need to preserve the bodies of their ancestors or local heroes. This was the case of the Inca rulers whose desiccated bodies were put in a shrine along with other mummies to be properly venerated and also paraded during religious festivities (fig. 6). Even more pronounced was the interaction of the Muisca Indians of Colombia whose mummified ancestors were brought to the battle fields in times of war (Cárdenas, in press).

Perhaps the first question to be asked is whether mortuary rituals are generally meant to satisfy the spiritual needs of those left behind or those of the deceased. One of the first anthropologists to address this question was Edward Tylor (1920) who argued in 1871 that complexity in mortuary rituals reflects the level of complexity of the society. In his view, fear of death led to the creation of the concept of the soul, and worship of ancestors led to the creation of religion. In contrast to Tylor's evolutionary approach, sociologist Emile Durkheim (1965) and anthropologist Bronislaw Malinowski (1948) saw ritual and religion as having practical and functional purposes. In their views, religious and mortuary ceremonies serve the function of healing the broken chain of life by creating

Fig. 6. Drawing representing the Inca celebration of the dead, showing a mummy paraded in public (drawing by Guaman Poma de Ayala, [1615] 1980, v. 1:230).

solidarity and group unification. They postulated that rituals reinforce and preserve the social structure of the group; religion was considered a buffer against human suffering.

Using another functionalist approach, sociologist Robert Hertz (1960) postulated that the continuity of society is threatened by someone's death and only through mortuary rites and mourning could balance be regained. In other words, Hertz believed that it is not the fate of the spirit or soul that put mortuary rituals into action, but rather that the rituals grew out of the anguish of those left behind over the loss of someone who was contributing or had the potential to contribute to society. In his view, mortuary rituals served the worthy purpose of reassessing the loss of the deceased and reassigning new roles to the living. Metaphorically, the mourners could be seen as generals regrouping their forces to come up with a new strategy for the battle over life.

In Hertz's view, the death of a stranger, slave, or child would not be felt, and no rituals would be undertaken because these individuals were not full members of society (Hertz, 1960:76). However, the deaths of many active adults place an immediate toll on social relations and the economy of any society. Why then do some societies give proper burial to newborns or the stillborn who have not yet had any active role in the society? Some societies give proper burial to the corpses of senile or sick individuals who have not contributed to their community for years. These types of behavior challenge Hertz's views.

Unlike Hertz, anthropologist Arnold Van Gennep (1960) interpreted death not as a negative economic force, but instead as social shock. Van Gennep called it a rite of passage that also deserved celebration. Death rituals, or any ritual of transition, are marked by a stage of separation, a period of uncertainties called liminality, and a stage of reincorporation of the mourners to their normal activities. Only through death rituals could the living regain harmony and the deceased join the ancestral pantheon of mythological forefathers and foremothers. And only through death rituals could the living stop being in limbo or feeling "betwixt and between" in Victor Turner's words (1970:93).

Death kills not only the individual but, to some extent, the group as well, because it destroys the harmony of everyday life. Death may trigger two different and opposite responses. At one extreme is the fear of dying, which can lead individuals to flee from the scene. At the other, individuals may feel a sense of worthlessness; thus, in an act of terrible pain and abandonment, the mourners could kill themselves to join the departed (Geertz, 1973:162). To avoid this scenario, rituals are performed to create comfort and console the living, and death is denied by belief in an eternal existence or through allusions to divine forces (Geertz, 1973:110). Death rituals, then, are beneficial because through participation the living emerge stronger from social uncertainties.

If death can shatter the group, creating deep emotional pain and uncertainties, can anything good come out of it? Anthropologists Maurice Bloch and Jonathan Parry (1982) interpreted death not as a malevolent force of destruction, but as a positive source capable of generating life. They maintained the socioeconomic perspectives of Hertz and

Van Gennep, but added the notion that death generates life by means of regeneration, fertility, and rebirth which are symbolized in funerary rites. Bloch and Parry argued that in many cultures ancestors held the knowledge and the power to propitiate fertility of plants, animals and human life and, thus, they must be venerated. These scholars, as well as anthropologists Martha Donavan (1985) and Frank Salomon (1991), envisioned death as a regeneration of life and as a rite of passage in which death and reproduction are central to human social life. In their views, without reproduction there is no gain, and without death which produces life, everyone would die. For example, many plants die to produce seeds and, in turn, a dried seed will produce life. Humans must die to give a place to others. It is the transformation of natural elements and things that provides continuity of life (Donavan, 1985:32).

Salomon (1991), using the foundations of Hertz, Van Gennep, and Bloch and Parry, argued that preservation of ancestors in the Andes, as in Inca society, was a way to achieve and maintain socioeconomic success. Using this model, Salomon discussed how in the Andes during Inca times, the mummies of ancestors were deeply venerated to obtain good herding and successful harvests. The mummies were considered *huacas* (deities). According to Allen (1988:59,63) and Salomon (1991), death in Andean cosmology can be seen as a transformation of soft material (childhood) into a harder inalterable substance (a mummy). From the mummy's tissues a spiritual entity rises (soul) and travels to the *Pacarina*, or the mythological place of origin of the group. The mummy *huacas* must be properly cared for, fed, and dressed to assure plenty of good harvests and herds because they hold the key to fertility. They are durable and immutable like deities (see also Allen, 1988:172).

In a similar sociopolitical perspective, anthropologists Richard Huntington and Peter Metcalf (1985) discussed how death rituals can be manipulated to legitimize the inheritance of power and maintain the structure of the social system. They pointed out that through lavish mortuary ceremonies, the heirs increase the importance of the dead leader to gain public recognition. In other words, the respectful son or daughter of the deceased leader not only would have the right, but also would deserve to rule.

In Bloch and Parry's words (1982:12) burial ceremonies can be seen as a mechanism to maintain seniority. Political symbolism of death, for example, was taken to an extreme in ancient Egypt, where the energy necessary to produce increasingly complex rituals for the dead is reflected in the size of their magnificent pyramids. However, the death of a beloved leader does not always unify the group; it may do exactly the opposite, creating an emotional abyss among followers and relatives (Allen, 1993). In the Andes, for example, the death of Inca Huaina Cápac caused a civil war between his sons, Huascar and Atahualpa, leading to the collapse of the Inca Empire.

But why do some less complex societies such as hunters and gatherers bury their dead and hold ceremonies, if there is no economic or political power to gain in doing so? And, in the case of the Chinchorro, why did they even mummify fetuses?

Need for Death Rituals

The nature of death has shaped societies since the dawn of humans. Rituals and burials seem to be archaic social behaviors that have shaped us emotionally for thousands of years. Evidence of death rituals has been associated with Neanderthals (ca. 100,000 years ago) who painted or sprinkled the corpses with red ocher during burial (Gowlett, 1993:102–103). Also, in the Shanidar Cave (Iraq) Neanderthal bodies were apparently covered with flowers. Even at this early time the dead could have remained among the living, in some cases as mental images and in other cases as tangible evidence (e.g., skeletal remains or frozen bodies), thus giving rise to spiritual ceremonies for the dead.

In early cultures the fear of dying and being possessed by or in intimate contact with supernatural forces was most likely the primordial force shaping mortuary rituals, rather than economic or political needs. Death needed an explanation. It is possible then that rituals may have emerged as a means for the living to regain their inner peace or to protect themselves from further death.

In modern hunter and gatherer societies in Africa that most closely parallel the simple political organization of ancient societies, death is feared because it is often associated with supernatural power such as witchcraft (Woodburn, 1982:192,195). Likewise, Yanomamo Indians of Brazil, for example, see the death of children as the work of sorcery, not as a result of disease (Chagnon, 1977:49,52,85). They need to protect themselves, not only from their enemy's arrows, but also from more powerful non-tangible evil spells. Therefore, shamans spend most of their time performing ceremonies to drive off evil spirits or sending evil spirits to enemies.

Death may be feared because it is seen as a sign of inferiority in the face of more powerful enemies. For example, when Amerindians succumbed to European diseases, their death was seen as a consequence of Europeans having a more powerful god.

Rituals minimize the fear of the unknown. It seems, then, more likely that mortuary rituals arose as a response to the uncertainties of life and the supernatural world beyond rather than as a consequence of economic and sociopolitical pressures. If death can be seen as a gradual phenomenon of losing life (Urioste, 1981), then the group, facing the growing void and fear of the loss of a loved one, finds strength in adversity.

Theories about death rituals have been heavily biased toward economic gain, and they often underplay the human emotional perspective. Perhaps mortuary ceremonies instead evolved initially as a mechanism to protect the living from evil forces and to bring people together for healing, and soon after to please ancestral or spiritual entities. Later, gains in personal power likely became another motive, especially in the case of stratified or complex societies. Humans learned how to adapt to the stress of death by creating rituals, and then they adapted these rituals to obtain spiritual and, later, economic advantages.

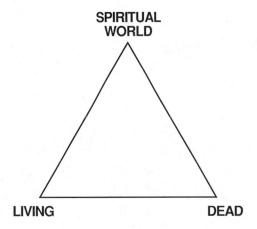

Fig. 7. Trilogy of death (drawing: T. Cantrell).

Trilogy in Death

How different cultures undertake the care of their dead is by no means uniform, but grief and some spiritual beliefs, such as ghosts or the existence of an afterlife, are experienced nearly universally when facing death. Some societies may not necessarily have understood from a biological perspective why someone died, but the rituals they performed ensured harmony for the living, the body, and the spiritual entities. Death rituals seemed to have evolved as a tridimensional ideological system that required perpetual and reciprocal feedback among its three components: the living (mourners), the corpse, and the spiritual world (fig. 7). The living properly honored and disposed of the body as the individual may have desired; in return, the liberated spirit interceded with the deities to satisfy the biological and social needs of the living. From this perspective, death rituals can be seen as very ancient adaptive phenomena that changed according to the social and ideological needs of the group. Funerary practices can then be analyzed from these different perspectives: first, a social intercourse to satisfy the needs of the mourners; second, a physical treatment for the needs of the corpse; and third, a spiritual treatment to fulfill the necessities of the spirit(s) or soul(s) of the deceased.

Rituals for Mourners

In many societies the days following the death of a member of a group may be considered an occasion of extreme danger and susceptibility, because a spirit has been unleashed. Especially after someone dies, some groups believe ghosts, demons, and wicked spirits are waiting for the opportunity to damage or devour the living (see Allen, 1988:62; Huntington and Metcalf, 1985:76). Priests or shamans may be called upon to perform rituals, and observance of taboos are often mandatory for the relatives as well as for the morticians in order to avoid harm. In addition, friends or group members are expected to cooperate in the rituals, otherwise they face the accusation that their witchcraft caused the death of the victim (Huntington and Metcalf, 1985:35). The potential danger for the living may be considered even greater if the person is believed to have had many souls that must be protected and pleased after death. Researchers Robert Habenstein and William Lamers (1960:684) noted that the Sioux Indians believed the individual had four souls, and archaeologists Jens Hansen, Jorgen Meldgaard, and Jorgen Nordqvist (1991:56–57) pointed out that the Greenland Inuk believed in many souls, most of which lived in the joints of the body.

Although some cultural groups perceive death as a natural process and do not fear the body, they may fear the spirits. Other groups may fear both. For example, Hansen, Meldgaard, and Nordqvist (1991) noted that the Inuk fear a dead body because the corpse may become impregnated with evil spirits. Habenstein and Lamers (1960) reported that the Hottentots of Africa avoid living close to the grave of a family member so as not to expose themselves to mean spirits. The Yahgan in Patagonia burned the huts and personal belongings of the deceased and quickly moved to a new place to avoid unwanted ghosts (Gusinde, 1937). Likewise, in Africa the Hazda (northern Tanzania) and Baka (Cameroon) people quickly abandon the camp when someone dies, and the !Kung hold night dancing ceremonies to ward off evil spirits (Woodburn, 1982). Many modern westerners are not immune to the notion of an evil corpse. For example, some fear that dead bodies may prey on the living, as reflected in the once-popular vampire television series, *Dracula* and *Dark Shadows*. Vampires were thought to cause consumption of the body or tuberculosis (Sledzik and Bellantoni, 1994). Thus, fear of vampires caused 19th century New Englanders to go to the extreme of exhuming cadavers of putative vampires to kill them once and for all. In Catholic mortuary ceremonies, wakes may be performed in the hope that the soul will not stay to haunt the living; in this way bad spirits will be kept at bay, and the dead will rest in peace.

Ceremonies are performed not only to provide social strength and reintegrate the mourners, both socially and spiritually, but more importantly to protect the integrity of the souls or spirits of the living, avoiding ailments and further death. Some cultures believe evil powers can cause loss of soul, resulting in sickness and death. In Latin America, for example, a temporary loss of the soul is called *susto* and is believed to be responsible for creating sickness and miseries, especially in children. Similarly, in Yanomamo ideology, evil spirits may devour one of the children's souls causing sickness or death (Chagnon, 1977:85). In Coltauco, Chile, for example, if a second death occurs soon after a first death, people blame the soul of the first person for not wanting to depart alone. Supposedly, company is desired for the unknown and frightening trip to the hereafter (see also Allen, 1988:62–63). For this reason, in many parts of the world family and friends devote much energy toward properly treating the body and soul(s) to avoid the soul(s) of the departed becoming possessive or angry and hurting the living (see Allen, 1988:61–62). Thousands of years ago people may have had similar or even stronger convictions about the existence of heinous spiritual entities surrounding them.

The treatment of the cadaver often includes ceremonies and purification rites for both the deceased and those who handled the corpse, as it is often considered unclean and dangerous (Malinowski, 1948:50). The corpse is feared, not because of the smell or decomposition, but because it has supernatural hidden powers. As Huntington and Metcalf (1985:63) synthesized: "The corpse is feared because, until its reconstruction in the beyond is complete, part of its spiritual essence remains behind, where it menaces the living with threat of further death."

Rituals for the Corpse

Habenstein and Lamers (1960) have described an amazing variety of ritualistic treatments for corpses. For example, in parts of India the body is publicly cremated on a large pyre. In Tibet the Lama monks intentionally dissect the corpse to ensure that scavenger birds and animals will eat the cadaver. The North American Plains Indians placed the corpse in a scaffold for about a year before a permanent ground burial was undertaken. In Western countries, where the idea of eternal youth and the maintenance of social status is an obsession, the body is well dressed and an elaborate make-up job is expected to give the dead an aura of tranquility and, ironically, vitality. The body is then deposited in an elaborate coffin and buried. Today, the face of the dead can even be given cosmetic treatments to resemble the person's favorite idol, such as Elvis Presley. As illustrated in these few examples, humans have a kaleidoscope of treatments for the corpse, varying widely from culture to culture. Treatment of the body, however, is not a random phenomenon. It is shaped by the rules of each society.

Rituals for the Spirits

Although humans dislike dying, they often regard the afterlife as a paradise, a continuation of terrestrial existence with plenty of leisure and pleasure, or as a place of spiritual enjoyment (Chagnon, 1977:48; Malinowski, 1948:160). Grave goods reflect the needs of life in the hereafter. From a spiritual point of view, it seems that mortuary ceremonies are performed for three main purposes: first, to insure that the soul (or spirit) leaves the body; second, to guarantee that the soul is purified and arrives safely at the hereafter or final resting place; and third, to ensure that the soul has a joyful and eternal existence in the hereafter. Thus, according to Habenstein and Lamers (1960), in India the body is cremated to release the soul which is trapped inside the skull, as well as to purify the soul. In Iran, relatives read sacred writings in the ears of the departed before the body is given to the vultures, in order to assure the successful departure of the soul. The body is placed in a special tower for the vultures to eat the flesh, because it is believed that human fluids contaminate land, water, or fire, which are considered immaculate substances. The Lamas from Tibet are also indifferent to the body. They give the body to the vultures because it is the soul that is important; the flesh is but a terrestrial burden. It is interesting that Catholics are concerned with the soul, too, yet they avoid destroying the body because it is necessary for resurrection. They believe that prayers are helpful for purifying the soul and shortening its time in purgatory, thus speeding its entrance to heaven. Novenas, or nine-day prayers, are considered necessary so the soul will rest in peace.

Today, the hectic daily lives of most cosmopolitan people interested in economic success make spiritual matters ephemeral. Modern city dwellers are not completely afraid of the spirits of the dead. In contrast, people of simple societies, or people living in rural areas, tend to be more concerned with evil forces. Thus, the observance of taboos, the performance of ceremonies guided to maintain a balance between life and death, and proper mortuary rituals to protect the living and to please the souls of the dead appear to be the emotional fuel that gives meaning to social existence.

But how do death rituals illuminate the social milieu of a group? In Hertz's view it is the trilogy of rituals for the dead, the mourners, and the supernatural forces that offers anthropologists an understanding of how the group may regain its social balance. In his view, for example, the fate of the deceased resembles that of the mourners who are facing a liminal or ambiguous period of social dysadaptation. The rotting of the body is analogous to the transformation and liminal journey of the soul to the hereafter. Exhumation of remains for secondary burial parallels the final resting of the soul. But, in contrast to Hertz's view that rites are for the sole benefit of society, mortuary rituals can also be interpreted as a mechanism of reciprocity between the living and the dead. Participation in such a system lies beyond logical explanation and is rooted in metaphysical beliefs on the nature of death. Death rituals are abstract (spiritual concepts), functional (creating solidarity), and plastic (they change according to social needs).

In summary, proper mortuary practices, across many cultures, may include prayer, songs, dancing, mourning, a dress code, body decoration, purification rites, orgies, or feasting. These ritualistic activities may be considered necessary for protection of the living and for the soul of the deceased to successfully reach its final destiny. More important yet, complex ceremonies are performed even years after burial because they are essential to please the spiritual entities and for continued protection of the integrity of the soul of the living.

Archaeological Theory

In archaeological mortuary theory, complexity of mortuary treatment is said to be primarily influenced by sex and age in hunter and gatherer societies, but in more socially complex groups (e.g., intensive agriculturalists), social position and social affiliation determine burial treatment (Binford, 1971). Archaeologist Joseph Tainter (1978) correlated complex mortuary treatment with high social rank. In Tainter's view, high burial energy expenditure is reflected in greater and better quality grave goods and in the complexity of body treatment. Along similar lines, archaeologist James Brown (1981) proposed that ranked societies arise from competition for wealth and mates. In Brown's view, inherited rank would be seen in the grave goods with the inclusion of symbols of authority that cross-cut age and sex. Other archaeologists such as Arthur Saxe (1970), Robert Chapman, Ian Kinnes, and Klavs Randsborg (1981), and Lynne Goldstein (1980) theorized that spatial patterns and cemeteries reflect social organization. Individuals are not buried at random in a cemetery, and corporate groups, such as clans, will maintain an area exclusively for themselves. These archaeological theories show the necessity of having a holistic approach toward mortuary studies. The grave, its location, the individual, the burial treatment, and the grave goods must all be taken into consideration.

The Chinchorro Model

Can these ethnographic and archaeological models be applied to the Chinchorros, who lived as modest fishers with a simple political organization? Most of the studies mentioned emphasized competition and socioeconomic needs, minimizing spiritual beliefs. The Chinchorros will be explored here using Hertz's trilogy: the living, the corpse, and the supernatural, incorporating Van Gennep's sociological model and Bloch and Parry's model of death as a regeneration of life. The Chinchorros were a politically simple fishing society with extraordinarily complex mummification practices that could not be based on economic gain. Thus, it will be argued that from the Chinchorro example, complex treatment of the dead can no longer be seen as a cultural phenomenon exclusively associated with the existence of rank or with the presence of complex societies. Complex mortuary practices may also be a part of simple and demographically small groups, as in the case of the Chinchorros. Chinchorro burial practices arose neither as a consequence of social shock as used by Hertz (1960) and Van Gennep (1960), nor as competition for resources or political power, but as a manifestation of love, emotions, grief, and spiritual beliefs. The model to be explored here is that the artificially prepared Chinchorro mummies were images of the dead. The Chinchorro mummies became "living" entities that used the same space and resources as did the living in a similar manner as the Laymi people of Bolivia, where the dead harvest chile peppers from the same fields (Harris, 1983:146). It will be argued in the following chapters that Chinchorro mummification practices can be interpreted as a system to achieve continuity with life, rather than regeneration of life as in the model of Bloch and Parry (1982). In other words, in Chinchorro ideology, the dead became an extension of the living. Chinchorro mummies could have been part of a belief system that negated death. Immortalization was gained through mummification, from which the body and spirit survived. That is, artificial mummification provided a resting place for the soul and therefore the mummies were considered living entities. As the mortuary practices evolved they became more sophisticated, likely stimulating creation and maintenance of sacred beliefs and social harmony. And finally, artificial mummification can also be interpreted as an adaptive ideological strategy for group survival to the arid Atacama Desert.

Chapter 4

Chinchorro Habitat

 The Chinchorros were bound by the Pacific Ocean and the Atacama Desert (pl. 4). The barrenness and solitude of the hostile desert environment are broken by narrow rivers that cut across the desert, bringing life and creating sharply contrasting patches of green against the brown sand. Among these shallow rivers that create green valley bottoms are the Sama and Caplina in southern Peru and the Lluta, San José, and Camarones in northern Chile (pl. 5). Where the rivers meet the Pacific Ocean, they provide a rich ecosystem of plants, birds, and animals forming what is called a fertile coast, and most of the Chinchorro sites have been found in the drainage of these Chilean rivers. This fertile coast is made up of swamps at the river drainages, sandy beaches, and rocky shores extending from Arica to Pisagua. South of the modern city of Pisagua the coast becomes more arid because fewer rivers reach the ocean; high cliffs are common there.

Wildlife was extremely abundant at the fertile coast, as evidenced by the mountains of bird excrement known as guano. These tons of bird feces have accumulated through thousands of years of deposition on cliffs and bluffs at the shore. Sea mammals were also abundant, as seen in the middens and burials that include sea lion and in some places whale bones. Thus, the Chinchorros had plenty of resources to exploit in the concentrated fertile coast ecosystems.

In northern Chile and southern Peru, the coastal temperature is pleasant year-round: 15.5 to 22°C (60 to 72°F) are the minimum and maximum temperatures. There is also an absolute lack of rain along the Atacama coast, which contributes to an abundance of amazingly well-preserved ancient cultural materials and mummies. It can be said that in some parts of the Atacama Desert it has not rained in thousands of years.

The cold Humboldt current of the Pacific Ocean inhibits evaporation, and the transverse winds push any collected moisture up and away from the coast to the higher altitudes of the Andes, where rain and snow are common. This creates at the coast a desert without rain, and as one ascends to the heights of the Andes one passes through, within only a few kilometers of altitude, a diversity of ecosystems due to increasing rain and cold weather.

The pampa is the dry desert coastal area. Except for an occasional oasis, it is an inhospitable, barren environment. Higher up in the sierras, about 3,000 meters (9,842 feet), fertile valleys are hospitable environments for a wide variety of plants and animals. Even further up into the Andes, about 4,000 meters (13,123 feet), in what is known as the puna, only small bushes and grasses are found, as this area is above the tree line. For the lowlander ascending to the puna, hypoxia, or low oxygen levels in the blood, can cause engorgement of the brain, acute headaches, fainting, and a general inability to function normally until the body adjusts. Today, the misery is compounded by the sight of puna locals engaging in a rough soccer match, while for most newcomers walking is a major undertaking.

The puna and sierra support a variety of native wildlife such as *parinas* (flamingo species), *ñandu* (the Andean ostrich), deer, camelids (*alpaca* and *llama*), and *viscachas* (a large rabbitlike animal). These species were exploited by the early hunters of the highlands (Rivera, 1991; Santoro, 1993).

It was here in the coastal and valley environments that the Chinchorro lived, between the modern cities of Ilo, Peru, and Antofagasta, Chile (parallels 17 and 24 south and 70 to 71 west longitude) covering a distance of about 900 kilometers (fig. 2). However, the best evidence of Chinchorro artificial mummification practices are found between the cities of Arica and Cobija, located along the fertile coast. Archaeological evidence suggests the Chinchorro existed north of Arica and south of Cobija, but further research is needed to substantiate the evidence of extended burial practices or artificial mummification in these peripheral areas.

South of the Morro 1 site in Arica are several archaeological preceramic sites showing extensive coastal human occupation, such as Quiani and La Capilla, but today there are no water sources there. In the past, freshwater springs must have existed in many places along the Atacama coast, otherwise human occupation would have been impossible. Only a few scholars have attempted to investigate the interrelationship between water resources and human occupation in the coast of northern Chile. One of them, archaeologist Alan Craig (1982), pointed out the existence of many large lakes in the Atacama Desert during the Pleistocene, about one million years ago. Today, these lakes are completely dried out and nature has transformed them into *salares,* or salt beds. According to Craig, these lakes were the product of tectonic plates and underground highland water that filtered out to lower altitudes, including the coast. Also, the highlands of northern Chile had a maximum pluviosity about 12,000 B.C., nourishing the rivers and the lowlands. Since then the coastal area has had a continuous decline in water availability, resulting in desertification of the environment (see also Crom, 1993). If water resources were abundant when the first Chinchorro people arrived, exploration, settling, and peopling of the Atacama coast would have been an easier task than under present-day desolation.

CHAPTER 5

CHINCHORRO: A SEDENTARY SOCIETY

 The Chinchorros have been viewed in the past as mobile hunters and gatherers or as a semisedentary society (Muñoz and Chacama, 1993:46; Núñez, 1989:91–92; Rivera, 1991, among others), but in light of new information coming from interdisciplinary research, it can be argued that the Chinchorro people instead had a sedentary maritime existence. They exploited the maritime resources year-round and not just seasonally. In other words, Chinchorro represents an early Andean society that quickly adapted to a maritime way of life along the Pacific coast, starting about 7,000 B.C.

Three models could explain why this sedentism occurred at this early date. First, thanks to several unique environmental conditions found in this arid region, such as a stable environment with mild seasonal changes, pleasant year-round temperatures, easy access to sources of fresh water, and plenty of marine food resources, the Atacama coast was an ideal place for early hunters and gatherers to settle. Second, if the early Atacama people were mobile coastal bands coming from Peru to more fertile coasts, then they already possessed the necessary maritime technology to adapt and live year-round at the Atacama coast. And third, if the original Atacama people were Andean highlanders, they could have been from the area of Lake Titicaca and thus already had knowledge of some fishing techniques. This would have made the coastal adaptation an easy task. In any case, the evidence coming from settlement patterns, cemeteries, mummification, maritime technology, and subsistence, which will be discussed here, indicates that the Chinchorros were an early sedentary maritime society.

Settlement Patterns

The best argument for sedentism is the formation of houses and villages as permanent structures. Although Chinchorro houses are rare, there are some descriptions available which lend at least partial support for sedentism. Settlements associated with the Chinchorros have been found in Arica (Acha 2 and Quiani 9 sites), at Camarones gorge (Conanoxa W(a)), Antofagasta (Cerro Moreno), and in the drainage of the Loa River (Caleta Huelén 42) (Llagostera, 1989; Muñoz, 1985; Muñoz and Chacama, 1982;

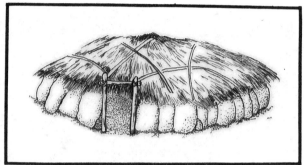

a

b

Fig. 8. Chinchorro-related houses: *a*, Acha 2; *b*, Caleta Huelén 42; *c*, Quiani 9. (After Muñoz and Chacama, 1982:65; Muñoz and Chacama, 1993:30; and Nuñez, 1989:92–93; drawing: D. Kendrick-Murdock).

c

Schiappacasse and Niemeyer 1969; Núñez, Zlatar, and Núñez, 1975). Remains of Chinchorro houses consist of circular or semicircular cobbles and vertical wooden posts. These wooden posts were obliquely placed to form the framework of the conically shaped huts. The exterior of the hut was likely covered with branches, reeds, or animal skins. The huts varied in diameter from one to three meters and a hearth was placed in the center (fig. 8).

The earliest coastal settlement found to date in the Arica area, Acha 2, had eleven circular huts dating to 7,020 B.C. (Muñoz and Chacama, 1993). If these huts were all contemporaneous, and if it is assumed that two to four persons lived in each hut, then the population at this site ranged from twenty-two to forty-four persons. The site itself occupies approximately 880 square meters (Muñoz and Chacama, 1993:25). Though middens from the area were not concentrated and stratigraphically deep, shell remains were found scattered everywhere, implying a long occupation rather than a base camp. The shells also provide evidence that the Acha 2 inhabitants primarily exploited coastal resources, though small amounts of faunal remains and animal feces indicate they still occasionally hunted some camelids (Belmonte, Torres, and Molina, 1993; Muñoz and Chacama, 1993; Vilaxa and Corrales, 1993).

More evidence for Chinchorro houses in Arica was found by archaeologists Iván Muñoz and Juan Chacama (1982) on the slope of a hill overlooking the Pacific Ocean. They excavated the remains of two semicircular huts at Quiani 9 (fig. 8c), which were dated to 4,420 and 4,165 B.C. The middens at this site were dated to 3,300 B.C., indicating an occupation of at least a thousand years. The huts were built of light posts and likely covered by skins of sea mammals (Muñoz and Chacama, 1993:45). Quiani 9 is about 100 meters up slope from a shell midden studied by Bird (1943) that is situated directly on the beach below. The Quiani site studied by Bird was dated to 4,220 B.C. and 3,680 B.C. (Mostny, 1964). Bird (1943:246) found one artificially prepared mummy at his Quiani site, and although the mummy itself was not dated, because it was artificially mummified it shows these fishers were clearly part of the Chinchorro culture. Considering the close dates and the short distance between these sites, the Quiani sites studied by Muñoz and Chacama (Quiani 9), and Bird (Quiani 1 and 2) may well be related. It could be argued that Quiani 9 was the actual settlement, while the middens at Quiani 1 and 2 represent debris left behind by the Chinchorro people during their daily activities on the beach. Besides the range in dates for these sites, the tremendous height of the shell middens (5–10 meters) is another indication that this coastal area was permanently occupied.

Later, about 2,830 B.C., and over 500 kilometers to the south of Arica, at the Caleta Huelén 42 site, twenty-two circular houses seem to have been built with greater permanence (Llagostera, 1989:71; Núñez, 1989:92; Núñez, Zlatar, and Núñez, 1975). These structures have compact, hard floors made up of a paste of seaweed ashes. Vertically placed stones were used as low walls (fig. 8b). The finding of various extended skeletons with mud facial masks indicate their cultural connection with the Chinchorro.

Dated much later, about 2,500 B.C., and in the Camarones Valley, about 100 kilometers south of Arica and 40 kilometers inland (Conanoxa site), is more evidence of circular houses (Schiappacasse and Niemeyer, 1969). They had stone bases with upright posts, and, according to Muñoz and Chacama (1993:45), they were similar to those found at the Acha 2 site in Arica.

The Chinchorro coastal houses were simple and partially made of perishable materials, but considering the mild climate they were fully adequate and could be considered permanent in this environment. The adequacy of light building materials is even reflected in modern Arican settlements, where houses made of perishable elements, such as cardboard and plastic sheeting, become permanent structures in poorer neighborhoods.

Few Chinchorro habitation sites have been found compared to the many cemeteries discovered along the coast. Three possible ideas, not necessarily exclusive, may explain this discrepancy. First, the Chinchorros lived on the beaches and the evidence of their housing could have been washed away long ago; second, the modern city of Arica now covers most of their settlements and cemeteries; and third, their settlement patterns have received little attention. Previous researchers assumed that early populations were nomadic, or at most semipermanent, so no research has been done to show otherwise. Although systematic settlement pattern studies are lacking, the few Chinchorro settlements that have been found could equally represent sedentary rather than semisedentary or nomadic lifestyles.

The type of circular huts found in these habitation sites apparently was common to many Andean preceramic populations. Circular and small huts have been found in the Peruvian sites of Asia, Chilca, and La Paloma (Quilter, 1989). About 420 reed huts have been counted at La Paloma site (Quilter, 1989:19), but it is not clear if all were contemporaneous. According to archaeologist Jeffrey Quilter (1989), local changes in climate probably forced the people of La Paloma to abandon their settlement after 2,500 B.C. In sum, the many preceramic habitational sites found along the coast of Peru and Chile starting about 7,020 B.C. indicate an increase in ocean-resources dependency and that these Andean populations had the potential to become sedentary.

Cemeteries

When someone dies among nomadic peoples, the corpse is disposed of with a simple ceremony or simply abandoned. For example, anthropologist Martin Gusinde (1937) reported that historic Yahgans from Patagonia placed the corpse inside the deceased's hut and burned it, then the group moved on. Likewise, anthropologist James Woodburn (1982) described several African hunter-gatherer groups (Hazda, Mbuti, and Baka) in which the corpses were simply abandoned. Sometimes, the body was left inside the deceased's hut, and the roof was pulled down to cover the corpse after a small ceremony. These African groups, like the Patagonian Indians from South America, avoid returning to the sites where the dead were left.

When people become sedentary, they develop cemeteries to bury their dead to avoid the foul smell of decomposing flesh and the visibility of dead loved ones, and to prevent scavengers from attacking the body. Chinchorros had formal cemeteries, which supports the argument that they were sedentary. Most of the Chinchorro cemeteries with artificially prepared bodies are concentrated along the coastal areas of Arica. Although Chinchorro-related cemeteries have been found in southern Peru by Wise (1991), the preservation is poor because the sites have undergone human and natural disturbances; thus, the existence of artificial mummies in this Peruvian area still requires confirmation.

Chinchorro cemeteries were small, but densely occupied (fig. 9), and there was no evidence of individuals with lavish grave goods, thought to denote the existence of an elevated social rank, as seen in later agricultural societies of the region. Chinchorro cemeteries vary in size from only a few individuals to more than 100, and they contain mummies of several types, such as black, red, bandage, mud-coated, and natural (pl. 6). The mummies were buried in shallow graves along the fringes of the Atacama coast.

The stratigraphy of most Chinchorro cemeteries was horizontal, meaning the bodies were placed next to each other. The Chinchorro mummies were often aligned and buried in groups according to their mummification styles. In some cases, however, the mummies of different styles were intermingled, indicating long periods of cemetery usage. In addition, radiocarbon dates from the cemeteries at Morro 1 and Camarones 14 span several millennia. The radiocarbon dates of many cemeteries found along the Atacama coast suggest many contemporaneous settlements even within the same oasis (table 3). Moreover, middens, cemeteries, places of preparation of the mummies, and house dwellings seem to have been near each other. This indicates a daily routine of sedentary people, rather than a semisedentary or highly mobile group.

Artificial Mummification and Energy Investment

The process of making complex Chinchorro mummies required the acquisition of distinct soils and plants. Probably weeks of work and ritual ceremonies were carried out until the mummies were finished (see Bittmann and Munizaga, 1977:163). This time and energy investment, along with the complexity and heavy physical weight of each adult mummy, means they were not made to be transported long distances; therefore, they were not the work of transhumant groups. Also, it would be unlikely, after such complex mummification treatment, that the body would be left behind as the group moved to a new place. The mummies were likely made to be worshiped at the village.

Technology

The initial hypothesis, that local ecological conditions and early maritime technology and subsistence allowed for sedentism, is supported by numerous findings from interdisciplinary research. For example, south of Arica, at Quebrada Las Conchas (Antofagasta, fig. 2), Llagostera (1979) found human occupation as early as 7,730 B.C. At this site, tool assemblages were already basically those of a fishing society oriented to maximize the exploitation of the shore and bathytudinal (ocean) resources. However, because no evidence of burials of Chinchorro mummies were found at Las Conchas, its association with Chinchorro is unclear. Despite some material at Las Conchas, such as geometric

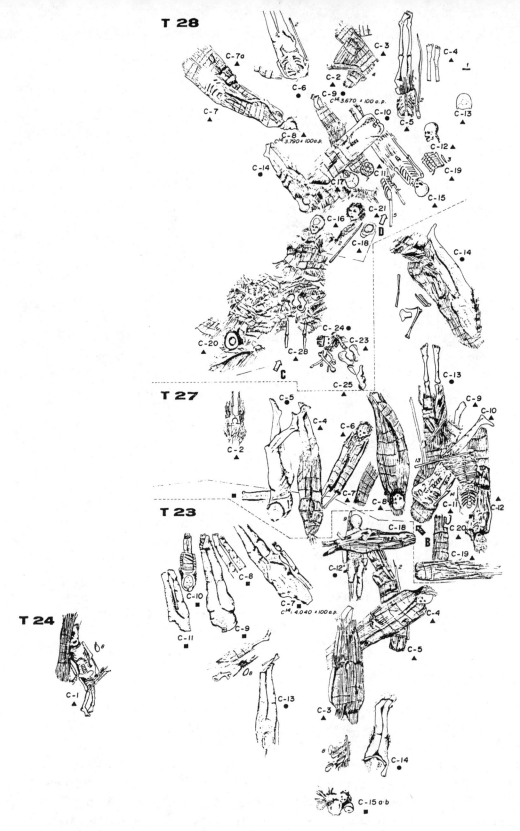

Fig. 9. Distribution of a group of mummies at the Morro 1 site (drawing: V. Standen).

Table 3. Chinchorro radiocarbon dates and associated sites

Site	Type of Site/Mummy	Radiocarbon and Calibrated Dates (B.C.)[1]	Sample	Lab No.	References
Camarones S	—	1110±380 2193 (1260) 368	—	RL-2055	Rivera (1991:17)
Camarones 15	Natural	1110±100 1505 (1260) 933	wood	GAK-5813	Rivera (1991:17)
Quiani 7 T16	Natural	1290±90 1677 (1440) 1261	muscle	I-13655	Lab record, Universidad de Tarapacá
Quiani 7 T12	Natural	1330±90 1734 (1510) 1311	muscle	I-13654	Lab record, Universidad de Tarapacá
La Capilla 1	Cave	1500 ±90 1928 (1730, 1690) 1510	bone?	I-11642	Muñoz and Chacama (1982:10)
Guasilla 1	—	1540±290 2562 (1740) 1009	—	B-3122	Bittmann (1984) in Rivera (1991:17)
Morro 1-6 T13	Natural	1610±100 2132 (1880, 1840, 1820, 1800, 1790) 1538	muscle	I-14-958	Focacci and Chacón (1989:46)
Quiani 7	Cemetery	1640±100 2140 (1880) 1625	wood	GAK-5814	Núñez (1976:122); Rivera (1977:200)
Camarones 15	—	1700±200 2553 (1940) 1450	—	RL-2054	Rivera (1985) in Rivera (1991:17)
Morro 1 T28C9	Mud-coated	1720±100 2281 (1970) 1698	muscle/lung	I-13651	Allison et al. (1984:163–165)
La Capilla 1	Cave	1720±160 2461 (1970) 1529	bone	GAK-8778	Muñoz and Chacama (1982:10)
Conanoxa W(a)	Camp	1790±130 2463 (2120, 2080, 2040) 1739	camelid feces	IVIC-175	Schiappacasse and Niemeyer (1969) in Núñez (1976:82)
Morro 1-6 T27	Natural	1800±140 2474 (2130, 2080, 2040) 1699	cartilage	GX-18261	Focacci and Chacón (1989:46); Aufderheide and Allison (1994)
Caleta Huelén 42	Natural	1830±90 2455 (2140) 1887	harpoon wood	GAK-3545	Núñez (1976:93)
Morro 1 T28C8	Natural	1840±140 2563 (2140) 1748	muscle	I-13656	Allison et al. (1984:163–165)
Morro 1 T28C22	Natural	1880±100 2474 (2200) 1923	lung	I-13652	Allison et al. (1984:163–165)
Morro 1-6 T39	Natural	1930±70 2468 (2280) 2041	muscle	GX-18259	Focacci and Chacón (1989:46); Aufderheide and Allison (1994)

Table 3. (*continued*)

Site	Type of Site/Mummy	Radiocarbon and Calibrated Dates (B.C.)[1]	Sample	Lab No.	References
Morro 1-6 T53	Natural	1945±75 2551 (2300) 2043	cartilage	GX-18262	Focacci and Chacón (1989:46); Aufderheide and Allison (1994)
Conanoxa W(a)	Camp	2020±120 2865 (2460) 2038	—	IVIC-876	Schiappacasse and Niemeyer (1969) in Núñez (1976:102)
Cañamo. Fsc. 1	Midden	2060±136 2882 (2470) 2041	—	—	Núñez and Moragas (1977) in Muñoz (1985:275)
Morro 1-6 T23	Natural	2060±75 2850 (2470) 2206	liver	GX-18263	Focacci and Chacón (1989:46); Aufderheide and Allison (1994)
Conanoxa W(a)	Camp	2070±110 2873 (2470) 2142	—	IVIC-875	Schiappacasse and Niemeyer (1969) in Núñez (1976:102)
Morro 1 T23C7	Red	2090±100 2873 (2490) 2200	wood	I-13543	Allison et al. (1984:163–165)
Playa Miller 8	Red	2140±105 2885 (2570, 2510) 2284	wood	GAK-5811	Núñez (1976:122)
Morro 1-5 (MI)	Red	2170±75 2879 (2590) 2457	liver	—	Guillen (1992)
Morro 1 T21C1	Natural	2250±100 2921 (2860, 2810, 2740, 2730, 2700) 2463	muscle	I-13541	Allison et al. (1984:163–165)
Morro 1-6 T9	Natural	2360±145 3342 (2890) 2468	liver	GX-18260	Focacci and Chacón (1989:46;. Aufderheide and Allison (1994)
Morro 1 T19	Red	2400±280 3649 (2910) 2140	charcoal/organ	I-13650	Allison et al. (1984:163–165)
Carrizal	Midden?	2440±110 3346 (2920) 2625	charcoal	—	Wise (1991)
Aragon 1	Camp	2530±170 3625 (3080, 3060, 3040) 2614	—	—	Núñez and Zlatar (1976) in Muñoz (1985:275)
Morro 1 T7C1	Red	2570±90 3493 (3260, 3240, 3100) 2904	muscle	B-40956	Standen (1991:288)

Site	Context	Date	Material	Lab No.	Reference
Morro 1 T25C6	Mud-coated (2)	2620±100 3513 (3330, 3210, 3200, 3150, 3140) 2915	muscle	I-13542	Allison et al. (1984:163–165)
Km 4	Midden?	2670±90 3619 (3350) 2929	—	—	Wise (1991)
Camarones 8 T1C1	Red	2685±90 3624 (3350) 3034	muscle	GX-15079	Aufderheide, Muñoz, and Arriaza (1993:191)
Guasilla 1	—	2780±180 3905 (3500, 3420, 3380) 2915	—	B-3121	Bittmann (1984) in Rivera (1991:17)
Maderas Enco C1	Black w/red	2800±155 3792 (3510, 3410, 3390) 2930	wood	GX-17464	Arriaza (1993a)
Caleta Huelén 42	Village	2830±100 3705 (3610, 3600, 3520) 3335	charcoal/bone	GAK-3546	Núñez (1976:92)
Caleta Abtao 1	Midden	2870±70 3699 (3630, 3570, 3540) 3369	—	—	Boissett, Llagosteras, and Salas (1969) in Muñoz (1985:275)
Cobija 1/S	—	2930±90 3792 (3640) 3374	—	B-3114	Bittmann (1984) in Rivera (1991:17)
Pisagua Viejo 4T2	Black?	2930±320 4339 (3640) 2780	wood/vegetal	IVIC-170	Núñez (1965:23)
Camarones P. N.	Midden	3000±210 4222 (3700) 3104	—	—	Dauelsberg M.S. in Muñoz (1985:275)
Arica	Black	3060±110 3981 (3760) 3524	wood	GAK-9903	Vera (1981:12)
Cobija 1/S	—	3110±120 4040 (3790) 3539	—	B-3117	Bittmann (1984) in Rivera (1991:17)
Caleta Abtao 1	Midden	3150±130 4220 (3930, 3880, 3810) 3547	—	—	Boissett, Llagosteras and Salas (1969) in Muñoz (1985:275)
Morro 1 T1C4	Black	3210±110 4224 (3950) 3669	lung/vegetal	I-13539	Allison et al. (1984:163–165)
Aragon 1	Camp	3220±200 4354 (3960) 3389	charcoal	GAK-5965	Núñez and Zlatar (1976) in Rivera (1991:17)
Pisagua Viejo 4T2	Black?	3270±170 4351 (3980) 3641	wood/vegetal	IVIC-170	Núñez (1965:23)
Caramucho 1	Midden	3270±130 4327 (3980) 3698	—	—	Sanhueza M.S. in Muñoz (1985:275)
Arica	Black	3290±230 4468 (3990) 3518	wood	GAK-9902	Vera (1981:12)
Quiani 9	Midden	3300±430 4946 (3990) 2919	charcoal/wood	GAK-8781	Muñoz and Chacama (1982:72)
Cobija 1/S	—	3490±150 4530 (4310, 4250) 3828	—	B-3115	Bittmann (1984) in Rivera (1991:17)

Table 3. (*continued*)

Site	Type of Site/Mummy	Radiocarbon and Calibrated Dates (B.C.)[1]	Sample	Lab No.	References
Cobija 1/S	—	3510±140 4530 (4320, 4290, 4260) 3961	—	B-3114	Bittmann (1984) in Rivera (1991:17)
Cobija 1/S	—	3560±60 4453 (4340) 4162	—	B-3934	Bittmann (1984) in Rivera (1991:17)
Chinchorro 1 T1C2	Black	3610±175 4771 (4350) 3973	wood	GX-15083	Aufderheide, Muñoz, and Arriaza (1993:191)
Camarones P.N.	Midden	3650±150 4763 (4430, 4360) 4040	—	—	Dauelsberg M.S. in Muñoz (1985:275)
Quiani 2	Midden	3680±145 4775 (4450, 4420, 4400) 4086	charcoal/fish	I-1349	Bird (1943); Mostny (1964)
Camarones S	—	3690±160 4794 (4460, 4410) 4046	—	GAK-8645	Rivera (1984) in Rivera (1991:17)
Camarones P.N.	Midden	3720±170 4895 (4460) 4048	—	—	Dauelsberg M.S. in Muñoz (1985:275)
Camarones P.N.	Midden	3800±170 4937 (4540) 4231	—	—	Dauelsberg M.S. in Muñoz (1985:275)
Camarones P.N.	Midden	3930±160 5068 (4720) 4351	—	—	Dauelsberg M.S. in Muñoz (1985:275)
Camarones P.N.	Midden	4000±130 5193 (4790) 4466	—	—	Dauelsberg M.S. in Muñoz (1985:275)
Cobija 1/S	—	4080±70 5056 (4900, 4880, 4850) 4722	—	B-3933	Bittmann (1984) in Rivera (1991:17)
Tiliviche 1b	Midden	4110±130 5248 (4920) 4592	—	—	Núñez and Moragas (1977) in Muñoz (1985:275)
Chinchorro 1 T1C1	Black	4120±285 5520 (4930) 4334	wood	GX-15084	Aufderheide, Muñoz, and Arriaza (1993:191)
Quiani 9	Camp	4165±280 5567 (4950) 4350	charcoal?	I-11643	Muñoz and Chacama (1982:75)
Quiani 1	Midden	4220±220 5446 (5060) 4517	charcoal	I-1348	Bird (1943); Mostny (1964)
Camarones P.N.	Midden	4290±160 5438 (5210, 5170, 5140, 5110, 5090) 4774	—	—	Dauelsberg M.S. in Muñoz (1985:275)
Camarones P.N.	Midden	4320±130 5433 (5220, 5160, 5150) 4841	—	—	Dauelsberg M.S. in Muñoz (1985:275)

Site	Context	Date	Material	Lab code	Reference
Quiani 9	Camp	4420±540 6189 (5270) 4006	charcoal	GAK-8782	Muñoz and Chacama (1982:75)
Camarones 14	Cemetery	4665±390 6176 (5450) 4628	charcoal	I-9816	Schiappacasse and Niemeyer (1984:26)
Camarones 14	Cemetery	4700±155 5733 (5520, 5510) 5256	charcoal	I-9817	Schiappacasse and Niemeyer (1984:26)
Camarones 17 T1C3	Black	4830±110 5772 (5600) 5438	wood	GX-15080	Aufderheide, Muñoz, and Arriaza (1993:191)
Tiliviche 1b	Midden	4850±90 5755 (5600) 5448	—	—	Núñez and Moragas (1977) in Muñoz (1985:275)
Tiliviche 1b	Midden	4955±65 5831 (5690) 5594	—	—	Núñez and Moragas (1977) in Muñoz (1985:275)
Camarones 17 T1C4	Black	4980±140 5986 (5710) 5490	wood	GX-15081	Aufderheide, Muñoz, and Arriaza (1993:191)
Camarones 14	Black?	5050±135 6040 (5770) 5579	muscle	I-11431	Schiappacasse and Niemeyer (1984:26)
Camarones 14	Cemetery	5470±225 6605 (6180) 5741	charcoal	I-999	Schiappacasse and Niemeyer (1984:26)
Morro 1 T7C1	Red	5860±180 7044 (6550) 6189	camelid fur	I-13653	Allison et al. (1984:163–165)
Tiliviche 1b	Mid/Hab	5900±280 7472 (6600) 6044	vegetal fibers	GAK-6052	Núñez (1976:123)
Aragon 1	Camp	6710±230 8081 (7580) 7048	charcoal	GAK-5966	Núñez (1976:123)
Acha 2	Camp	6950±150 8122 (7940) 7541	charcoal	—	Muñoz and Chacama (1993:28)
Acha 2 T1	Natural	7020±255 8475 (7980) 7448	muscle	GX-15082	Muñoz and Chacama (1993:28)
Tiliviche 1b	Midden	7180±365 9044 (8080) 7428	—	—	Núñez and Moragas (1977) in Muñoz (1985:275)
Q. Las Conchas	Midden	7450±160 8990 (8410) 8038	charcoal	—	Llagostera (1979:314)
Q. Las Conchas	Midden	7730±160 9244 (8950) 8348	charcoal	—	Llagostera (1979:314)

1. Calibrated ages are from Stuiver and Reimer (1993) using Method A, where the calibrated ages are in parentheses, and the 2-sigma minimum and maximum dates are outside the parentheses. Forty years were deducted from the original radiocarbon dates for southern hemisphere atmospheric samples.

Total number of radiocarbon dates = 85

Total number of dated mummies = 32

stone artifacts, that was unique and not found at other Arica sites, the consistency and long duration of fishing technology, rather than the tool diversity required of transhumant migrants, argue for stable coastal traditions.

Later (about 7,020 B.C.) findings at the Acha 2 site in Arica also demonstrate the development of coastal technology. Sinkers and cactus hooks were some of the elements of the fishing kit found (Muñoz and Chacama, 1993). Certainly, coastal gathering strategies and fishing required proper tool and technical abilities, as well as dedication, in order to make a successful living. In other words, maritime life required energy investment and specialization to survive. The sophistication of the tool technology (fishing gear and harpoons) found at the Chinchorro sites (fig. 10) implies a complete coastal adaptation, which contributes to the notion that the Chinchorro were permanent coastal dwellers as early as the seventh millennium B.C.

Subsistence and Diet

If the Chinchorros were permanently dependent on coastal resources, then their garbage and human bone chemistry should show high percentages of consumption of maritime products. Studies of ancient garbage mounds in northern Chile, and in oases from southern Peru that are not directly associated with the Chinchorro, indeed suggest this was the case and that early migrants quickly shifted their survival strategies. They gave up hunting land mammals and focused on fishing and hunting sea mammals and coastal birds (Muñoz and Chacama, 1993; Sandweiss et al., 1989). Chinchorro subsistence was indeed based on a systematic exploitation of ocean and coastal resources. For example, the excavations and analyses of faunal remains from several Chinchorro coastal middens have revealed that fishing, mollusk gathering, and hunting of sea lions and coastal birds produced the bulk of their food resources. The excavations also show that their diet was complemented only partially with terrestrial plants and land mammals available in the nearby river valleys (Aufderheide and Allison, 1992; Bird, 1943; Llagostera, 1989; Standen, 1991; Vilaxa and Corrales, 1993). At the Morro 1 site, the presence of whale bones indicates that scavenging for beached whales occasionally added to their food resources. The use of beached whales has also been noted in other cultures contemporaneous with the Chinchorros, such as in the cases of the Peruvian sites of Huaca Prieta and Chilca (Quilter, 1989:74,76).

The analyses of the Chinchorros' bones also point toward a coastal economy. In fact, trace mineral analyses indicate that the bulk of Chinchorro diet was maritime (Aufderheide and Allison, 1992). The presence in Chinchorro skulls of external auditory exostoses, an activity-induced pathology related to diving or fishing in cold water (Standen, Allison, and Arriaza, 1985), also reinforces the notion that harvesting from the sea was a major Chinchorro activity. This pathology (pl. 7) was already observed in the earliest skeleton found at Acha 2 (Arriaza, Muñoz, and Aufderheide, 1993). In addition,

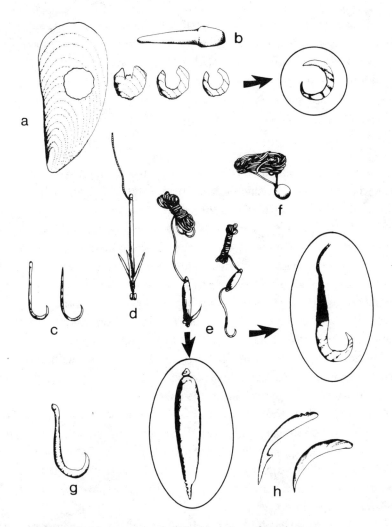

Fig. 10. Fishing gear: *a*, shell fishhook manufacturing steps; *b*, stone file to polish the shell hooks; *c*, two hooks made of cactus thorns; *d*, composite hook; *e*, two types of hooks with sinker stones and cords. The encircled details show a hook (*right*) and a sinker stone (*left*); *f*, cord with round sinker stone attached; *g* and *h*, bone hooks. (After Llagostera, 1989:62, 64; Muñoz, 1985:280; and Schiappacasse and Niemeyer, 1984:29; drawing: D. Kendrick-Murdock).

the teeth of the Chinchorros had substantial dental abrasion and paucity of cavities, signifying presence of sand and grit in their diet. In summary, the faunal remains, direct analyses of dietary intake, and bone pathology all suggest the existence of a full-time coastal economy, and thus permanent coastal settlements.

Comments

If the forbearers of the Chinchorro were highlanders, they had discovered a new paradise along the fertile coast of the Pacific Ocean, which marked the end of their journey and perhaps the edge of the world for them. The impression of the great contrasts of a narrow green valley and a barren desert extending to the very edge of the ocean would have been astonishing. In the fertile coastal oases, the abundance of marine food resources, fresh water, and the ease of acquisition of essential foodstuffs must have been attractive for the early nomadic hunters and provided them with the opportunity to settle along the coast. Acha 2 could represent one of these groups because its lithic technology, such as rhomboidal and lanceolate lithic points, are associated with a highland tool tradition (see Muñoz and Chacama, 1993; Santoro and Chacama, 1982). Also, the radiocarbon dates obtained for Acha 2 (7,020 and 6,950 B.C.) are contemporary with various hunting camps in the highlands, such as those of Patapatane and Las Cuevas studied by archaeologists Calogero Santoro and Juan Chacama (1982).

On the other hand, if the Chinchorro were maritime people coming from the coast of southern Peru to the Arica-Camarones area, then sites with artificially made Chinchorro mummies in southern Peru should be much earlier than those in Arica. This has not been found to be the case. Instead, the few sites and dates that could possibly be associated with Chinchorro in southern Peru, as reported by Wise (1991, in press), are contemporaneous with those found in northern Chile.

If there was time for specialization, what prevented the Chinchorro culture from developing solid houses, communal public structures, or a stratified society? Perhaps the combination of low population density and the abundance of food sources created little conflict between groups for control of essential resources and, as a result, there was no need for strong political organization. In the event serious conflicts did arise, most likely one group moved further down the coast to another oasis. Apparently, there was little pressure for greater social or political organization to control resources or populations; had there been, it might have led to the development of fortifications or temples as seen in central Peru at La Galgada and El Paraiso sites dating from about 2,500 B.C. These settlements also had a rich maritime subsistence which in these cases allowed for the construction of public monumental buildings (Moseley, 1975; 1992; Quilter, 1989). It is interesting to note that pottery and true loom weaving began about 1,700 B.C. to 1,500 B.C. in Peru, while in northern Chile similar technology began to appear about 800–500 B.C., long after the Chinchorro culture.

In Arica, the development of a maritime technology, with little evidence of terrestrial hunting implements, and the existence of coastal cemeteries extensively occupied for thousands of years imply that the Chinchorros had a sedentary way of life from a very early period. Moreover, the rather dry environment and patchiness or long distances between the Atacama freshwater riverain resources could have created a deep sense of territoriality, discouraging frequent and large nomadic movements along the coast. But apparently a strong sense of territoriality was not the case, as there are no fortifications. Also, the accumulation of several mummified relatives within the settlement would have literally weighed them down and limited their coastal movements as well. Obviously, coastal movements did occur, as similar mummy styles are found at different and distant coastal sites that today lack water. These movements would have been facilitated by the use of wild gourds as canteens for water storage when traveling along the dry desert coast in the conquest of the littoral. Moreover, water resources seem to have been more abundant in the Atacama region during the preceramic, but have been decreasing continuously since (Craig, 1982).

Although the Chinchorros were sedentary, trade with distant groups, or movements of people, occurred between the coast and the highlands using the small transverse Atacama valleys. The valleys provided accessible routes of connection between distant places for the acquisition of nonlocal resources. Throughout the Chinchorros' existence, continuous or semicontinuous contact with the highlands, or places even further removed, such as the Amazon jungle, seems to be indicated by the evidence of tool technology (rhomboidal points) and the occasional use of camelid furs, rhea skins, tropical plants (*Mucuma eliptica*) and feathers from tropical birds (Allison et al., 1984; Rivera, 1991; Standen, 1991). Perhaps a more formalized contact with highland groups also could have provided for exchange of mates. Just as the Chinchorros made use of some highland resources, there is some evidence that highlanders made use of coastal resources. Las Cuevas and Patapatane sites (ca. 7,550–6,000 B.C.), both about 5,000 meters above sea level, contain evidence of fish and shellfish remains (Santoro and Chacama, 1982). In Tiliviche (ca. 7,810–5,900 B.C.), forty kilometers inland, maritime products were abundant in the middens (Núñez and Moragas, 1978). Early long-distance travel was not exclusive to the Chinchorros. It is also evident at the Peruvian coastal site of La Paloma, where obsidian used for lithic points was brought from 400 kilometers inland (Reitz, 1986, in Quilter, 1989:24). Unfortunately, to date, no investigation has fully addressed whether the Chinchorro coastal-highland-tropic connection was through direct acquisition or through trade.

The absence of monumental architecture would make some scholars uneasy with the idea that the Chinchorros were a sedentary society. But as more evidence of settlements accumulates, the argument for early coastal sedentism is becoming clearer. Chinchorro settlement patterns vary and seem to be either dispersed or concentrated, ranging from a few huts, such as at Acha 2, to about 180 at Caleta Abtao in Antofagasta (Llagostera, 1989:70).

In summary, the settlement of the Atacama coast and conquest of the littoral was possible because fresh water in the form of rivers, springs, and swamps brought patches of life to the arid desert. Thus, the Chinchorros had plenty of natural resources to exploit. In Arica, this abundance and the development of maritime technology allowed for the formation of sedentary fishing communities beginning about 7,020 B.C. In turn, sedentism led to better food procurement and extra time to devote to spiritual matters. Having their basic biological needs satisfied, the Chinchorros could concentrate much of their energy on the intentional preservation of the dead. These maritime and mortuary specializations would have been highly unlikely if they were mobile hunter-gatherers or seminomadic populations. The richness of the environment led the Chinchorro people to settle the coast permanently and develop a maritime specialization long before agriculture was introduced to the area.

Plate 1. Chinchorro "family" number 7, during excavation at the Morro 1 site. This "family" included six mummies (photo: B. Arriaza).

Plate 2. Natural mummy from Arica (M1T21C1, subadult female) (photo: B. Arriaza).

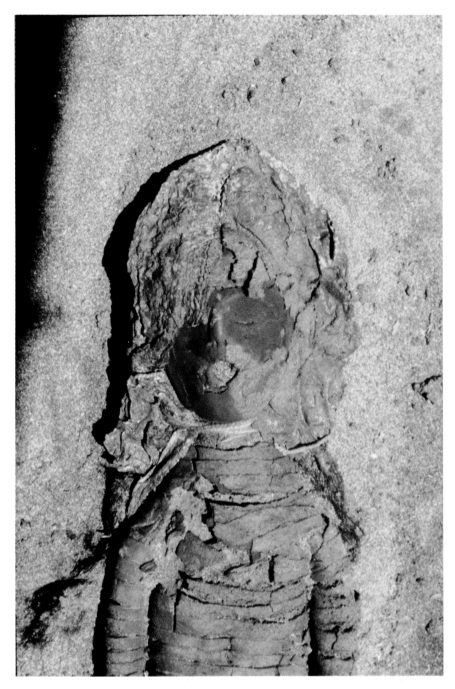

Plate 3. Artificially mummified child from Arica (M1T23C10, bandage style) (photo: B. Arriaza).

Plate 4. View of the arid Atacama coastline, Arica, Chile (photo: B. Arriaza).

Plate 5. View of the Lluta valley in Arica showing the sharp contrast of the valley river bottom and the desert (photo: V. Cassman).

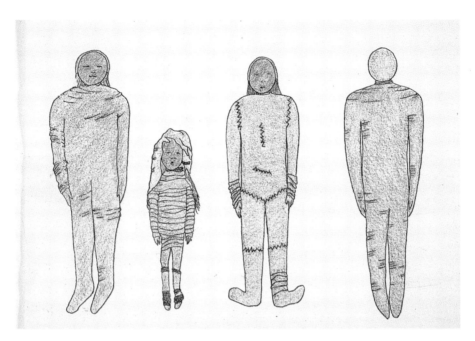

Plate 6. Most common artificial Chinchorro mummies. From left to right: black, bandage, red, and mud-coated mummies (drawing: B. Szuhay).

Plate 7. External auditory exostosis in the skull of the Acha man caused by continuous underwater activities (photo: B. Arriaza).

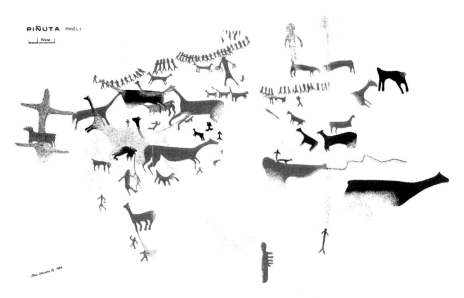

Plate 8. Rock painting from Piñuta Cave, in the highlands of Arica (from Santoro and Chacama, 1982, courtesy of C. Santoro).

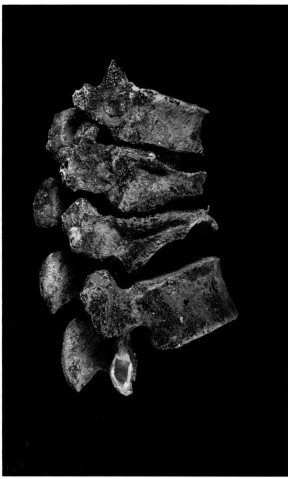

Plate 9. Segment of spine showing a compression fracture of vertebrae due to osteoporosis (M1T27C8, adult female, natural mummification) (photo: B. Arriaza).

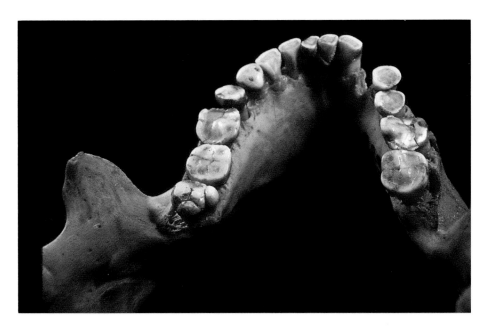

Plate 10. Mandible showing dental abrasion and absence of cavities. Note unusual extra cusp on lingual surface of left third molar (M1T27C9, adult female, natural mummification) (photo: B. Arriaza).

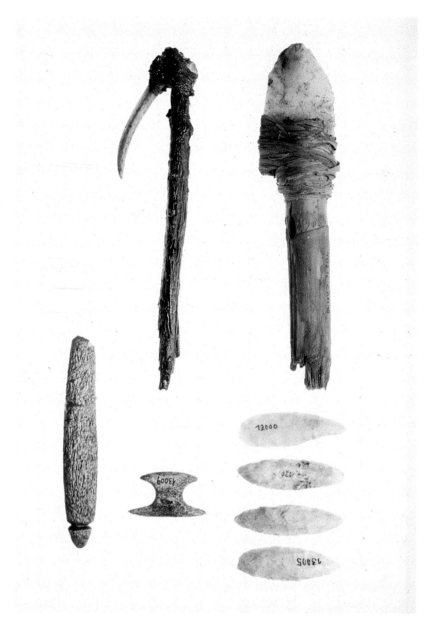

Plate 11. Lithic tools from the Camarones 14 site. Museum of Natural History, Santiago (photo: B. Arriaza).

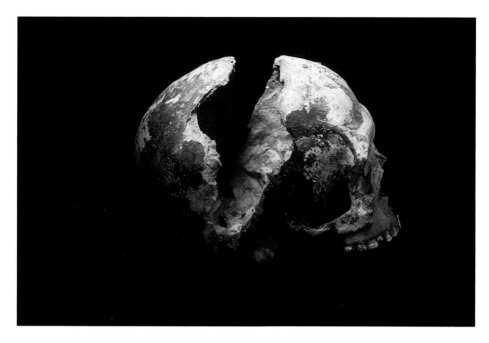

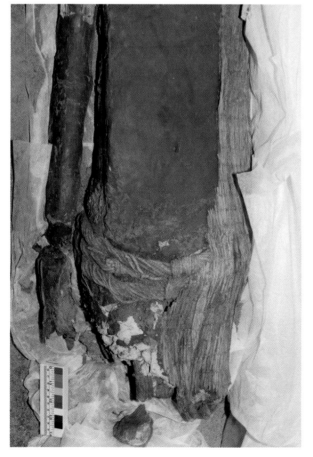

Plate 12. Opened skull of a black mummy, illustrating one of the methods used for evisceration of the brain (M1T1C4, adult male) (photo: B. Arriaza).

Plate 13. Lower trunk of a black mummy, illustrating manganese coat and minimal clothing, worn around the hips. Note umbilicus and reed mat or blanket (M1T1C1, adult female) (photo: B. Arriaza).

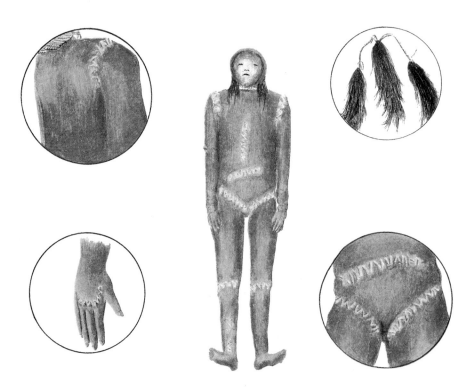

Plate 14. Red mummy showing incisions and hair tufts for wig (drawing:
D. Kendrick-Murdock).

Plate 15. Red mummy head showing helmetlike covering (M1T7C5, subadult)
(photo: B. Arriaza).

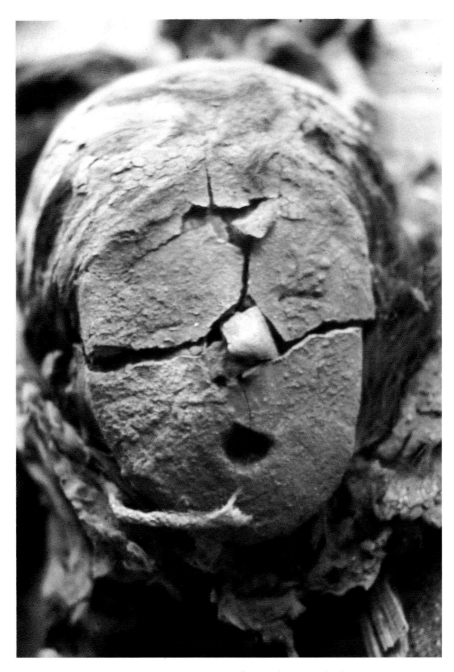

Plate 16. Red mummy head (M1T22C1, infant) (photo: B. Arriaza).

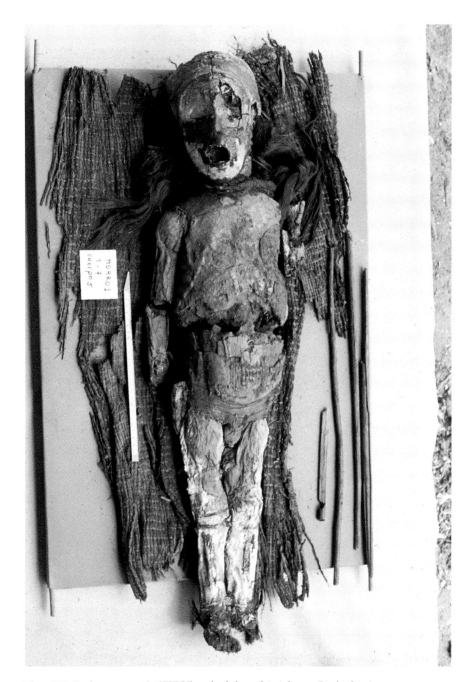

Plate 17. Red mummy (M1T7C5, subadult male) (photo: B. Arriaza).

Plate 18. Mud-coated mummy without evisceration (M1T23C12, adult female) (photo: V. Standen).

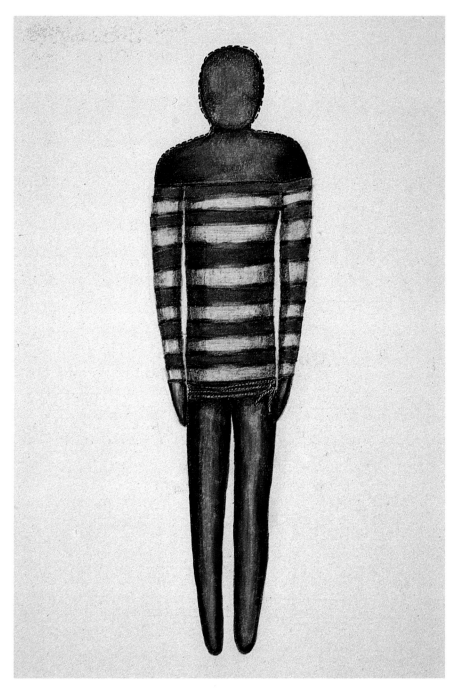

Plate 19. Drawing of a black mummy with red and yellowish stripes (Maderas Enco C1, young adult?). Note cord at hip level (drawing: D. Kendrick-Murdock).

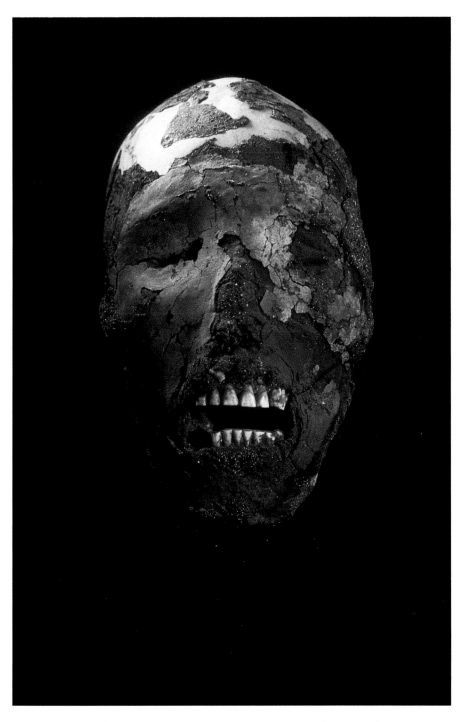

Plate 20. Red mummy head, PLM8 Cr1, showing black manganese mask with external layers flaking off (photo: B. Arriaza).

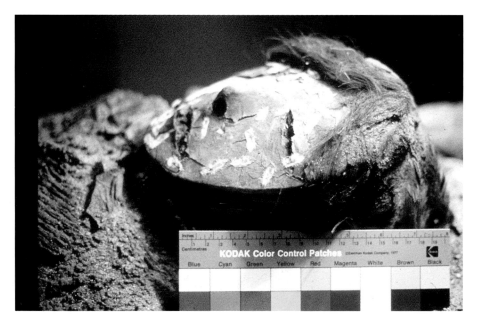

Plate 21. Head of a black mummy during conservation to prevent further surface losses (photo: B. Arriaza).

CHAPTER 6

ORIGIN OF THE CHINCHORROS AND THEIR MUMMIES

 The origin of the Chinchorro culture is still unknown because few researchers have addressed this topic. It must also be stressed that the Chinchorros' biological origin and the origin of their artificial mummification practices can no longer be treated as a single subject. This has created confusion rather than clarifying the Chinchorro roots. These two sources need to be analyzed separately because they are not necessarily related. One is a genetic problem and the other is ideological-social. It will be argued in this chapter that the founder Chinchorro populations had a highland origin and that they did not practice the custom of complex preparations of the dead when they first settled along the coast of the Atacama Desert. Despite past scholarly thought, it also will be argued that artificial mummification was not an external cultural influence. Artificial mummification was a coastal cultural phenomenon that developed in the Arica-Camarones area.

Biological Origin

There are four logical geographic locations from which the Chinchorro could have migrated to the Atacama coast. Listed starting with the least probable, they are the South Pacific islands, northern or southern Peru, an area south of Arica-Camarones, and the east or the highlands of northern Chile (and the Amazon even farther east). Each of these possible locations will be explored.

The first insular option is highly improbable. The Chinchorro did not have boats, especially boats that could withstand high sea navigation. In addition, Easter Island, the closest Pacific south sea island from which they could have emigrated, was unpopulated until about 500 B.C.

Any of the three other continental origins are more likely. Uhle (1917, 1919), the pioneer in Chinchorro studies, influenced by the logic of cultural diffusion of his time and by the fact that the Chinchorros lacked ceramics, placed the Chinchorros as a primitive society that derived from more advanced "Protonazca" Peruvian cultures. Núñez (1969) and Muñoz (1985), basing their studies on similar maritime adaptations observed in Peruvian and Chilean coastal populations, believed that the Chinchorros migrated along the coast from Peru. But if the early Chinchorro settlers were already part of a maritime tradition coming from southern Peru to Arica, then the Chinchorro sites in southern Peru should be much earlier than those in Arica. So far, this is not the case. The few dates from Ilo (Peru) associated with Chinchorro (Wise, 1991) are contemporaneous with the radiocarbon dates found in northern Chile.

A coastal migration from south of the Arica-Camarones area could also have given rise to the Chinchorro culture. Llagostera (1989) described human occupation at Quebrada Las Conchas (Antofagasta, fig. 2) from 7,730 to 7,450 B.C., much earlier than any date for Arica or Camarones. Today, this date from Las Conchas is the oldest one known for the peopling of the Atacama coast. The Las Conchas site had evidence of a coastal adaptation (fish consumption) as well as a unique manufacturing of geometric stone artifacts, but it offered no evidence of mortuary practices that would associate it with the Chinchorro culture. The possibility of a south to north population movement by Las Conchas people toward Arica-Camarones in the north has not been explored.

The most in-depth study to date has been carried out by archaeologist Mario Rivera and geneticist Francisco Rothhammer (1986). They believe the Amazon area was the "mother land" for the Chinchorros. They support their view by comparing late Chinchorro and late Amazonian craniometric data, as well as genetic markers between modern populations from the Andes and the Amazon. The Jivaro shrunken head practice was also used to illustrate cultural similarities between the Chinchorros and the Amazonian people. This Amazon origin could be possible, but owing to the nature of the data (e.g., late cranial samples), their findings may shed light onto the last Chinchorro populations, but not necessarily their beginnings. Though we have no solid evidence to date for Chinchorro social interactions, it is possible that the founding populations were genetically different than late populations owing to interbreeding with other groups.

The biological origins of the Chinchorro people are most likely to be found in the highlands of present-day northern Chile, on the basis of chronological evidence, similarities in lithic technology, early presence of coastal goods in the highlands, and early presence of highland goods on the coast. In fact, Rothhammer and collaborators (1983:163) using craniometric studies found that late Chinchorro skulls cluster closer with late highland Peruvian populations (ca. 1300 A.D.) than with late coastal Peruvian groups. Although no contemporary cemeteries or mummified remains have yet been found in the Chilean highlands, owing to the humid environment, numerous cultural representations left by archaic hunters and gatherers indicate that this region was occupied as early as 8,000 to 7,000 years B.C. For instance, rock overhangs and caves with early rock art depicting hunting scenes are common in Arica's highlands (Dauelsberg, 1983; Santoro and Chacama, 1982) (pl. 8).

Santoro (1993) has suggested that seasonal climatic changes forced the highland hunters to be highly mobile and even to search for lowland resources as a subsistence survival tactic. Although ecological catastrophes such as droughts likely existed, they may not have been the only or the primary force driving early highland populations toward the coast. It is possible, though more difficult to prove archaeologically, that another simple reason brought them to the coast–human curiosity. History is full of examples of explorations and trips by thrill seekers, so why should early humans be the exception? It seems quite narrow to believe that exploration by "White Europeans" was due to curiosity and adventure, while attributing population movements observed in prehistoric or nonwestern groups solely to functional necessities, such as searching for food.

Early hunter-gatherers from the Andes must have had inquisitive minds in order to survive. The magnificent view from the highlands, especially the dramatic sunsets to the west, certainly could have invited exploration of lowland and coastal territories. The early hunters could have easily discovered new environments by moving to lower lands following the trails worn by camelids (alpacas, llamas, guanacos) or cervids. It seems possible that the Andean geography led early exploratory bands to rivers like the Lluta and San José that now cut through the modern city of Arica. The riverain environment certainly would have provided the necessary food and drinking water to sustain the early explorers on their trip to the lowlands. In two or three days a group of hunters could have traveled the approximately 150 kilometers from more than 5,000 meters above sea level to the ocean, discovering a new horizon and wildlife to exploit. Whether the driving force was ecological change or human curiosity, there should be cultural evidence to prove or disprove that early population movement from highlands to the coast did in fact take place. In other words, if highland hunters and the Chinchorro fishers were part of a continuum, highland and coastal tool production (e.g., lithic technologies) should share some similarities. Tool kits would not be expected to be identical, however, because very different ecological settings might require modifications of some tools. Although no formal quantitative comparative stylistic analyses of highland and lowland technologies have been undertaken yet, some evidence indeed suggests a highland-lowland cultural continuity. Acha 2, the earliest Arica site (ca. 7,020 B.C.), had lithic points suggesting a highland interaction, especially the rhomboidal points (fig. 11; Muñoz and Chacama, 1982:54). Rhomboidal points, also called "Tambillo" (see True and Crew, 1980:70–73), were common in other early highland sites (ca. 4,000 to 5,000 meters above sea level), such as in the Salar de Atacama, Patapatane, and Las Cuevas sites (ca. 7,550–6,000 B.C.). The last two sites are from the Arica highlands (Santoro and Chacama, 1982). Even early preceramic highland sites, far from the ocean, such as Las Cuevas and Patapatane, provided evidence of coastal resources like shells (*Choromytilus chorus*) and shark teeth (Santoro and Núñez, 1987; Santoro, 1989:41,43).

The ocean and coastal resources furnished early hunters with access to abundant food year-round. Acha 2 site likely represents early highlanders adapting to the coast, yet an almost completely maritime subsistence was found there. Acha 2 is only six kilometers inland, in the Azapa Valley. This camp was composed of eleven circular huts. The huts varied from one to five meters in diameter and had a hearth in the center. One of the hearths was radiocarbon dated to 6,950 B.C. (Muñoz and Chacama, 1993:28). A naturally mummified body buried lying on one side with legs semiflexed and wrapped in a

52

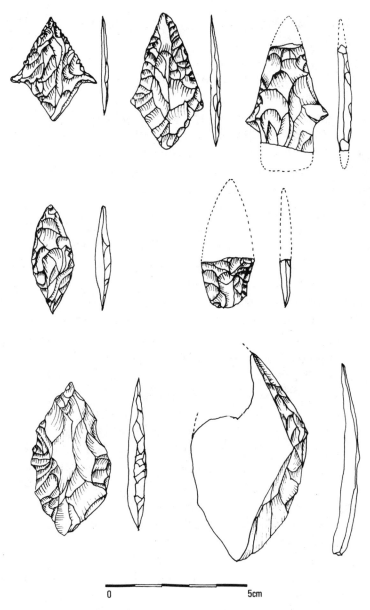

Fig. 11. Lithic points from Acha 2 site (after Muñoz and Chacama, 1982:54; drawing: D. Kendrick-Murdock).

reed mat and camelid fur was also found at this site. The body was radiocarbon dated to 7,020 B.C. (Muñoz and Chacama, 1993:28). Both dates corroborate the antiquity of the site. Although Acha 2 is an early site, it provided evidence of a maritime tool technology (sinkers, cactus fishhooks, and harpoon heads), although hunting instruments (lanceolate and rhomboidal lithic points) were also present. Evidence of fishing gear, numerous shell remains at the site, trace elements from human bone in concentrations associated with a maritime diet, and auditory exostosis also indicate that the people of Acha 2 had an intense maritime subsistence.

The Acha site represents the earliest evidence of the peopling of the Arica coast found to date. It is also associated with the origin of the Chinchorro culture on the basis of continuity of maritime technology and subsistence and the style of burial disposition, which is of an extended body wrapped in a shroud of twined reeds, similar to that of later Chinchorro mummies (Arriaza, 1993a). Recently, two more naturally mummified bodies buried in an extended position and each wrapped in a reed mat were found about 500 meters from Acha 2. These bodies date to about 6,000 B.C. (Santoro and Standen, pers. comm., 1993). Standen (pers. comm., 1993) also commented on the incredible morphological resemblance of the facial features of these three individuals. Perhaps the newly discovered individuals also belonged to the Acha 2 settlement.

The Morro 1 site (6,000 B.C. to 2,000 B.C.) contains evidence of camelid fur and rhea remains (Allison et al., 1984; Standen, 1991). This suggests a coastal and highland interaction. Both species today are native to highland habitats, although in the past both species may have inhabited the lowlands as well.

All the material evidence taken together—the Acha 2 lithic evidence, the acquisition of maritime food by early highland hunters, and the highland camelid and rhea remains found at the Morro 1 site—suggests that, possibly starting as early as 7,020 B.C., the Chinchorro people interacted with highlanders. Continued contact with the highlands may indicate the Chinchorros had a highland origin instead of a coastal one. Future analysts need to consider further the possibility of studying the Chinchorros not only as a sedentary coastal group, but also as a group originating from the highlands.

Origin of Chinchorro Mummification Practices

The origin of Chinchorro artificial mummification practices is puzzling and open to interpretation. An Amazon origin for this anthropogenic practice has been suggested by Rivera (1975, 1991) on the basis of some tropical feathers and seeds found at the site of Camarones 15 (ca. 1,110 B.C.). Even if the biological origin of Chinchorros can be traced back to hunters and gatherers from the Amazon, it still does not answer the question of whether they practiced artificial mummification before moving to the coast.

It seems unlikely that artificial mummification practices began before the Chinchorro settled at the coast. The nomadic way of life of early hunters and gatherers in the highlands of Arica and Camarones or even farther northeast in the Amazon would make elaborate time-consuming death ceremonies such as artificial mummification unlikely and impractical. In fact, no highland cemeteries have been found to support the argument of a highland origin for the complex mortuary practices of the Chinchorros. Contemporaneous Amazon skeletal remains are as rare as they are in the highlands, and the few found so far do not show evidence of artificial mummification (Standen, pers. comm., 1990).

Bittmann and Munizaga (1977:125–126) argued that Chinchorro artificial mummification was a nonlocal cultural phenomenon. Instead, they asserted, it came from the coast of southern Peru. Artificial mummification, they argued, required exceptional anatomical knowledge and high energy to prepare the mummies, and they noted the simultaneous appearance of various new cultural traits such as postmortem trepanation, bow and arrow, and intentional skull deformation. The sudden occurrence of these traits led them to argue for external influence. However, no evidence of these traits in preceramic Peruvian populations was given.

Nor do preceramic coastal cemeteries from Ecuador to southern Peru show evidence of artificial mummification. A brief description of these sites follows to illustrate that this lack of evidence also supports the hypothesis that artificial mummification was not an imported cultural trait, but rather a local Arica-Camarones cultural phenomenon.

Early Coastal Ecuadorian and Peruvian Sites

The earliest reported site associated with a cemetery from the Andes comes from southern Ecuador (Santa Elena Peninsula), Las Vegas site. The earliest dates for this site range between 8,890 B.C. and 8,150 B.C., but cemetery usage appeared about 6,000 B.C., lasting until 4,000 B.C. (Stothert, 1985, 1988). Archaeologist Karen Stothert dug up 192 individuals who were buried with legs flexed and lying on their sides and probably wrapped with a twined mat blanket that was tied closed. None of the bodies exhumed showed evidence of artificial mummification. Stothert noted that most of the interments were secondary burials (N = 157). The skeletons were disarticulated and the bones piled next to a newly buried individual. This most likely took place when a subsequent individual was being buried; thus all the bone piles must be older than the primary burials associated with them. It is interesting that grave goods were rare, but shell spoons, shell containers, perforated shells, and polished pebbles were present. Although some stone flakes were present, projectile points were not found. Analysis of faunal remains indicated that Las Vegas people subsisted by harvesting mollusks that live around mangrove trees, collecting wild gourds, and doing a large amount of deer hunting. Fishing was minimal (Stothert, 1985).

Farther south, at the Paijan camp in northern Peru, dating from 10,845 B.C. to 6,000 B.C., the remains of two skeletons were found buried with legs flexed and lying on their sides (Chauchat, 1988). Bifaced points, Paijan points (points with a long and narrow base), denticulated tools, perforators, and grinding stones were the main artifacts found at the site. According to archaeologist Claude Chauchat, the Paijan people had a maritime and terrestrial subsistence.

Near Lima, archaeologist Frederic Engel (1981:32–33; in Quilter, 1989:71) dated Camp 96 of the Paracas site from 7,000 B.C. to 6,000 B.C. Two burials were found there. One was an extended adult with hands on face and wrapped in a reed mat. Textiles were also present. The other burial was flexed and wrapped in penguin hides. Reed mats covered this body, too. Neither showed evidence of artificial mummification.

More evidence of coastal occupation and cemeteries comes from the site of La Paloma (near the city of Lima). According to archaeologists Robert Benfer (1984) and Jeffrey Quilter (1989), La Paloma dwellers were preceramic and precotton people who lived in a small village about 5,700 B.C. to 2,800 B.C. and took advantage of rich lowland oases known as *lomas*. Over 200 burials were recovered at La Paloma, but none showed evidence of artificial mummification. These bodies had their legs flexed and the hands placed on the face or at the side of the body. Remains of mats indicate the bodies were wrapped before burial, but they were buried with few artifacts. These scholars also found inhumations inside some houses, which could have taken place before or after the houses were abandoned. The Paloma people used maritime resources complemented by gathering terrestrial plants.

In the Chilca site (near Lima, Peru) dating from 3,650 B.C. to 2,550 B.C., fifty huts and fifty-six burials were found by Engel (1984:31–32; in Quilter, 1989:74). The Chilca people buried the bodies in an extended position, lying on their backs and wrapped in a mat shroud. This horizontal mode of interment resembles Chinchorro mortuary practices. Some Chilca people were buried inside the huts in an extended position (Donnan, 1964:141). Some Chilca burials have flexed legs with hands over their faces (House 6), which is reminiscent of the interments from La Paloma. Also, both Chilca and La Paloma sites had evidence of burned skeletons. The Chilca people exploited the ocean resources using shell fishhooks and compound fishhooks (Lanning, 1967), which is similar to the technology found in the Arica area.

The burial pattern of Chilca (ca. 3,650 B.C. to 2,550 B.C.) with bodies buried in an extended position and wrapped in reed mats, was associated with Chinchorro by Llagostera (1992). This association of Chilca with Chinchorro seems unlikely, however, because by 3,000 B.C. in Arica-Camarones, the Chinchorro were at their peak in the development of their most sophisticated mummification techniques (black mummies), but the bodies at the Chilca site showed no evidence of artificial mummification. These dissimilar but contemporaneous mortuary practices between Chilca and Chinchorro may represent not only different groups but also different religious ideologies. The similarities observed in technology between these two groups are likely explained by the similarities in their subsistence bases. Moreover, Chilca and Arica sites are separated by about 1,000 kilometers. In addition, none of the preceramic mummies found between the cities of Lima and Ilo in southern Peru shows any indications of artificial mummification.

A more Chinchorro-like burial pattern can be found in the coastal site of Huaca Prieta (northern Peru), at the mouth of the Chicama valley, where a total of thirty-three burials were found by Bird (1985). Although bodies dating to 3,000 B.C. were buried in a flexed position, three were covered with solidified ashes. This must have been an aqueous ash solution dropped onto the bodies in the grave pit during the burial ceremony. A similar burial pattern was observed at the site of La Paloma (Quilter, 1989:76). These burial types and their associated dates somewhat resemble those of the late Chinchorro style from Arica (ca. 1,700 B.C.), known as mud-coated, although body positions were not the same. Was there any connection between these cultures, and if there was, were the Chinchorros influencing northern cultures or were northern cultures influencing the Chinchorros to cover their dead with mud? Further investigation of this matter is warranted.

In Ilo, at the Villa del Mar coastal site, Wise (1991) reported the findings of six skeletons, poorly preserved, but buried in an extended position. Charcoal samples taken from the associated hearths were dated to 5,850 B.C. and 4,250 B.C. Although no bodies with obvious complex artificial mummification have yet been found north of Arica, the geographical proximity of the Ilo site to Arica and the fact that the bodies studied by Wise were buried in an extended position and had what seemed to be facial paint make the Ilo skeletons culturally closer to Chinchorro burial practices than the skeletons from Chilca, La Paloma, or Huaca Prieta. This association is more probable when the late date of 4,250 B.C. from Villa del Mar is considered, because at this time, classic black Chinchorro mummies were present in Arica (ca. 4,120 B.C.) and Camarones (ca. 4,980 B.C.) (see table 3).

More skeletons have been found in the Asia coastal site (1,500 B.C. to 1,225 B.C), a few kilometers south of Lima. Here the bodies were buried with the legs flexed. An important technological achievement is found at this time: the bodies began to be dressed with cotton textiles, though they still were preceramic people (Engel, 1963, in Quilter, 1989). Moreover, an increase in technological sophistication is also seen in their monumental architecture. Fishing gear in the form of hooks, stone weights, and shell knives were some of the tools used by the Asia people. Coiled basketry and awls were also present. By this time Chinchorro artificial mummification practices were disappearing in the Arica-Camarones area.

In summary, as early as 8,000 B.C., many early and contemporaneous preceramic coastal cultures from Ecuador to Peru reveal a maritime adaptation but no evidence of artificial mummification. Most of the bodies of these more northerly coastal cultures were buried in a flexed position and lying on one side (Quilter, 1989; Stothert, 1988), and by the definition used here a Chinchorro mummy has an extended body position.

The Chilean Evidence

In Chile in Quebrada Las Conchas human occupation has been dated to as early as 7,730 B.C. and 7,430 B.C. (Llagostera, 1989). The Las Conchas people had a maritime-based economy. No evidence of cemeteries or artificial mummies were found. Another early Atacama site with evidence of maritime influence but no evidence of artificial mummification is Tiliviche (ca. 7,810–5,900 B.C.), located about 130 km south of Arica and 40 kilometers inland (Núñez and Moragas, 1978). Although a few bodies were found buried in an extended position, resembling Chinchorro burial practices, most bodies were buried lying on one side with arms and legs flexed (see Standen and Núñez, 1984:138).

The absence of artificial mummification practices in other areas indicates this mortuary treatment was a local Arica-Camarones coastal development. To date, the earliest unequivocal evidence of artificial mummification is from Camarones 14. Here Schiappacasse and Niemeyer (1984) excavated twenty-three burials and found five children with artificial mummification; one was dated to 5,050 B.C. Although the preservation of the bodies was not the best, it was noted that they had facial masks, wigs, sticks in the trunk, and filling materials like twigs. At Camarones 17, Aufderheide, Muñoz, and Arriaza (1993:191) dated two more children with artificial mummification to 4,980 and 4,830 B.C. These sites are so near to each other that they are basically the same site. Not surprisingly, the radiocarbon dates of the artificially prepared bodies are also close. The earliest artificially mummified bodies from Camarones 14 are the simplest found so far; the arms and legs were not elaborately treated compared to later ones. It is doubtful that mummification started much earlier than 5,050 B.C. and improbable before 6,000 B.C. Therefore, the anthropogenically made Chinchorro mummies from Camarones 14 appear to mark the genesis of artificial mummification. From Camarones this practice then spread to Arica, where bodies with complex mummification (black style) from Chinchorro 1 site have been found to date from as early as 4,120 B.C., if a controversial red mummy (M1T7C1) is excluded (table 3). This controversial mummy from Morro 1 yielded two different dates. The oldest radiocarbon date was 5,860 B.C. (Allison et. al, 1984:165). The more recent date of 2,570 B.C. was obtained by Standen (1991:288). Despite this large discrepancy, the more recent radiocarbon date seems to be the correct one, as it clusters well with other mummies of a similar red style from the Morro 1 site that dated about 2,400 B.C. (table 3). This inconsistency could be explained by sampling differences. The first sample consisted of camelid skin, which possibly was as old as it dated and may simply have been a case of reuse of an earlier animal skin by the Chinchorros; the second dated sample was of muscle taken from the actual mummy.

Today, most of the artificially prepared mummies have been found in Arica (fig. 12). So it appears that when artificial mummification reached Arica from Camarones, it found fertile ground and developed to amazing levels of sophistication. In this area, and to a lesser extent south of Camarones, artificial mummification developed to its fullest expression with a succession of different styles of mummification (black, red, bandage, and mud-coated styles).

The Arica-Camarones coastal region, therefore, can be considered as the cultural epicenter of the Chinchorros. From the Arica-Camarones area artificial mummification

58

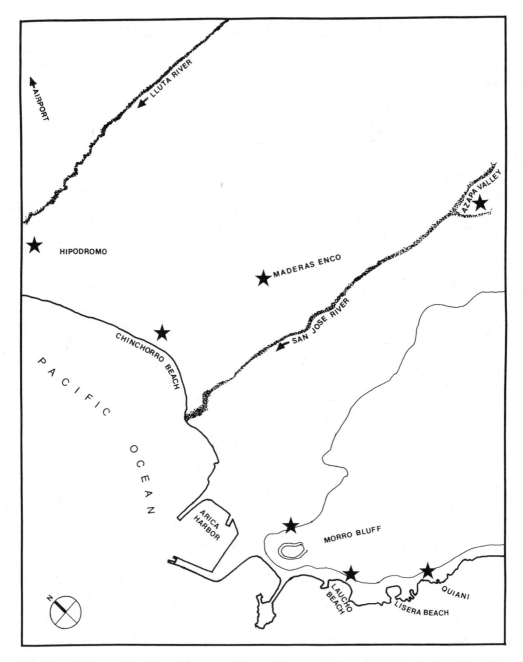

Fig. 12. Main Chinchorro sites in Arica with mummies (drawing: R. Rocha and D. Kendrick-Murdock).

likely spread north and south, because radiocarbon dates for the mummies are later as one moves away from this center, especially from Camarones. In Pisagua, for example, about 150 kilometers south of Arica, the earliest Chinchorro mummies have been dated to 3,270 B.C. (table 3). Nearby in Punta Pichalo there is also evidence of Chinchorro mummies, but unfortunately there are no dates. South of the modern city of Iquique, the sites of Bajo Molle (likely 2,000 B.C); Patillos (likely 2,000 B.C.), Caleta Huelén 42 (ca. 1,830 B.C.) and possibly Antofagasta (no dates) show evidence of Chinchorro burial practices (table 3; fig. 2). (Bittmann, 1982; Núñez, 1969; Olmos and Sanhueza, 1984).

Why Artificial Mummification Developed

Of equal interest as the antiquity and place of origin of Chinchorro mortuary practices is the question of why the Chinchorros developed artificial mummification. Even though hypotheses explaining why artificial mummification developed are not testable, it is useful to speculate on the reasons for its development. Artificial mummification was central to the culture and what made it unique. Child mummification practices, ecological factors, and ideological needs will be explored as possible models for explaining the beginnings of artificial mummification.

Adoration of Children

At the oldest site in Arica, the adult male body from the Acha 2 settlement was naturally mummified (Arriaza, Muñoz, and Aufderheide, 1993; Muñoz, Arriaza, and Aufderheide, 1993). No contemporary subadult human remains have been found there, so it cannot be determined yet if children were artificially mummified as early as 7,020 B.C. But as discussed above, artificial mummification this early is not likely. Schiappacasse and Niemeyer (1984) found children were the earliest (ca. 5,050 B.C.) and only artificially mummified bodies in the cemetery they studied, Camarones 14. Muñoz, Arriaza, and Aufderheide (1993) found a similar pattern at Camarones 17 (ca. 4,980 B.C.). Later, at the Morro 1 site in Arica, adults of both sexes, as well as children, were artificially mummified and buried next to each other. The mummies from Arica (ca. 3,290 B.C. and 3,210 B.C; table 3), however, are much later than those of Camarones.

If in a given cemetery children with complex mummification are found to be contemporaneous with adults without artificial mummification, then this would substantiate the idea that artificial mummification started with children. This seems to be the case at Camarones 14 and Camarones 17, where naturally mummified adults and artificially mummified children were buried together; unfortunately, only the children were radiocarbon dated at both sites. Cemetery reuse can be another explanation for mummies of different styles being buried together. This reveals the importance of dating all bodies buried together with different mummification techniques. The hypothesis that artificial mummification began with children still requires confirmation.

The importance of mummification of children is especially fascinating inasmuch as, generally and cross-culturally, children receive less mortuary attention, especially those who never lived, such as the stillborn. It seems that the Chinchorros put little emphasis on material goods, as these are rarely found along with the earliest artificial mummies. Their focus was entirely on the bodies, and the children may have been especially important members of this egalitarian society. The Chinchorro seemed to honor all human beings, whether they had contributed materially or not to society. It appears initially they gave more emphasis to those who never achieved their potential, like seeds that never germinated. When a fisher catches a small fish, it is customary to return it to the ocean for a second chance at life. This image fits aptly the Chinchorro preparing their dead children for a second chance.

Many reasons could explain the death of Chinchorro children, but because the Chinchorros relied heavily on maritime subsistence, almost certainly the ocean exposed them to many hidden dangers. For example, today in Arica, where the Chinchorro lived, a beach called *Las Machas* is rich in shellfish, but strong currents often take a toll on daring youth who swim or collect shellfish there. It seems likely that drownings or fatal coastal accidents, such as falling when surprised by a large wave while standing on slippery rocks, could have been common among the Chinchorros. The agony of losing a relative, especially a child, probably contributed to the development of special treatment for the dead.

However, not all coastal South American or other maritime populations developed artificial mummification; each culture reacts differently to death, according to its members' beliefs and particular situations. So why did artificial mummification develop? This question is not answered by the evidence pointing toward its origination for treating children. Every group grieves over the loss of a family member, or close friend. But this grief is exacerbated by the loss in a small group, on which the death of one person takes a higher toll. It seriously threatens the integrity of the group. Death becomes genocide. When Chinchorro children died they could have been preserved as an act of love and caring by afflicted parents and relatives, but other factors such as spiritual beliefs could also have contributed.

Spiritual Concerns
Artificial mummification may have developed from purely spiritual needs without involving environmental influences. Preservation of the body was perhaps considered necessary for the individual to travel and enter the afterlife successfully. In other cultures that practice artificial mummification, it is believed the soul cannot survive if the body is not preserved (Cockburn and Cockburn, 1980).

Artificial mummification may have originated as an instrument to reinforce a sense of community or as a way to keep deceased kin "alive" as "active" family members and as interlocutors to communicate with the supernatural to help the living with their daily needs. This model is taken from Inca times when, according to Spanish chroniclers, the mummies were preserved and venerated (Cieza de Leon, [1553] 1959:183; Guaman Poma, [1615] 1980). Consequently, maintaining the mummies to communicate with supernatural forces may have been a consoling response in the face of danger or uncertainties, and the proper and continuous worship of the ancestors might have emerged as a central social function for the Chinchorro people. The millennial duration of Chinchorro artificial mummification practices demonstrates that mummies were functional, and indeed served as powerful instruments of group identity and as means for assuaging communal grief.

Ecological Factors

If Chinchorro artificial mummification started with children, why did it later expand to include adults as well? One possible explanatory model is based on ecological determinism. The dry Atacama Desert predisposed bodies to become natural mummies; thus, the Chinchorros must have observed naturally desiccated cadavers, both on the surface and below ground. This experience may have triggered a desire to improve upon nature, and they manipulated cadavers to achieve even greater preservation than that achieved naturally. The observation of natural mummification could be one factor, but perhaps it is too simplistic an explanation: it does not address why the mummies were maintained or spiritual factors that motivated these unusual practices.

The peaceful Atacama may hold some answers. Earthquakes and tidal waves frequently strike in this area, suddenly creating a place of terror for everyone. For example, in historic times the cities of southern Peru and northern Chile were severely devastated by earthquakes in 1604, 1868, 1877, and 1987. In addition, large tidal waves nearly destroyed the city of Arica in 1868 and 1877. The waves were so huge that some ships landed in the middle of the city. Modern Aricans always fear that a big tidal wave (tsunami) will hit again, just as Californians in North America are afraid of having a powerful earthquake they refer to as "The Big One." Natural disasters like this also occurred in the past (see Schiappacasse and Niemeyer, 1984:21–26), likely generating terror and desperate searches for answers to the cause of these cataclysms.

The direct impact of natural phenomena on the lives of ancient Andean people has been documented elsewhere. For example, about 700 B.C. a tsunami apparently devastated the ancient Peruvian site of Huaca Prieta (Bird, 1985; Moseley, 1992:17; Quilter, 1989:9).

From an ethnographic point of view, the devastating nature of earthquakes and tsunamis as experienced by Andean people were so vivid and powerful that they became incorporated in their mythology, as illustrated in the historical document called the Huarochiri manuscript, from a Peruvian community. "In ancient times the sun died. Because of his death it was night for five days. Rocks banged against each other. Mortars and grinding stones began to eat people. Buck llamas started to drive men" (Salomon and Urioste, 1991:53,#35).

This passage describes not only the horror of an earthquake, but perhaps an eclipse of the sun as well. Another description illustrating the forces of nature in Andean life can be seen in the following quote from the same text: "A llama buck, aware that the ocean was about to overflow, was behaving like somebody who's deep in sadness. . . . The waters covered all those mountains and it was only Villca Coto mountain, or rather its very peak, that was not covered by water. . . . Five days later, the waters descended and began to dry up" (Salomon and Urioste, 1991:51,#30–34).

These quotes, and additional paragraphs in the original Huarochiri manuscript, depict an event that may be equated with the Old Testament Flood; they give a graphic description of people's anxiety in the face of natural calamities. Similar situations may have been faced by the Chinchorros. Some Chinchorro cemeteries appear along the slopes of hills at higher elevations away from the ocean. The hills protected them in the face of tidal waves and provided a sanctuary for the dead. Perhaps this can partially explain why mountains are still highly venerated in Andean cosmology.

The Niño phenomena, which are cyclical changes in the ocean temperature due to warm tropical currents moving into the cold Humboldt current, may be added as another natural phenomenon that created dramatic oceanic disturbances along the coast and upset marine subsistence. Assuming the Chinchorro experienced one or all of these natural phenomena, then hypothetically, any one of these natural disasters costing human lives could have played a significant role in the search for existential arguments and in the development and maintenance of artificial mummification practices. For example, the sudden occurrence of thousands of fish and birds dying as a result of the arrival of a warm Niño current could have been a perplexing event that created enormous psychological and subsistence stresses leading to a search for spiritual help and answers. The creation of a communication medium, a preserved mummy of a deceased relative, now living in the supernatural world, would have been one strategy to find explanations to cope with these mysterious phenomena. In summary, it can be speculated that artificial mummification developed as a sociological response to these natural disasters.

To summarize, the origin of Chinchorro artificial mummification practices was probably multifactorial. Environmental conditions leading to the creation of natural mummies could have been the first visual stimulus. Also, a belief in an afterlife, high frequency of infant and adult mortality (frightening events for a small group of people), natural disasters, tragedies such as drownings, and ecological changes may have all intertwined, influencing the Chinchorros in their need to preserve the cadavers of departed relatives. Maintaining the bodies as a sign of mourning or as a spiritual link to supernatural forces might have paved the way to artificial mummification and to continuous worship of the dead.

CHAPTER 7

HEALTH

 The health of the Chinchorro people can be inferred through the scientific study of their soft tissue and bones. For artificially mummified bodies, most of the soft tissue and organs were destroyed so mainly the bones tell their story. Many illnesses leave permanent imprints on the bones which allow physical anthropologists to reconstruct past health conditions of prehistoric populations. The following evidence was based primarily on the study of mud and natural mummies (ca. 2,000 B.C.) associated with the later stages of the Chinchorro culture from the Morro 1 site.

Physical Appearance

The bones of the Chinchorro people reflect strong muscle insertions, a product of heavy work related to their subsistence economy. However, they were not extremely stocky. The Chinchorro people were relatively short: females averaged 1.60 meters (5'3") and males, 1.62 meters (5'4"). This is generally consistent with the low stature of Andean people, both past and present. The Chinchorro had wide faces without much prognathism, that is, the face did not project forward. Their noses and eyes were narrow (fig. 13). Their heads were mesocranial, that is, neither long nor round. The cranial vault was high, and the cranial capacity averaged 1400 cc, which is the human average today.

Chinchorro males and females had straight hair at various lengths, but males had shorter hair than females. They did not braid their hair as did later cultures from Arica. Braiding did not appear until the disappearance of Chinchorro artificial mummification practices when the Quiani phase began (ca. 1,500 B.C.) (Arriaza et al., 1986a,b). As ornamentation for the head, the Chinchorro children and adults wore headbands made of thick multiple camelid fiber yarns. The tight headbands worn during infancy created a circular depression around the head in the still-malleable bones, producing a permanent skull deformation of annular shape, lasting throughout the individual's life. The cultural practice of elaborate artificial skull deformation became commonplace in later agropastoral communities from this area, with all kinds of shapes and even increased height of the skull. Thus, the local origin of annular skull deformation may be traced

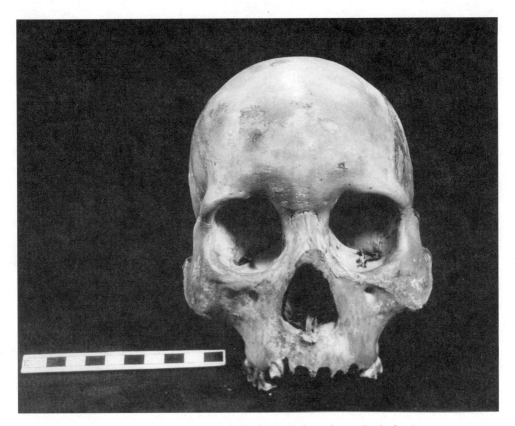

Fig. 13. Frontal view of the Acha man's skull (7,020 B.C.) (photo: B. Arriaza).

back to the Chinchorro culture to about 2,000 B.C. when headbands became evident. The Chinchorro people did not practice any other modifications of the head, such as perforated ear lobes, as did later agricultural groups from Arica (see Allison et al., 1983; Arriaza, 1988).

Demography

At the Morro 1 site about 44% (42/96) of the mummies were subadults, revealing a high incidence of infant and childhood mortality. Twenty-six percent (N = 23) of the mummies were below one year of age (fig. 14). At the Camarones 14 site, 21% died between birth and two years of age (Kamps, 1984:165). This high incidence of infant mortality appears not to be exclusive to Chinchorro, but common to many other prehistoric populations from the Andes. For example, at the contemporaneous site of La Paloma (Peru), 42% died during childhood (Quilter, 1989:20).

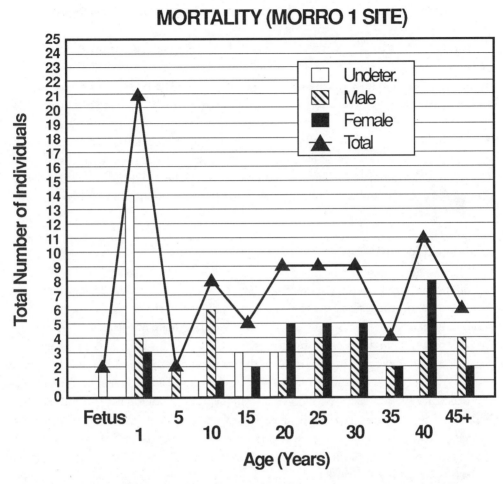

Fig. 14. Mortality curve for mummies from the Morro 1 site. Ages are in intervals of about five years except for the two youngest and the oldest age categories (numbers indicate upper end of each interval, that is, 1 equals 0–1, 5 equals 1.1–5, 10 equals 5.1–10, etc.). Connected triangles represent totals for each age group (graph: T. Cantrell).

The high incidence of infant death decreased the average expectancy of life among Andean populations. In the case of the Chinchorros, if all individuals from Morro 1 are pooled, the average Chinchorro life expectancy was only eighteen years. If only those above one year of age are considered then their average life expectancy increased to twenty-four years of age. Although most individuals clustered between fifteen and thirty years of age, some lived well beyond age forty. At Camarones 14, the average life expectancy for the population of this cemetery was about twenty-six years (Kamps, 1984:166). This may seem to be a short life expectancy, but it is not unusual when compared to contemporaneous people from La Paloma, who lived on average twenty to thirty-five years after the critical risk of childhood death had passed (Quilter, 1989:20).

Analysis of the Morro 1 sample also revealed a similar incidence of male and female death rates (m = 33.3%, f = 35.4%, undetermined = 31.3%), but incidence of female deaths was slightly higher during the childbearing years. The high frequency of fetuses and newborns found in Chinchorro cemeteries suggests a high incidence of miscarriages and maternal death. A maternal death rate as high as 25% has been reported by Arriaza, Allison, and Gerszten (1988) for post-Chinchorro populations. In the face of high infant mortality the Chinchorros must have had many children in order to assure the survival of some. However, if more Chinchorro children were born, then Chinchorro mothers faced greater risks of dying due to childbirth and puerperal infections with each pregnancy.

Childhood Health

Childhood health problems are evident in some subadult skulls that present *cribra orbitalia* or cribriform lesions on the eye sockets. This is related to an anemia, most commonly an iron deficiency type, caused either by inadequate nutritional absorption of iron due to intestinal disorders or by a shortage of iron in the diet. Iron is a fundamental mineral, a central element in hemoglobin, the compound within red blood cells that is responsible for carrying oxygen from the lungs to the cells of all body tissues. When there is a deficiency of iron each red blood cell contains less hemoglobin than normal. The body then produces more red cells in an effort to keep up with the tissue cells' demand for oxygen. The increase in marrow red cell production consequently creates an expansion of the diploe or inner layer of the skull bones, which leads to a destruction of the outer table of the bone, resulting in a skull with a pitted surface. This abnormality can be seen in the eye orbits as well. In more severe cases, the top of the skull can be affected, a condition known as *porotic hyperostosis*. Radiographically, the latter condition is known as a "hair-on-end" morphology because the top of the skull appears like a "crew cut" hairstyle. Twenty-four percent of the children from the Morro 1-6 site had porotic hyperostosis (Aufderheide and Allison, 1994; Focacci and Chacón, 1989:61). This is surprising because marine foods are considered to be very rich in iron, especially shellfish. Therefore, instead of nutritional deficiencies, parasitic infections such as fish tapeworms seem most likely to have caused the anemia. However, the cases of porotic hyperostosis seem to be insignificant when compared to the incidence and severity of late post-Chinchorro populations. A 21% to 30% frequency of porotic hyperostosis was seen in children of agropastoral groups from Arica (Fouant, 1984:176).

Another way to gain insight into Chinchorro childhood health is through the study of changes in bone formation, a condition known as *Harris' lines*. These are observable transverse radiopaque lines seen on radiographs of the long bones. They are related to metabolic stresses that took place while the individual was growing. The etiology of these lines is multifactorial: acute infections, fevers, and nutritional deficiencies could all produce these lines. Despite the lack of specificity, they are still a useful tool for deciphering health in prehistory. About 86% of both adults and children had these lines (32/37 and 12/14, respectively). Chinchorro females had one and a half times more lines than males, but both peak in morbidity (disease intensity) at the age of ten to twelve years. The high incidence of female lines can represent a different pattern of morbidity or an artifact of greater bone remodeling in males.

The average for the Morro 1 site was 4.8 Harris' lines/per positive individual. Other contemporary preceramic populations reveal similar findings. Individuals had 2.2 lines/per positive in Huacho (Peru); 4.8 lines/per positive for Camarones 14; and 6.4 lines/per positive for Tiliviche (Allison et al., 1982a; Quevedo, 1984; Standen and Núñez, 1984). In comparison the incidence of Harris' lines in later agricultural populations from Arica was much higher: some had as many as 20 lines (Allison et al., 1982a:267). Allison and co-workers also found that coastal populations from the Atacama had an average of 1.5 lines but inland farmers and herders had 6.3 lines/positive. The differences in the incidence of Harris' lines indicate that childhood at the coast was healthier than it was inland in the villages of later groups (Allison et al., 1982a; Arriaza, Allison, and Standen, 1984b).

Subsistence-induced Pathology

The range of activities that humans perform is culturally and environmentally dependent. Many of these activities are learned during childhood and practiced throughout adulthood; one example is the selection of types of food and food preparation. Subsistence activities can leave permanent imprints in the soft and hard tissue, providing essential clues for reconstruction of daily life activities in prehistoric populations (table 4).

Zoonosis

Humans can acquire infections and parasites from animals. The Chinchorro were dependent on maritime resources, from which they derived sustenance but were simultaneously exposed to helminth parasites. Paleopathologists Karl Reinhard and Arthur Aufderheide (1990) analyzed the intestinal tract of late Chinchorro mummies and found that 19% of them were infected by eggs of *Diphyllobothrium pacificum*, a tapeworm found in sea lions and fish. Sea lions (*Otaria flavescens*) are the primary host, and fish and humans are the intermediate hosts. Reinhard and Aufderheide believe that the Chinchorros' parasite infections most likely occurred because they were eating raw or poorly cooked fish. After consumption of contaminated food, especially fish, these eggs will adhere to the human intestinal tract where the adult tapeworms can grow four to fifteen meters in length (Vik, 1971:574). Tapeworms absorb nutrients from the body increasing the chances of anemia and resulting in porotic hyperostosis.

Table 4. Synthesis of Chinchorro pathology

Pathology	Total sample	Male	Female
Zoonosis	19% (4/21)		
Auditory exostosis	21% (10/48)	36% (9/25)	4% (1/23)
Spondylolysis	10% (5/51)	18% (5/28)	0% (0/23)
Osteoarthritis	38% (14/37)	33% (5/15)	47% (9/19)
DISH	7% (1/14)		
SNS	4% (2/51)		
Osteoporosis	13% (6/45)	4% (1/23)	19–30% (4/21)
Trauma	16% (12/75)		
Dental cavities	5% (2/41)		
Treponematosis	39% (12/31)	36% (5/14)	35% (6/17)
Tuberculosis	0% (0/66)		

Note: Where number of males and females do not add to the total sample, some
individuals could not be sexed accurately.

The inland people of Tiliviche (ca. 4,110 to 1,950 B.C.) also were infected by
Diphyllobothrium pacificum (Ferreira et al., 1984). This is not surprising inasmuch as the
middens from Tiliviche already pointed toward a maritime subsistence (Núñez and
Moragas, 1978). According to Reinhard (1992:236), this type of helminthic infection
was common to many Andean coastal populations from 8,000 B.C to 2,000 B.C., but as
populations shifted their subsistence to agriculture, the infection of *D. pacificum* declined.

More direct evidence that the Chinchorro hunted and consumed sea lions is found in
the skeletal remains of these animals with lithic points embedded in their bones (see
Schiappacasse and Niemeyer, 1984:71; Standen, 1991:262). Moreover, sea lion ribs
were used to make essential tools (*chopes*) for shellfish gathering, and this tool tradition
persisted until late agricultural times. Helminth parasites, faunal remains, and bone tool
manufacture all reinforce the notion that the Chinchorros were heavily dependent on sea
lions as a subsistence resource.

External Auditory Exostosis

A study of forty-eight skulls of the Chinchorro people from the Morro 1 site by Standen,
Allison, and Arriaza (1984) revealed that approximately 21% of the adult Chinchorro
population, after about 2,500 B.C., suffered from multiple ear inflammations that finally
led to a bony growth in their ear canals. This condition is known as external auditory
exostosis (pl. 7). The bony exostoses are related to chronic irritations and infections of
the ear canal due to exposure to cold water, wind, and diving. The external auditory

exostoses can be round or oval and are found in the anterior or posterior wall of the auditory meatus. This ear problem was an occupational disease, or subsistence-induced pathology, in the Chinchorro people. It was the price they paid for the continuous extraction of marine foods from the cold Pacific Ocean.

The external auditory exostoses were a chronic pathology that worsened with age. Bone irritation started as early as age twenty, and would have led to a loss of hearing and eventually deafness as the exostoses grew with subsequent irritations until they completely obliterated the ear canals. The hearing capabilities of older individuals would have been substantially affected.

If the population is divided by sex, 36% of Chinchorro males had auditory exostoses, while females had only 4.3%. Thus, this pathology was typically a Chinchorro male illness, with a male to female occurrence ratio of nine to one. This suggests that men were doing most of the daily marine food procurement. In the Camarones 14 cemetery, physical anthropologist Silvia Quevedo (1984) found that 16% of the Chinchorro skeletons had external auditory exostoses. Most of them were also males. Even the earliest Chinchorro individual found to date—the Acha man, who was about twenty-five to thirty years of age—presented evidence of well-developed bilateral auditory exostoses (Arriaza, Muñoz, and Aufderheide, 1993).

This ear pathology was also common in other coastal populations from Chile and Peru, but normally absent among inland groups (Bonavia, 1988; Standen, Allison, and Arriaza, 1985). For example, auditory exostoses were common in the preceramic Peruvian coastal villages of La Paloma and Huaca Prieta (Benfer, 1977, and Tattersall, 1985, in Quilter, 1989:21). Consistent with the sex pattern observed in Arica, the cases observed in Peru were also all males. In Las Vegas, the early culture from Ecuador, physical anthropologist Douglas Ubelaker did not find auditory exostoses (Stothert, 1988). This is not surprising as the Las Vegas people exploited maritime resources only superficially. Thus, this chronic ear pathology, along with the evidence of fish and sea lion tapeworms, are direct indicators that the Atacama coastal populations practiced an early and intense exploitation of marine resources. These observations are consistent with the maritime tools found associated with the Chinchorro mummies.

Spondylolysis

My examination of twenty-eight Chinchorro males' spines indicates that about 18% suffered from a particular type of microtrauma in their lower back called spondylolysis. It was found in males as young as twenty years of age. This condition was absent in the twenty-three Chinchorro females studied; hence, it appears to have been an unusually common ailment of Chinchorro men.

Spondylolysis is defined as a separation of the neural arch from the vertebral body and typically affects the fourth or fifth lumbar vertebra. Spondylolysis is not a congenital anomaly, the individual is not born with it, as it has not been observed in newborns.

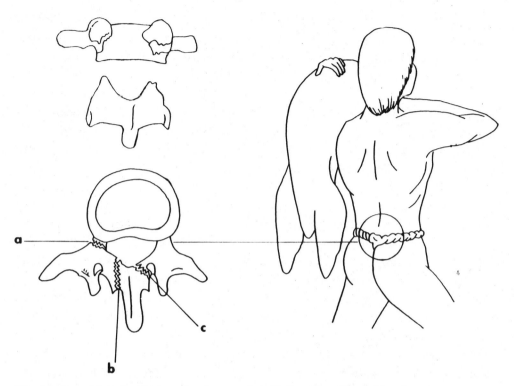

Fig. 15. Spondylolysis affecting a lumbar vertebra. Unilateral or bilateral breaks may occur at: *a,* pedicle, *b,* lamina, or *c,* pars interarticularis. Top detail illustrates bilateral breakage at the pars interarticularis (drawing: B. Szuhay).

Rather it is a type of spinal fracture resulting from accumulative microtrauma that subsequently leads to a fracture of the vertebral arch (Merbs, 1989). The fracture may be unilateral or bilateral. If the latter condition is present, then the vertebra becomes completely separated into two pieces: the vertebral body and most of the vertebral arch. As illustrated, the fracture may take place in various parts of the vertebra, but most commonly it occurs at the pars interarticularis (see fig. 15 for location). In some people, this separation causes extra problems because the vertebrae slip forward, a condition known as spondylolisthesis.

Andean paleopathological studies addressing the presence of spondylolysis are lacking. Perhaps this is because spondylolysis has been considered a congenital anomaly rather than a pathological condition. The frequency of this pathology varies among populations; physical anthropologist Charles Merbs (1989) reported that the highest frequency of spondylolysis is found in Eskimos and Aleuts with 15% to 54% and 23% to 25%, respectively. A high incidence was also found by Arriaza (in press), 21%, in ancient Chamorros from Micronesia. In arctic populations, acute trauma from sledding stresses may account for their high incidence (Merbs, 1989), and in the Chamorros, lifting large stones for house construction was likely the contributing factor (Arriaza, in press). Merbs (1989) suggested that this pathology may even be beneficial to the individuals because the spine gains flexibility.

These spinal fractures or stress-related microtraumas indicate that the Chinchorro men were doing physically demanding tasks. Scrambling over and falling on the rocky coastal areas, and the stress of hyperextension of the back in throwing harpoons and sticks with the atlatl while hunting could certainly have created the necessary stress to produce a vertebral fracture such as spondylolysis. The degree of pain and disability varies from person to person: some feel no pain at all, while others have severe back pain (Merbs, 1989; Resnick and Niwayama, 1988).

Degenerative Diseases

Osteoarthritis

A study of thirty-seven adult Chinchorro individuals by Standen, Allison, and Arriaza (1984) showed that about 38% had osteoarthritic changes of the spine. These changes are typically seen as horizontal bone growths (osteophytosis) on the edges of the vertebral body (fig. 16) or as degenerative changes in the articular facets of the vertebra (osteoarthrosis). Osteoarthritic changes were seen in 47% of the adult females and in 33% of the males. The Chinchorro females were affected mostly in the neck and lumbar areas. In contrast, the arthritic changes in males were predominately in the lower thoracic and lumbar vertebrae. Osteoarthritis of the lower back was also common to the Paloman people (Quilter, 1989:21).

Osteoarthritis of the spine and other joints is usually associated with aging. Accumulative stress during the individual's life results in the wear and tear of the normal structure that protects the joints. This is common in both ancient and modern populations. The severity of the arthritic changes increases with age and abuse of the joints. Osteoarthritic changes of the spine, shoulders, elbows, and knees were also noted in the Chinchorros.

As in spondylolysis, degenerative osteoarthritis can be associated with the hardships of daily life, such as engaging in strenuous physical labor or carrying heavy loads of daily catch back to their settlement. As there was no evidence of camelid domestication at this early time, carrying cargo home must have been a cooperative effort by adults and children. For instance, to bring back the daily ocean catch to a settlement, such as that of the Acha site, the walk with a heavy burden would have been about six kilometers long. For the people of Tiliviche, situated forty kilometers inland, this would have been even more strenuous. Standen and Núñez (1984) pointed out that some of the Tiliviche skeletons had severe osteoarthritic changes. Within a person's lifetime, such daily activity would cause permanent osteoarthritic changes on the bones. The different areas affected in Chinchorro males and females may again denote a division of labor by sex.

72

Fig. 16. Degenerative arthritis of the spine (AZ8 T23, adult female, post-Chinchorro) (photo: B. Arriaza).

When compared with later agropastoral populations from Arica, the degenerative spinal arthritis seen in the Chinchorros was milder and did not start at such a young age. Well-defined arthritic changes were evident in Chinchorro skeletons thirty years of age or older. In contrast, when agricultural practices became intensive, individuals developed spinal osteoarthritis in their early twenties as a consequence of carrying heavy baskets (tumplines) on their backs (Allison, 1985a:124).

Idiopathic and Inflammatory Arthritides

A study carried out by this author shows that the Chinchorro people faced other kinds of arthritides. About 7% had a mild case of a condition known as DISH (diffuse idiopathic skeletal hyperostosis) and 4% had erosive or inflammatory arthritides, specifically seronegative spondyloarthropathies (SNS) (Arriaza, 1993b). These are all conditions that affect the spine and various other joints. The DISH condition is an age-related phenomenon and does not cause much discomfort, as compared to other articular disorders. The seronegative spondyloarthropathies, however, are more severe joint diseases than osteoarthritis and DISH because they cause swelling, pain, destruction, and eventually fusion of joints. Although clinically the etiology of the seronegative spondyloarthropathies is not clearly understood, an infectious component and genetic predisposition are suspected to play major roles in their development (Arriaza, 1993b; Rothschild and Woods, 1989).

Of the Chinchorro cases affected by spondyloarthropathies, one case of a male, M1T27C4, is particularly noteworthy for the severity of his lesions. He was at least thirty-five years of age. The study of his joints reveals a dramatic arthritic condition involving most of his joints with well-defined symmetric erosive lesions. The hands were severely and symmetrically affected. This inflammatory arthritis was severely crippling to him; thus, his contributions to food gathering in this fishing society must have been seriously limited in his adult life. His case testifies to a charitable side of Chinchorro society that provided help to those unable to provide for themselves.

Osteoporosis

The Chinchorro women also suffered from osteoporosis, a metabolic/endocrine disease that causes gradual reduction of bone density and predisposes individuals to bone fracture. Osteoporosis is a common disease in females of advanced age in modern society. Aging and postmenopausal hormone deficiencies are factors that predispose modern women to developing osteoporosis. A less active life may create more fragile bones, inasmuch as bone that is not used is weakened. As the disease progresses the bones become dramatically thinner and structurally weaker. Spontaneous bone fracture may then occur (pl. 9). Because the spine bears most of the weight of a person, a weakened spine resulting from loss of bone density is not able to support the body weight and typically one or more vertebrae will eventually collapse, giving the individual a "hump-back" appearance. Osteoporotic fractures are also common in the hip bones.

In a study of forty-five adult spines from late Chinchorro, about 13% of them were found to have fractures of the vertebral column due to severe osteoporosis. The fractures normally affected the lower thoracic and upper lumbar vertebrae. Females had about 19% vertebral fractures, but considering the thinning of bones, roughly 30% of the Chinchorro females suffered from osteoporosis. In contrast, males had fewer vertebral fractures, only 4%. Fractures were common in individuals forty years or older. Osteoporosis is considered a rather modern disease, thus it is intriguing that at least 4,000 years ago, women were already suffering from osteoporosis, and the reason for this has not been studied in detail. It can be hypothesized that Chinchorro osteoporosis was caused by frequent childbearing, long-term nursing, and possibly culturally induced nutritional deficiencies. Infant mortality was high in Chinchorro so Chinchorro females must have had many children for group survival. In a recent clinical study, researcher Mary Fran Sowers and co-workers (1993) demonstrated that women who breast fed their babies for six or more months lost a significant amount of calcium and bone density in their lower spine and hip bones. Most Chinchorro females had vertebral fractures in the lower spine. Sowers and co-workers demonstrated that the loss of bone density and recuperation was directly proportional to the number of nursing months: the longer the nursing time the higher the loss of bone density. Contrary to expectations, they found that different diets, physical activities, and age did not play a significant role in bone loss. However, undernourished teenage mothers will obviously be at higher risk of developing osteoporosis after menopause, especially if they had several children. The Chinchorros were sedentary rather than nomadic, so Chinchorro females would have had more time and food resources to produce and care for their children. More children meant continuous breast feeding, which, in turn, prevented the Chinchorro females from completely recuperating their normal bone density levels. And if they started to have children at an early age, mineral loss would have increased.

Unbalanced diet may also play an important role in the development of osteoporosis. A diet low in calcium and phosphorus, vital elements for bone formation and maintenance, will increase risks of osteoporosis. Moreover, even if a balanced diet was available, some cultures have food taboos for pregnant or nursing women, unknowingly depriving them of nutrients and predisposing them to osteoporosis (see Spencer, 1977). In consequence, a high birth rate, and likely low intake of calcium and phosphorus, put the Chinchorro females at high risk of developing osteoporosis in their later years.

Although osteoporosis seems to have a long history, it is interesting that its osteopathological pattern has changed through time. In both antiquity and modern times, vertebral fractures are common, but hip fractures are a modern phenomenon. Even today, however, vertebral fractures are far more common than hip fractures. This can be explained, in part, by the anatomy of the vertebral bodies which have spongier bone tissue, making them more likely to be compressed or fractured than the denser hip bones. The absence of hip fractures in antiquity might be explained by the lower life expectancy of Chinchorro people. As a person reaches an advanced age, there are hormonal changes and a natural decrease of bone cell activity; thus, the skeleton becomes structurally weaker. The paucity of hip fractures in prehistory is one example illustrating the price modern populations pay for living longer—the predisposition to many more skeletal health complications than our forbearers.

Bone Injuries

Along the coast where the Chinchorro lived, rugged rocky areas were in places hard to access. But tide pools formed there, and shellfish could have been easily gathered, making the risk worth the effort. The wet rocks and splashing waves could have easily toppled a member of their group, resulting in a bone injury or fracture. Swimming and diving along the rocky coast also predisposed them to accidents. Of seventy-five Chinchorro skeletons studied by Standen, Allison, and Arriaza (1984), 16% had bone trauma that was probably occupationally related. Most of those injured were males.

Dental and Bone Infections

Dental Pathology

The Chinchorro people had a number of ailments as a consequence of their adaptation to a maritime and sedentary lifestyle. However, they did not suffer as much from tooth decay as did later Arican populations. Physical anthropologists Marc Kelley, Dianne Levesque, and Eric Weidl (1991:207) found the percent of individuals with dental cavities in the Chinchorro people was low (4.9%), and the cavities were small (<1mm), but in post-Chinchorro groups, up to 87% had cavities, most being quite large. They also found that Chinchorros lost an average of 1.4 teeth during their lifetime, but in various later agricultural groups from the same region, tooth loss was as high as sixteen per person. Chinchorros had an average of 1.2 dental abscesses per person, but agropastoral groups had 1.6 per person. Overall they found the frequency of cavities and tooth loss increased dramatically, nearly exponentially, with time as reliance upon agriculture increased (figs. 17, 18).

The Chinchorro had a hard abrasive diet that included a great deal of shellfish with only a few carbohydrate-rich plants. Starchy foods and their sugars, such as maize and potatoes eaten by agropastoral societies, increased the chance of cavities. Maritime products, on the other hand, have little or no sugar and have a lot of sand which acts to clean, as well as abrade, the teeth. This decreased the ridges and natural depressions found on

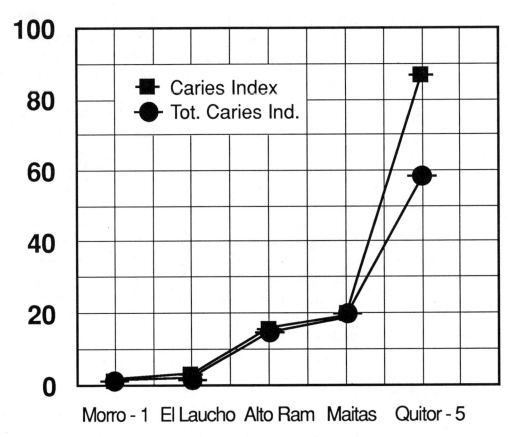

Fig. 17. Caries index for various prehistoric Chilean populations (after Kelley, 1991:208; graph: T. Cantrell).

the occlusal surface of the teeth, thus lessening the likelihood of cariogenic bacteria accumulating in the craggy surfaces. In older Chinchorro individuals the teeth were so worn down that the crowns were completely gone (pl. 10).

Chinchorro dental health was relatively good, but not perfect; the high dental abrasion predisposed them to more dental abscesses. Also tartar accumulation and periodontia, or reabsorption of the bone sockets that hold the teeth in place, were present, predisposing them to tooth loss.

Treponematosis

Other health problems observed in the Chinchorro people include infections, especially in the lower leg bones. Standen, Allison, and Arriaza (1984) described nine Chinchorro individuals with tibial infections; three cases were quite severe. Allison and co-workers

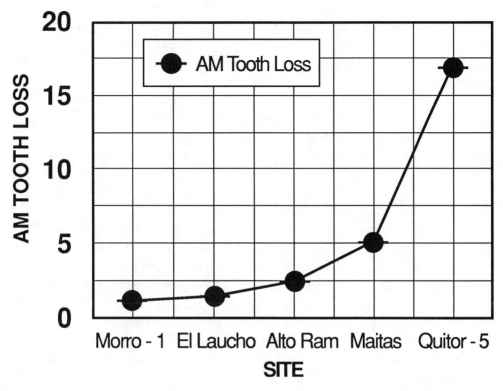

Fig. 18. Percentage antemortem tooth loss for various prehistoric Chilean populations (after Kelley, 1991:209; graph: T. Cantrell).

(1982b) described another Chinchorro specimen in which the skull and long bones had signs of severe chronic periostitis (inflammation).

Unfortunately, the materials used in the artificial mummification process do not allow for adequate radiographic evaluation of the legs and skull of each artificially mummified body. But in a more recent study of thirty-one Chinchorro individuals from Arica, including the previous cases and those whose legs have lost some of their mummification materials, it was found that about 39% of the Chinchorros had evidence of severe periostitis of their tibias. When divided by sex 35% of Chinchorro females were affected and 36% of males. These high percentages contrast markedly with post-Chinchorro populations in which leg inflammations are rare. For example, Allison and co-workers (1982b) described only six cases from agropastoral people among hundreds of mummies examined from Arica.

The affected long bones of these Chinchorros show new bone formation, especially in the anterior part of the tibia, creating an abnormal forward curvature of the lower leg known as "saber shin" or "boomerang" leg. Some Chinchorros have mild leg bone inflammations, while others were greatly affected. In a few cases the bones of the arms were also affected. Radiographically, in most long bones, especially tibias, the medullary cavity was infected and reduced considerably by new bone formation, but the cortex was thickened. During life the legs must have been swollen, ulcerated, and painful.

The bone lesions resemble those caused by the spirochete bacteria belonging to the genus *Treponema*. Today, *Treponema pallidum* causes venereal and congenital syphilis, but out of the four kinds of treponema infections (pinta, yaws, endemic syphilis, and venereal syphilis), only one, the venereal type, is sexually transmitted (Ortner and Putschar, 1985). Yaws and endemic syphilis are transmitted basically through contamination of food, water, and skin contact. They are acquired mainly during childhood, but may remain active through adulthood. Pinta, yaws, and endemic syphilis, unlike venereal syphilis, do not usually affect the central nervous system or the cardiovascular system. All but pinta cause severe bone lesions in later stages. The treponematosis of pinta (Spanish for paint or stain) affects only the skin, leaving colored patches and thereby deriving its name. Among the Aztec, the *pintados,* people with pinta, were valued for their unique skin patterns and colors. The general term *treponematosis* is preferred here since it is not possible to diagnose accurately which kind of treponema strain was causing the infection. The Chinchorro suffered from a treponematosis-like disease because they have the typical signs of treponema infection, the "saber shins" of the lower legs. Mostly young adults were affected. Severe cases were observed even in subadults. One fifteen-year-old male had a chronic infection with dramatic deformation of his lower legs (figs. 19, 20).

The evidence that younger individuals were severely affected by chronic long-bone infections indicates a childhood onset of the disease. From this evidence alone it would seem either endemic syphilis or yaws were more likely the type of treponematosis affecting the Chinchorro. Wounds and abrasions acquired from the areas of the slippery, rocky littoral environment could have added another port for the entrance and subsequent spread of infections on the lower legs.

Recent studies by geneticists Peter Rogan and S.E. Lentz (1994) have found evidence that these osteopathological lesions were caused by treponema bacteria. They were able to extract ribosomal DNA (rDNA) of the treponema bacteria from four prehistoric Arican individuals whose bones had lower leg inflammations resembling treponematosis. Two of the individuals tested were late Chinchorros and two represented post-Chinchorro periods. The rDNA sequence of the Arica spirochetes was not identical to modern spirochete strains, however, but interestingly enough, *Treponema pallidum,* which produces venereal syphilis, was the closest genetic match. This genetic study confirms the osteopathological analysis that the Chinchorros had treponematosis-like infections. This finding may be the breakthrough needed to begin to understand the genesis of modern venereal syphilis.

Fig. 19. Right and left lower leg bones showing treponema-like inflammation and deformities of the diaphyses (shafts) (M1T22C6, young adult, mud-coated mummy) (photo: R. Rocha).

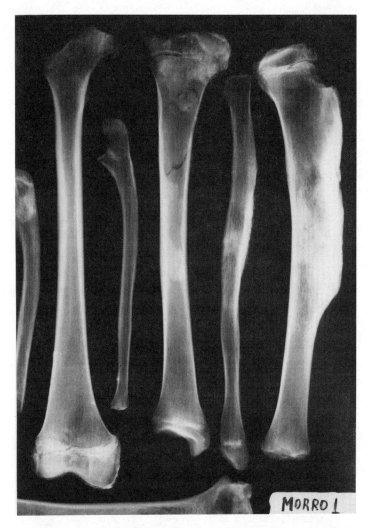

Fig. 20. Radiograph of long bones showing treponema-like inflammation and deformities of the diaphyses and medullary cavities
(M1T22C6, young adult, mud-coated mummy) (photo: R. Rocha).

Tuberculosis

Another disease that leaves a dramatic imprint on the bones is tuberculosis. Many
cases of tuberculosis have been reported for ancient Amerindians (see Buikstra, 1981),
but it is interesting that no evidence of bone tuberculosis was found in the analysis of
sixty-six Chinchorro skeletons. The absence of skeletal tuberculosis in the Chinchorro
contrasts with late Arica populations, in which a frequency of 2% has been found for

agropastoral societies (Arriaza, Salo, and Aufderheide, 1994). The absence of skeletal tuberculosis lesions in Chinchorros may be used as another argument to support the hypothesis that the Chinchorros lived in small groups, as tuberculosis prevails in crowded conditions.

Spread of Infections

The Chinchorro handled cadavers extensively, and many diseases could have been easily spread by mummy-makers who dissected infected cadavers. Potentially, any one of the Chinchorros could have run the risk of acquiring infections, as the diseases could be passed easily from mummy-makers to others. In fact, nine out of twelve tibias with periostitis and osteitis are from mummies that were prepared artificially, thus exposing others to their disease. Of these nine cases, two belonged to the red style and the others were of the mud-coated style. It is possible to hypothesize then that the incidence of the treponema-like infections, which were observed even in the bones of young adults, were either triggered or increased by mortuary practices. It is unlikely children were doing the mummification, but children might have been near mature females who were cleaning the cadaver. For example, if women were working with a contaminated body and a child was hungry or crying, a mother might have interrupted her work to feed, clean a scraped knee, or wipe tears with her infected hands, thus passing the infection to the child. Modern epidemiologic studies have established a precedent for mortuary practices and the spread of infections. The Fore people of New Guinea left the cadaver to decompose, and later, women dug up the corpse and cleaned the bones. Adults from this group suffered from severe paralysis, dementia, and death due to the contraction of a slow-growing virus known as kuru. Physician Carleton Gajdusek, who won the Nobel prize in 1976 for his work on slow viruses, postulated that kuru was the product of cannibalism. But anthropologists Lyle Steadman and Charles Merbs (1982) have argued against this, claiming that kuru was a disease acquired through mortuary practices. They hypothesized that while females were handling the decomposed cadaver, they were also wiping their children's noses, consequently infecting the children with the slow and lethal virus that did not show up until adulthood. A similar hypothesis based on mortuary practice-induced pathology can be argued for the treponematosis-like infection observed in the Chinchorro population.

Consequently, the Chinchorro people probably were continuously exposing themselves to many infections through the handling of cadavers, which may have seriously affected their health. The treponema-like infections were observed in red mummies as well as in the later mud-coated types, so the spread of infectious diseases was endemic or present in the area for thousands of years.

This manner of transmitting germs is not uncommon. Before the understanding of the transmission of infectious diseases in the last century, secondary infections acquired in the hospital were a common cause of death. In the 1700s, doctors were spreading lethal germs by performing autopsies, then proceeding to attend their patients without even washing their hands (Hempel, 1966).

Health, Subsistence, and Sedentism

Anthropologists Mark Cohen and George Armelagos (1984) postulated that the advent of agricultural practices produced a general deterioration in health, and this seems to be the case for the agriculturists of Arica starting about A.D. 100. Agriculture, however, was not the only cause of a general decline in population health. Sedentism also led to health problems. The Chinchorros were a preagricultural society, and the data synthesized here indicates that sedentism, nucleation or village formation, and a maritime subsistence also produced negative effects on a prehistoric population's health long before the development of agriculture. External auditory exostosis, arthritis, spondylolysis, osteoporosis, parasites, and bone infection were common in Chinchorro people, negatively affecting their health and daily life. Moreover, the Chinchorro practice of artificially mummifying their dead may have added another dimension to the spread of infections.

With aging, daily life of the Chinchorro people was far from idyllic. For the elders, the worries of attaining daily provisions and the physical burdens of cold-water diving, fishing and hunting, hearing problems for males, and osteoporosis for females placed them under continuous physical and social stress. The arthritic changes would have caused great discomfort and pain in the joints of those affected, slowing them down.

Not everyone in Chinchorro society suffered from all these ailments. The sexual dichotomy observed on bone pathology and anomalies such as external auditory exostosis, bone injuries, and spondylolysis indicate an obvious division of labor among the Chinchorro people. Males did the fishing and diving while females worked on other types of tasks, including childbearing. However, subsistence was a cooperative effort and both sexes present evidence of degenerative arthritis on their bones.

Unfortunately, when reconstructing the health profile of a population, an extremely negative image is created. It leaves the impression that all these ailments were found at once in every member of the group. This was not the case. As a culture, the Chinchorro people were able to thrive for thousands of years. The Chinchorros represent a remarkably early biological and cultural adaptation to the otherwise formidable environment of one of the world's most desolate deserts, the Atacama.

CHAPTER 8

SUBSISTENCE AND TECHNOLOGY

Chinchorro Diet

The study of the Chinchorro people provides not only knowledge of Andean prehistory, but a clearer picture of early fishing societies in general. Because food is essential to life, pursuit of dietary needs can become a primary determinant of behavior. Hence, the dietary reconstruction of an ancient population provides valuable clues that help define many aspects of its daily activities.

Traditional methods for deducing a group's diet involve predictions based on the study of the environment, tool technology, available plants and animals, and bone and dental pathology. Remains in middens, shelters, tombs, and skeletons provide clues for this study. More specialized studies involve coprolites, pollen, and phytolith (grass crystals) identifications. These methods can now be complemented by analyzing human remains chemically and quantifying individual food groups through measurement of bone or soft tissue content for a chemical unique to certain dietary items.

The soils and some water sources of northern Chile contain high concentrations of minerals, including arsenic. If ingested these can be eliminated through the urine or stored in the body. Toxic doses can cause severe poisoning and chronic damage to the skin and internal organs. Chemist Leonardo Figueroa and co-workers (1988) studied the environment from Camarones and its inhabitants, both ancient and modern, and found high levels of arsenic. At the Camarones gorge, arsenic levels are quite high in the soil, water, and food resources, and it is especially high in riverain shrimp. From autopsies and chemical analyses of thirty-one mummies from Camarones dating to 1,300 A.D., Figueroa's team found skin lesions associated with chronic arsenic ingestion. All the internal organs of the mummies revealed high levels of arsenic accumulation; a concentration of as much as 342 times the normal was found in kidneys (Figueroa et al., 1988:39). The people from Camarones developed a system of high tolerance to arsenic. Eighty-four percent of the mummies presented skin lesions varying from one to five millimeters in diameter, starting as early as age five. In all the affected mummies, the lesions were concentrated in the trunk area, increasing in severity with age. Arsenic is endemic to this area, so the Chinchorros who inhabited the Camarones gorge were likely at risk of chronic arsenic poisoning and related health problems, though no direct evidence has been reported so far for the Chinchorro from Camarones. Late Chinchorros from Morro 1, whose skin was visible, and post-Chinchorro mummies from Arica do not have skin lesions reflecting toxic levels of chronic arsenic (Figueroa et al., 1988). These Arica populations were fortunate because they lived in an ecosystem where the water and the soil had a low arsenic content.

Strontium, another soil element, becomes concentrated in plants. When plants are eaten, nearly 100% of the strontium accumulates in the animal's bones and almost none in the meat. A carnivore, therefore, will accumulate little strontium in the bones, but the bones of an herbivore, such as a llama or deer, will contain a large amount of strontium. Because humans eat both animals and plants, their bone strontium content usually lies between these two extremes. By comparing the human value with that of an herbivore from the same region, the vegetal portion of the human's diet can be estimated, and the remaining fraction represents the meat and dairy product components of the diet. Marine foods such as fish, shellfish, sea lions, and seaweed also have strontium. However, the ocean levels of strontium have a constant value; thus, the relative contributions of strontium from marine and terrestrial sources to the total bone strontium content can only be separated by measuring bone strontium isotope ratios (Aufderheide, 1989; Byrner and Parris, 1987).

The ratio of the minor isotope of carbon ^{13}C to the major fraction ^{12}C differs in the two principal categories of plants: those that synthesize three carbons (C3) and flourish in cool or temperate conditions, such as potatoes, wheat, barley and many fruits, and those that synthesize four carbons (C4) and grow best in warm and tropical climates, such as maize and sugar cane. This carbon isotope ratio value can be used to predict how much of each type of plant category was eaten. For example, a high absolute value of $^{13}C/^{12}C$ generally indicates a heavy dependency in maize consumption. Ingestion of a mixture of these plants will result in a ratio intermediate between the two. However, large consumption of seafood may also result in high levels of $^{13}C/^{12}C$ ratio. The measurements of isotope ratios of nitrogen ($^{15}N/^{14}N$) and sulfur ($^{34}S/^{32}S$) can then be used to separate the terrestrial versus marine component of the diet. High values of nitrogen and sulfur isotope ratios will indicate a diet rich in marine protein, from fish, sea mammals, and shellfish, for example (Aufderheide, 1989; Aufderheide and Allison, 1992; Kelley, Levesque, and Weidl, 1991:212).

Recently, Aufderheide and Allison (1992) outlined the chemical dietary reconstruction of several Chinchorro groups. A total of sixty-two adult Chinchorro individuals dating from 4,000 to 2,000 B.C. were sampled (mostly rib cortex) for strontium analysis and stable isotope ratio determinations. Using the principles outlined above, they found that most of the strontium in the Chinchorro bones had come from marine foods. Indeed, 89% of the Chinchorro diet consisted of shellfish, sea lions, fish, seaweed, and other marine foods. Only 6% of the diet was derived from plants. The Chinchorros did not practice agriculture, so these plants were from wild sources growing along the mouths of the valley rivers. Their dietary terrestrial meat fraction was equally low; only 5% of the diet was made up of nonmarine meat, most probably camelids. Thus, the almost exclusive marine diet of the Chinchorros, supplemented only minimally by botanical and terrestrial meat products, defines a population committed to harvesting from the sea.

The dietary values from Chinchorros living around 2,000 B.C. were essentially identical with those of the early Acha 2 specimen. This suggests little change in their subsistence over an impressively long period of several millennia. Little change in Chinchorro subsistence is also reflected by the continuous use of the same tool technology for thousands of years, the tons of shell midden remains, and the presence of auditory exostoses in all coastal populations.

Technology

Chinchorro maritime technology was simple, efficient, and ingenious. In an environment with no drastic seasonal changes, the middens and grave goods indicate that Chinchorro daily activities revolved around shellfishing, fishing, hunting sea mammals and birds, collecting wild plants, food preparation, and equipping themselves with other material needs. The Chinchorro had a highly conservative maritime tradition, as their tool kits did not change much over five millennia (Llagostera, 1992; Rivera, 1991; Schiappacasse and Niemeyer, 1984; Standen, 1991; Uhle, 1922). This absence of drastic technological changes was probably a reflection of their specialization and success in obtaining marine foods. Also, technological changes were minor because the stable coastal environment did not require new technologies for survival.

The following is a synthesis of the Chinchorro tools and artifacts found in their cemeteries, which reflect their daily life. Artifacts are described by probable-use category, but obviously some could have been multipurpose. The Chinchorro culture was preceramic and presmelting, as these technologies do not appear until after 1,500 B.C.

Shellfishing and Fishing

The Chinchorro collected shellfish in tide pools by diving for underwater varieties, as the activity-induced pathology in their ears suggested. To extract the mollusk from the rocks they used a *chope,* a bone instrument made of a sea lion rib. Similar instruments are still used by local fishers. One end of the *chope* was wrapped with vegetal cords to provide a handle with a firm grip and the other end was somewhat sharpened to remove the mollusk from its shell. To collect the shellfish the Chinchorro people used nets made of totora reeds. These nets were made with plied vegetal string looped in a simple fashion, sometimes applied to several bent sticks that together formed a rounded frame (fig. 21). These nets were also probably used to catch small fish. These types of bags are also locally referred to as "Chinchorro." Reeds to make these bags grow at the river mouths and were easily gathered and spun into cords (fig. 22). For fishing, the Chinchorro used fishhooks

86

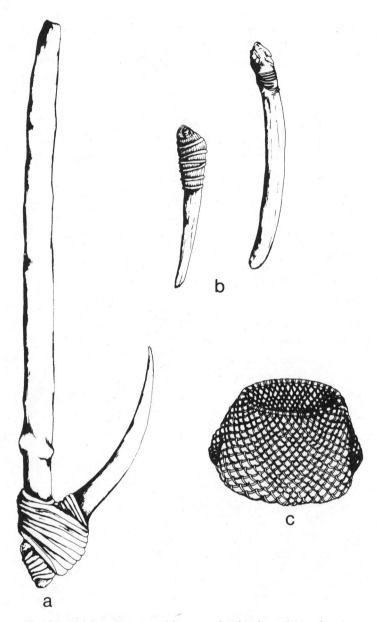

b

c

a

Fig. 21. Fishing gear: *a,* multipurpose hook (about 16 cm long); *b,* two bone shellfish openers (average length 16 cm); *c,* net basket for shellfish and fish collecting (24 cm by 16 cm). (Partially after Llagostera, 1989:62; and Schiappacasse and Niemeyer, 1984:36; drawing: D. Kendrick-Murdock).

87

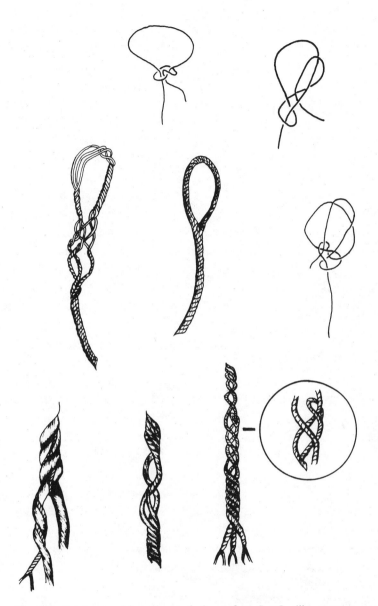

Fig. 22. Cordage and knotting techniques from La Capilla cave, Arica (after Muñoz and Chacama, 1982:24; drawing: D. Kendrick-Murdock).

made of cactus needles or shells, or made composite fishhooks of bone and wood to catch larger fish. The cactus hooks were probably bent while the needles were green and possibly hardened using heat. These cactus hooks have a long shaft and a sharp, nicely rounded hook. The shell fishhooks were manufactured from a core or disk cut from a type of large mussel shell (*Choromytilus chorus*). The shell disks were abraded and polished with stone files until a circular fishhook was formed (fig. 10). These hooks were small, ranging from ten to forty millimeters in length (Schiappacasse and Niemeyer, 1984:27–35). A fishing line was wrapped and tied around one end of the hook. The shape of the shell hook was not ideal, but the mother-of-pearl-like iridescence shimmering in the water and the movement of the small hook would have enticed fish to swallow it.

The composite hooks were made by wrapping and tying sharpened pieces of bone, shell, or cactus needles to a wooden shaft. Fishing lines were made of plied reeds and/or camelid hair, sometimes mixed with human hair. Elongated stone sinkers with a notch at one end were tied to the fishing line to help sink the hook. Sharpened pieces of bone were also attached to a wooden shaft forming a hook, likely for snapping up crabs or other seafood (fig. 21).

Hunting

Sea lions and birds were hunted with harpoons, throwing sticks, and darts. At the Morro 1 site the harpoon heads were about twenty centimeters long, and correspond to the detachable segments of a harpoon. Most of these harpoon heads lacked their lanceolate lithic points; only the resin which had been used to affix the points was left. Lithic lanceolate-shaped projectiles and bone tips were also probably used with spears. Besides hunting birds and sea mammals, the Chinchorros scavenged for larger animals that washed up onto the beach, as evidenced by graves that contained whale bones. The whale skin and bones most likely were used to provide shelter. Whale bones were also used by other Andean cultures. At the Chilca site (Houses 6 and 12) and Huaca Prieta, whale bones were used for house structures or as ornaments to accompany the dead in funerary structures (Bird, 1985:74; Donnan, 1964). Occasionally, land mammal hunting was also practiced by the Chinchorros, likely using the same harpoons and spears (figs. 23, 24, pl. 11) as evidenced by the occasional remains of camelid bones and skin found in the Morro 1 site.

Ornaments and Clothing

Artifacts for personal adornment were few. Most of the late Chinchorro people used small headbands made of spun and plied camelid yarns (z-spun and s-plied) which were then z-plied into thick cords and wrapped several times around their heads. Necklaces of

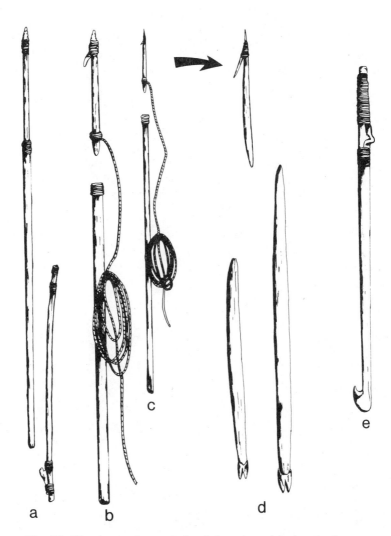

a   b   c   d   e

Fig. 23. Hunting tools: *a,* atlatl and throwing stick; *b* and *c,* harpoons and detachable points (*a–c* about 100 cm long); *d,* two detachable harpoon heads without stone tips (average length 25 cm); *e,* atlatl with thumb holder (length 46 cm). (Partially after Llagostera, 1989:62; drawing: D. Kendrick-Murdock).

90

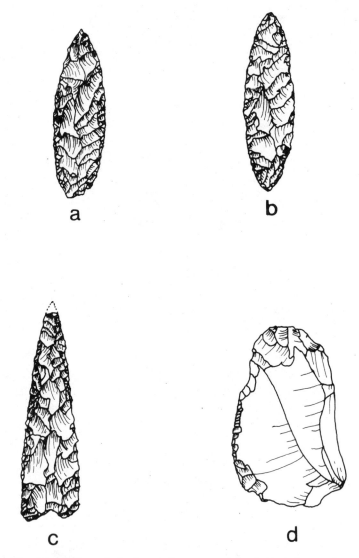

Fig. 24. Lithic tools (*a, b* and *d* are approximately 5 cm long; *c* is approximately 8 cm long) (after Schiappacasse and Niemeyer, 1984:45–55; drawing: D. Kendrick-Murdock).

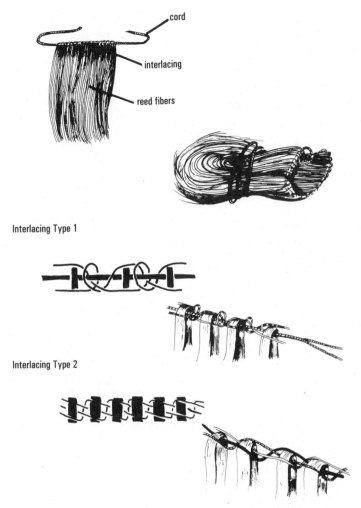

cord

interlacing

reed fibers

Interlacing Type 1

Interlacing Type 2

Fig. 25. Grass skirts from La Capilla cave, Arica (after Muñoz and Chacama, 1982:26; drawing: D. Kendrick-Murdock).

shells were additional ornaments, but were not very common. The few garments worn by the mummies indicate that their clothes were made of macerated reeds, animal skin, or camelid hair. If clothes were worn, males had skin breech cloths while females wore short, above-the-knee "grass" or fringed skirts (fig. 25).

The black and red paint so essential for the artificially prepared mummies may have been used to decorate the living as well. Ethnographically, body painting is common cross-culturally, especially for initiation and religious ceremonies. For example, body painting among the Patagonia inhabitants was extremely elaborate during burial ceremonies (Gusinde, 1937).

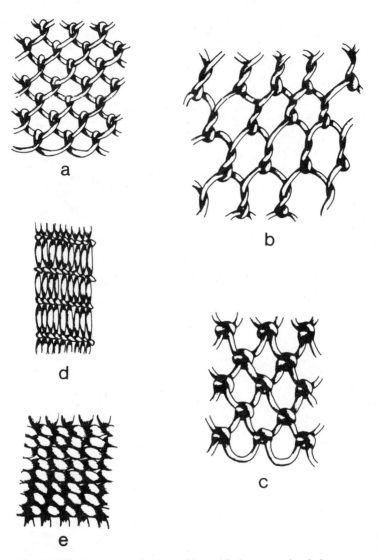

Fig. 26 Netting and reed mat-making techniques: *a*, simple looping; *b*, simple looping with a twist; *c*, simple looping with a knot;
d, spaced twining; *e*, compact twining. (After Schiappacasse and
Niemeyer, 1984:65; drawing: D. Kendrick-Murdock).

General Technology

Long bones from birds, possibly pelicans, were converted into containers likely used as hallucinogenic kits. Similar tubes were commonly used in post-Chinchorro cultures to aid in storing or sniffing hallucinogenic powders.

The Chinchorro also made large twined reed blankets that they used to wrap the dead, but these blankets probably had other general uses too, such as mats to sit or sleep on (fig. 26). One of the smaller mat blankets found at the Morro 1 site had little embroidered geometric designs in purple and yellow-dyed camelid yarns, but all the rest were plain with two fringed ends (Vicki Cassman, pers. comm., 1994; Standen, 1991). Uhle (1922:64) described a similar mat decorated with a red and black ladderlike pattern. Mats may also have served as roofing materials for their huts, but there is no direct evidence for this.

Hearths have been found in the few remains of Chinchorro huts. Does this indicate the Chinchorros cooked their food? The Chinchorro used some form of hot ashes and glowing coals, or smoking process, for the artificially prepared bodies; therefore, it seems quite likely fire was used for cooking, too. Also, the archaeological evidence from the Morro 1 site indicates they had used a fire drill composed of two sticks. One stick was held in place on the ground, with the feet, while another stick was placed perpendicularly, and quickly and continuously rotated either with the hands or with a bow until enough friction produced sparks to light dry grass or tinder (fig. 27). Although clear evidence exists to confirm the association of fire with the process of mummification, no objects associated with boiling or cooking have been found.

Uhle (1922:52) and Bittmann and Munizaga (1979) have suggested that the Chinchorro used the bow and arrow. However, Allison and co-workers (1984) believe that previous scholars were misled by the sharpened sticks used to reinforce the mummies, which may look like bow shafts. Allison and co-workers are likely correct, as the bow that Uhle (1922:52) described was found inside a mummy, and even he commented that the bow lacked the "shoulders" needed to tie the string.

In summary, Chinchorro subsistence technology maximized the exploitation of ocean and coastal resources. The abundance of wildlife, such as shellfish and fish, and a stable environment did not require new innovations for food gathering and survival. Consequently, technology was simple and efficient, with minimal changes thorough time.

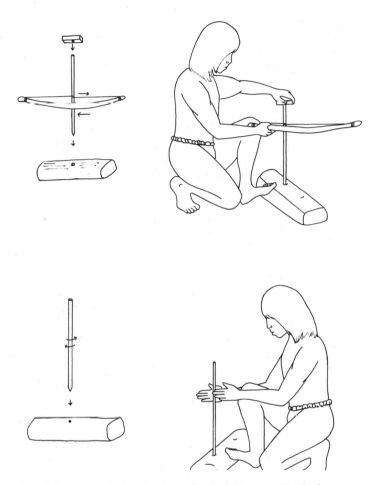

Fig. 27. Two methods of using a fire drill (drawing: B. Szuhay).

CHAPTER 9

MUMMIFICATION TECHNIQUES

 Uhle's (1919) classification of the Chinchorro mummies into three main types, natural, complex, and mud-coated, has served as the guide for the descriptions of most Chinchorro mummies found to date. Although variations from Uhle's typology have been noted, few attempts have been made to update it. In 1983, the cache of mummies found at the Morro 1 site provided an excellent opportunity to check Uhle's typology. His three-way classification system was found to be still valid, but numerical subtypes were created to illustrate the variation found within each category (Allison et. al., 1984; Arriaza et al., 1986a). These numerical subtypes, although useful, lacked attributes to make them easily recognizable, and they were not of practical use to scholars unfamiliar with the Chinchorro mummies. Thus, in 1993 Arriaza introduced a new classification system changing numerical categories to names related to color and mummification type (Arriaza, 1993a). The new typological approach includes black, red, bandage, mud-coated, and natural mummification styles (table 5, pl. 6, fig. 28). In this classification the black, red, and bandage mummies fit within Uhle's complex mummy category, and Uhle's mud and natural categories have basically remained the same. Additionally, in Arriaza's view there are two main types of artificial mummification: the complex mummies and mud-coated styles. This more inclusive view of artificial mummification contrasts with previous studies that have monopolized the term Chinchorro mummies for the complex artificial mummies only (e.g., black style). Chronologically, the complex types were the oldest, followed by the mud-coated types. The naturally mummified bodies were found to both predate and postdate the mummies with artificial mummification.

Of all the styles of artificial mummification, the black was the most complex. The black mummies were like statues that were internally built up from a reinforced skeletal framework. In contrast, many of the red mummies were stuffed without disarticulation, and the bandage mummies were a variation of the red. The mud-coated style was the simplest form of artificial mummification, and as the name indicates, involved plastering bodies with a special mud layer. Two types of mud mummies were found: one with evisceration and one without.

Table 1 shows that of a total of 282 Chinchorro mummies mentioned in the literature, it can be estimated that about 47% (133/282) were naturally mummified and

Table 5. Basic features of Chinchorro mummies by type

Treatment	Black	Striped	Red	Bandage	Mud 1 evis.	Mud 2 no evis.	Natural
HEAD							
Headband	—	?	X	—	?	X	X
Nonhuman skin head cap	X	?	—	X	?	—	—
Face:							
Presence facial features	X	X?	X	X	?	—	X
Removal of facial tissue	X	X	X	X	X?	—	—
Black face slip (Mn)	X	X?	X	X	X?	—	—
Embedded human skin	X	X?	X	—	—	—	—
Ash paste modeling below facial skin	X	X?	X	—	—	—	—
Skull:							
Cranium cut open	X	X?	X?	?	—	—	—
Cranium evisceration	X	?	X	X	—	—	—
Cranium filling	X	X	X	X?	—	—	—
Skull tied closed	X	X?	X?	?	—	—	—
Mn skull cap painted red	—	?	X	X	?	—	—
Short hair/scalp replaced	X	X?	—	—	—	—	—
Human hair wig	—	—	X	X	?	—	
Long hair (> 20 cm)	—	—	X	X	—	—	—
TRUNK & EXTREMITIES							
Mud layer head to toe	—	—	—	—	X?	X	—
Body painted black (Mn)	X	X	—	—	—	—	—
Body painted red (Fe)	—	X	X	X	—	—	—
Sex organs visible	X	X	X	—	—	—	X
Sex organs modeled	X	X	—	—	—	—	—
Genital covering	X	—	X	—	—	X?	X
External cord/skin joint wrappings	—	—	X	X	—	—	—
Interlaced cords at fingers & toes	—	—	—	—	—	X	X
Incisions/sutures	—	—	X	—	—	—	—
Evisceration	X	X	X	X	X	—	—
Trunk stuffing	X	X	X	X	X	—	—
Trunk modeling	X	X	—	X	—	—	—
Total skin removal	X	X	—?	X	—	—	—
Skin replacement	X[1]	—	X?	X	—	—	—

Table 5. (*Continued*)

Treatment	Black	Striped	Red	Bandage	Mud 1 evis.	Mud 2 no evis.	Natural
Ext. patches sea lion skin	X	—	X	—	—	—	—
Partial bone defleshing	—	—	X	—	—	—	—
Total bone defleshing	X	X	—	X?	—	—	—
Bone condyles abraded	X	X?	—	—	—	—	—
Internal joint wrapping	X	X	—	—?	—	—	—
Extremities modeled with ash paste/cord/mat	X	X	—	—	—	—	—
Extremities stuffed misc.	—	—	X	—	—	—	—
Stick spine splint	X	X	X	X	—	—	—
Skeletal framework sticks and reeds	X	X	—	X?	—	—	—
Longitudinally inserted sticks for arms, legs & spine	—	—	X	—	—	—	—
Twined vegetal shroud	X	X	X	?	—	?	X
Total # observations	28	24	27	19	5	4	6

Codes: X = presence of treatment; X? = probable presence of treatment; — = absence of treatment; —? = probable absence of treatment; ? = not enough evidence to tell

1. In some black mummies, the skin seemed to have been replaced in patches; in others, no human skin was found between the ash-paste modeling surface and the black manganese slip.

53% (149/282) were artificially mummified. The following detailed description of the main Chinchorro mummy types synthesizes previous studies (after Allison et al., 1984; Arriaza, Allison, and Standen, 1984a; Arriaza et al. 1986a; Bittmann, 1982; Bittmann and Munizaga 1976; Núñez, 1969).

Simple Treatment (Natural Mummification)

This particular treatment refers to mummies produced by exposure to the desiccating environment of the Atacama Desert. In this arid region, after burial, body fluids evaporate quickly owing to the dryness of the climate, especially when the corpse comes in contact with the soil and desert salts that exert an osmotic effect and act as natural preservatives, retarding decomposition. In these corpses no special additives were used to intentionally preserve the body. These mummies were found buried in an extended position and wrapped with reed mats and camelid furs. They were buried lying on their

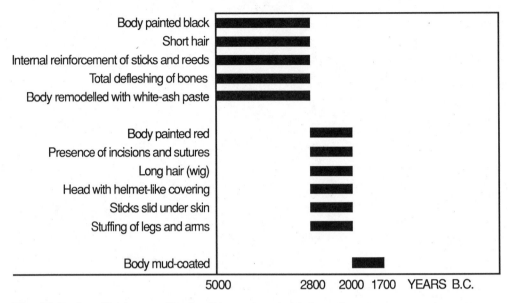

Fig. 28. Basic artificial mummification features (graph: T. Cantrell).

backs, some with the legs slightly flexed. Grave goods such as stone knives, shells, fishhooks, and fishing nets were included with some. A minimum of 133 mummies of this type have been found. Most come from the Morro area and Camarones 14 site (table 1).

Complex Treatment (Artificial Mummification)

In the complex Chinchorro mummies the entire cadaver was treated both internally and externally. The three subtypes of Chinchorro complex mummies—*black, red,* and *bandage*—can be loosely considered as the "typical" Chinchorro mummies. They are differentiated not only by their external appearance, but by their internal treatment as well (table 5, fig. 29). Even fetuses were artificially mummified, and these are referred to as *statuette mummies* (fig. 3). Most of these complex mummies come from northern Chile, from Arica to Iquique (fig. 2).

Black Mummies

Black mummies were externally painted with a black manganese coating, hence their name (fig. 29). They were the most complex of all. To make these black mummies, the

Fig. 29. Upper trunk of an artificially prepared black mummy from Arica (M1T1C1, adult female). Note inner layer of unbaked white-ash paste and reeds in destroyed area of right shoulder. Breasts were modeled (photo: B. Arriaza).

body was altered to such an extreme that they were converted into sophisticated statues or death images because of the reinforcement of their inner skeletal structure and removal of most of the soft tissue. They were literally disassembled and reconstructed bodies.

The following is an anatomical description, starting with the head, of how the mummification process may have proceeded for this black style; however, mummy makers may have worked simultaneously on different anatomical parts of the cadaver rather than in the same order as given here. The basic steps involved were as follows. The head was decapitated and extremities removed from the trunk. Often the skin was completely removed, except for areas which were difficult to deflesh or where there was less muscle, such as in the fingers and toes. The hands and feet could have been dried by heat, temporarily buried to induce desiccation or salted to avoid decomposition. The body was completely defleshed and eviscerated, leaving a clean skeleton that was dried with hot ashes or glowing coals, as the evidence of some burned bones indicates. Using stone knives, the head was scalped, defleshed, and then the skull was cut in half on a transverse plane, and the brain extracted (pl. 12). Later, after the cranial cavity was dried and filled with grass, ashes, soil, animal hair, or a mixture of these materials, the two halves of the

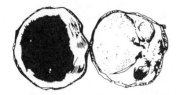  

Fig. 30. Steps taken in the assembly of the head of a complex, artificially mummified black mummy. *Top: left,* skull opened, brain extracted, and filled; *center,* skull tied together; *right,* application of white-ash paste. *Bottom: left,* facial skin replacement and wig addition; *center,* manganese coating; *right,* external reinforcement with ropes. (Drawing: R. Rocha and D. Kendrick-Murdock).

skull and the mandible were tied together to secure them (fig. 30). A white-ash paste was spread on top of the facial bones to model the face and bring back the original volume.

In some mummies, the prominent parts of the defleshed bones, such as those of the humeri and femora, were abraded or cut away in order to reduce bulk and facilitate reassembly (fig. 31). The joints were wrapped or bound together with vegetal cords (fig. 32). Three longitudinal sticks, roughly 1.5 centimeters in diameter, were used to secure the body, one for each leg and one for the spine. The sticks for the legs extended from the ankle of each leg, passing through the pelvis, chest, and along the neck to insert into the head through the foramen magnum, at the base of the skull (fig. 32). The stick for the spine extended from the foramen magnum to the sacrum. The tips of the three sticks were wrapped with cords and introduced into the foramen magnum, in order to reattach the head to the trunk. White-ash paste on the neck filled out and hid the manner of reattachment.

In the legs the sticks and bones were tightly wrapped together with cords made from reeds to provide rigidity to the skeletal framework (figs. 32, 33). Sometimes, pieces of mats were also added along the legs to give the limb strength and volume before being wrapped with cords. Similar procedures were used on the arms, except that twigs or

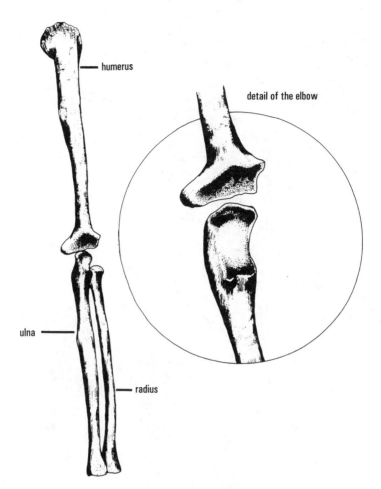

Fig. 31. Filed eminences of long bones which allowed them to be overlapped and wrapped tightly (drawing: R. Rocha and D. Kendrick-Murdock).

reeds, instead of sticks, were occasionally used to secure the arms to the trunk. The bundles of reeds, originating at the wrist level of one arm, extended up through the length of the arm, passed through the chest, across the shoulders and clavicles, and then descended to the other wrist. At this point, the hands and feet, if disarticulated, were tied back together and secured at the wrists and ankles, respectively.

In general, after reinforcement of the skeleton with sticks and cords and reattachment of the head by means of the longitudinal sticks and cord wrapping, the face, neck, trunk, extremities, and genitals were modeled with white-ash paste, embedding the bones, sticks, and cords (figs. 33, 34). This paste restored to some extent the volume taken away by initial processing. Following this, the skin was put back in patches. In a few cases the skin appears so intact it seems as though it had been rolled off along the extremities and

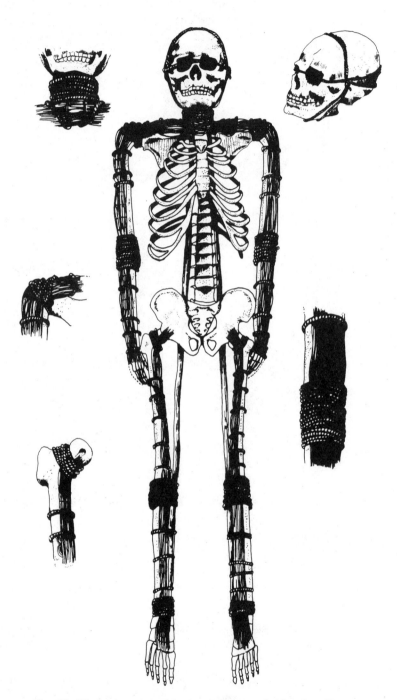

Fig. 32. Black mummy and its inner framework (drawing: R. Rocha and D. Kendrick-Murdock).

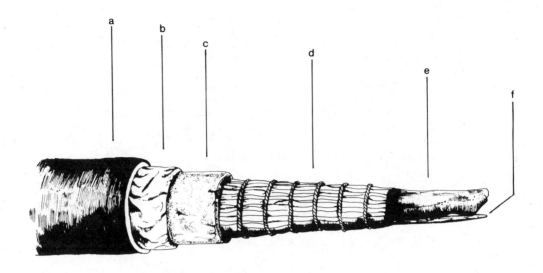

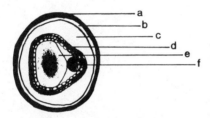

Fig. 33. Detail of a black mummy's long bone, showing various layers: *a*, manganese slip; *b*, skin; *c*, white-ash paste; *d*, reed wrapping; *e*, bone, *f*, wooden stick (drawing: D. Kendrick-Murdock).

then rolled back on again. In other cases, especially children, the skin appears to be missing.

After the facial volume was restored with the ash paste, in some cases the intact facial skin was skillfully replaced. A scalp with short black human hair was placed on the head. It was most probably the individual's own hair because in some cases patches of hair were still attached to the skull. Ash paste and pieces of sea lion skin were added to secure the replaced scalp to the head. In some mummies, patches of sea lion skin were also added to the rest of the body, under the final manganese coat.

After the head was in place, the finished mummy was completely painted black with a thick coat of manganese paint. In the case of the children, who are missing the skin, the black paint was applied directly on top of the white-ash paste. A thicker black paint was generally used over the replaced facial skin permitting some modeling of the eyes, nose, and mouth. In some mummies, the black facial coat is thin and the original skin can be

104

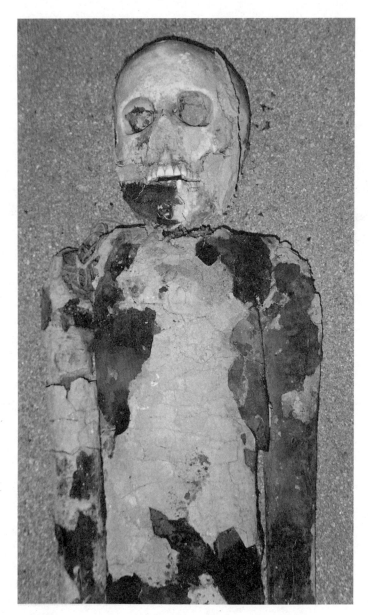

Fig. 34. Black Chinchorro mummy from Arica (adult male) showing white-ash paste filling. Museum of Natural History, Valparaiso, Chile (photo: B. Arriaza).

seen; in other mummies, however, it is thick and where the outer manganese paint layer has chipped off, older layers of the paint can be seen. Finally, in a few cases, a breech cloth or fringe skirt was added to the body after the manganese paint had dried (pl. 13).

Comments

Fishers are extremely skillful in skinning and dismembering their catch; as a consequence, the Chinchorro men and women had a basic anatomical knowledge that helped them manipulate cadavers. The skinning and dismembering of the bodies in preparation for making black mummies was expertly done. It is worth pointing out that no obvious cut marks from dismembering have been found, such as those related to defleshing and tendon removal. Either the morticians were extremely skilled at removing soft tissue without leaving any signs, or after the skin was removed, the body was allowed to decompose, possibly in a location where insects, birds, and humidity could speed up the cleaning process. In either case the end result was a skeletonized and disarticulated body. Unfortunately, the cut marks have not been studied in detail because most of the bone joints are still covered by mummification materials; therefore, it is difficult to say with certainty how the bodies were dismembered. Meanwhile, the removed skin could have been dried or preserved in a tide pool of salty water before replacement, or not preserved at all, as may have been the case with children. Skin removal and replacement on the faces of some black mummies were carefully done. In contrast, it appears that skin from the back of the trunk of adults was not always removed. Perhaps leaving the skin from the back in place in some way facilitated the stuffing and reassembly process. Skin from the extremities was not always replaced. It is also interesting that no obvious sutures have been observed in these black mummies. The ash paste and manganese paint would have acted as natural adhesives to keep the replaced mummy's skin in place.

The treatment that produced a black mummy was not identical in each case. The slight idiosyncratic variations among these mummies may correspond to different periods of preparation, the personal style of the mummy makers, or intergroup variation. The sticks for the spine, for instance, were placed either inside the spinal canal, anterior to the vertebral body, or next to the spinous process of the vertebral column. A few black mummies have been found without the black coat of manganese on the face. This may represent individual variations, or for some unknown reason, the mummies may not have been completely finished. Or perhaps the outer thick coating had simply flaked off.

The subadult black mummies also show variation; they tend to have a tubular or rectangular form, unlike their original anatomical shape. This could be because bodies of younger individuals have a more fragile infrastructure, so the morticians were not always able to maintain the normal anatomical proportions. Therefore, extra bones or sticks sometimes were added to give rigidity and attempt to somewhat restore anatomical proportions.

When the black mummy was finished, it was rigid enough to be easily transported to a ceremonial place. Some of the mummies show signs of repainting, suggesting that they were probably kept as death images in the settlement for long periods. And the mummies appear to have been buried in family groups after a certain period of time elapsed. They were wrapped or deposited in a mat shroud and then buried in a shallow grave, lying on their backs; some were unclothed.

In a technical sense, a black mummy, with its skeletal and wooden inner frame, intermediate reeds and ash paste layers, and external layers of human or sea lion skin covered with black paint, was more like a statue or a death image than a true mummy. Despite the simplicity of the mummification elements, these anthropogenic figures were beautiful and complex works of art.

The black treatment was given to adults and subadults of both sexes. At least twenty indisputable black mummies have been found, from five sites: the best preserved examples are eight mummies from the Morro 1 site (Allison et al., 1984), three out of four mummies from Arica described by Vera (1981), five from Chinchorro 1 and Camarones 17 sites (Aufderheide, Muñoz, and Arriaza, 1993), three from Maderas Enco, and one from the Arica hippodrome area (tables 1, 6).

Today, these black mummies are extremely fragile owing to disintegration of the unbaked clay pastes (fig. 34). But in the past they were obviously solid and heavy. They must have equaled the weight of the living individual. It is important to indicate that the dry unbaked ash paste could crumble away easily leaving no obvious signs that the clean bones were once a part of a complex mummy. However, cut marks and abrasions of the eminences of the long bones may provide clues that the bare bones belonged to a complex black mummy.

Red Mummies

The morticians utilized a variety of sophisticated procedures and techniques in making the red mummies. Using stone knives, incisions were made at the shoulder, abdomen, and groin level to partially or completely remove the inner organs and sometimes most of the muscle tissue from the body. The corpses were not disarticulated to the same extent as those of the black mummies. In the red mummies the cavities appear slightly burned, indicating they were most likely dried with glowing coals, as evidenced by charred remains found in the body cavities. As with the black mummies, in some cases it appears as if the skin of the legs and arms was rolled down, like a sock, and rolled back up again. In most cases, however, the skin was not completely removed; incisions were made through the skin for organ and muscle removal and then sewn back together. The head was separated from the trunk. The bones of the arms and legs were not abraded as in the black mummies, and apparently the body of a red mummy was not completely dismembered. The skull was usually emptied through the foramen magnum and stuffed with the same materials used for stuffing the body. Along the legs, arms, and trunk, sticks were slid under the skin to add rigidity to the body.

The body was then stuffed with a mixture of materials which may have included white or black ashes, camelid hair, feathers, grass, animal and bird skin, and soil, in an attempt to reshape the body to its original form. The metacarpal and metatarsal area of hands and feet, respectively, were cleaned of the muscle and stuffed with camelid fiber or soil to give them added volume.

At this point the head was reattached and the face modeled with white-ash paste as seen in the black mummies. The facial skin was replaced on top of this paste, and a coat of manganese paint was added on top of the skin. On the head a long wig made of tufts of black human hair, some as long as sixty centimeters, was added (pl. 14). It was affixed with a thick layer of manganese paint following the contour of the head. The result looks like a tight-fitting black helmet (pl. 15). This black clay helmet was subsequently painted red, as was the rest of the body. The face was left black, but other colors such as reddish black also can be found (pl. 16).

One of the last steps was to sew up the incisions at the shoulders, wrist, abdomen, and groin using thread of human hair or reed yarns (pl. 14). This contrasts with the black mummies in whom neither main incisions nor sutures have been observed, since they were completely disarticulated. The external joints of the red mummies were reinforced and bound with thin strips of animal skin (rawhide) or reed cords, especially at the wrists, ankles, and neck. This helped prevent the extremities from falling off. Sometimes loincloths were added, either before or after the application of red paint. In some cases, this cloth also served the function of giving extra support to the trunk. The finished red mummies were found wrapped in a vegetal mat shroud or camelid furs (pl. 17).

Comments

X-ray fluorescence analysis by Janice Carlson, at the Winterthur Museum Analytical Laboratory, indicates that the red paint used on the mummies was basically iron oxide and the black was manganese. These minerals were obtained locally. In general, the treatment of the red mummies' heads was more complex than that of the black mummies'. The wig of a red mummy held in place with a black manganese helmet is quite distinct from the scalp of a black mummy attached with sea mammal skin and ash paste. However, the face of both red and black mummies was commonly painted black. Also both the red and black styles shared the use of sticks for reinforcement (figs. 35, 36), but the internal treatment of the black mummies was far more complex.

The red mummies, like the black, were solid, heavy, and easily transportable. Likewise, adult and subadult red mummies of both sexes have been found. At least eighty-two red mummies can be counted in the literature from seven sites (tables 1 and 6): nine at Morro (Uhle, 1922), twenty-seven from Morro 1 (Allison et al., 1984), sixteen from Morro 1-5 (Guillen, in press), nine at Playa Miller 8 (Alvarez, 1969; Vera, 1981), one from Quiani (Bird, 1943:246), one from Punta Pichalo (Bird, 1943:246), one from Camarones 8 (Aufderheide, Muñoz, and Arriaza, 1993), five from Bajo Molle (Schaedel, 1957:71–72), and thirteen from Patillos (Nielsen collection). Variations within the red mummy types include those with treatment concentrated mostly in the trunk or with red painted surfaces only, such as seen at the Morro 1-5 site (figs. 37, 38).

108

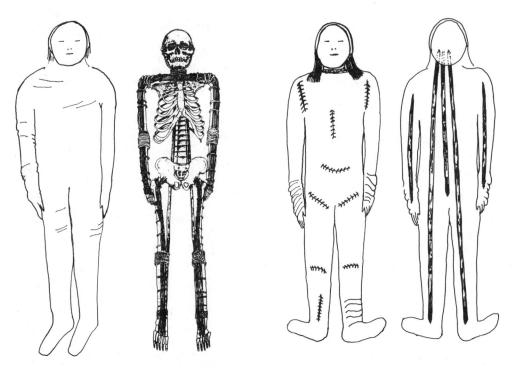

Fig. 35. Black mummy and its inner framework reconstructed (*two left figures*) and a red mummy illustrating its simpler inner structure (*two right figures*) (drawing: R. Rocha).

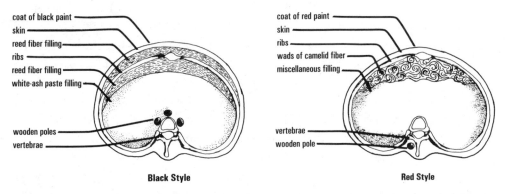

Black Style

Red Style

Fig. 36. Transverse sections at the level of the thorax of a black and a red mummy (drawing: J. Chacama and D. Kendrick-Murdock).

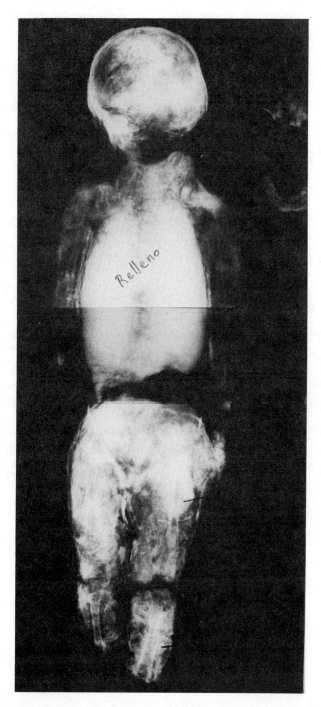

Fig. 37. Radiograph of a red mummy. Note complete filling of body (M1T7C6, subadult) (photo: R. Rocha).

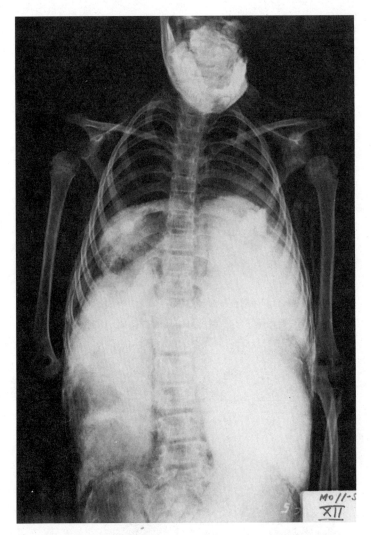

Fig. 38. Radiograph of a red mummy. Note partial filling of body (M1-5T12, subadult) (photo: R. Rocha).

Bandage Mummies

These bodies were given wrappings using various materials. The initial processing appears to have been a combination of that used for the black and red mummies. The body was completely skinned and longitudinal sticks were used to reinforce the body. After this, strips of either animal or human skin, about two centimeters wide, were used to wrap the body (fig. 39). The head and face were not bandaged but treated in a style similar to that of the red mummies. The bodies were also painted red, except for the face,

Fig. 39. Drawing of a bandage mummy (M1T23C10, infant) (drawing: R. Rocha).

which was painted with the typical black manganese paint. In one case from Morro 1 (M1T27C17), pelican skin was apparently used for wrapping the small body of an infant (fig. 40). Cords had been used to secure the bird skin to the body, but the cord had fallen off leaving only impressions of it behind.

Comments

This type of mummification was observed only in three infants. There are no radiocarbon dates for these mummies, but, from the technique of manufacture, they most probably can be grouped with the red mummies. At least one adult red mummy has its legs in a bandage style, lending credence to the contemporaneity between bandage and red mummy types.

Statuette Mummies

Chinchorro statuette mummies have received little attention. Only two detailed descriptions exist: one by scholars Sergio Martinez and Carlos Munizaga (1961) and the other by archaeologists Delbert True and Lautaro Núñez (1971). The statuettes may contain a partial or complete skeleton of a human fetus, along with bird bones or animal bones (see True and Núñez, 1971). Sometimes artificially mummified children are included under the category of statuette mummies. In this book, however, only artificially prepared mummies of fetuses or those with small animal bones are considered statuette mummies (figs. 3, 41). These anthropomorphic statuette mummies have a large head, but many

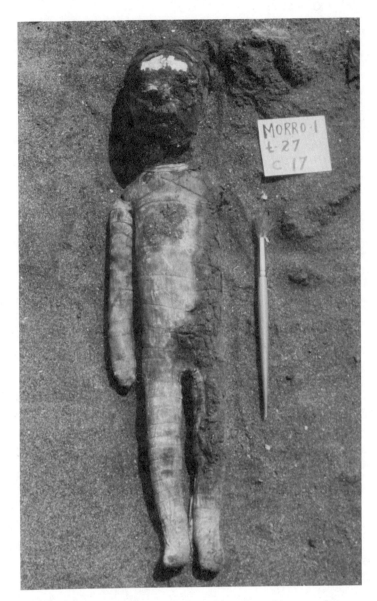

Fig. 40. Bandage mummy probably with pelican skin wrappings (M1T27C17, infant) (photo: V. Standen).

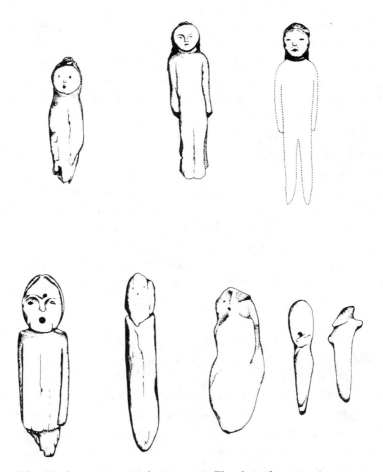

Fig. 41. Statuette mummies (*top row*). Figurines (*bottom row*): materials are wood, wood, clay, wood, clay. (Drawing: D. Kendrick-Murdock).

lack arms and legs. The body is tubular and its distal portion may finish in a point. Sexual organs are not modeled. These statuette mummies vary in size and shape ranging from about seventeen to thirty centimeters in height. Eight Chinchorro statuette mummies were found at the Playa Miller 8 site in Arica (Alvarez, 1969) and at least five from Patillos in Iquique (Martinez and Munizaga, 1961; True and Núñez, 1971:66–67). These statuettes were found buried next to red mummies (see Bittmann and Munizaga, 1977:120–121).

The manufacture of the statuette mummies was nearly identical to that used in the preparation of the complex mummies. The little mummies even have long wigs. By their appearance and reddish color, most of these statuettes seem to be related to the red mummies rather than the black style.

The Chinchorro people also created carved, anthropomorphic wooden figurines, similar in height to the statuette mummies. A few were found at Playa Miller 8 in Arica. Facial features were insinuated on these wooden figurines (fig. 41). It is interesting that clay and wooden figurines are also found in later Atacama cultural groups, but they are buried in residential areas. True and Núñez (1971:83–84) suggested that these figurines represent either a continuity of Chinchorro-like mortuary tradition or a fertility cult in post-Chinchorro cultural phases.

In the Andes, when treating sick people, a modern shaman might use a small doll like a fetish called a *Conopa*. Núñez (1965) and historian Juan Lastres (1951) commented that these figurines could be used in the event of an abnormal childbirth. In the case of dystocia a shaman would remove the clothes of the Conopa and place it over the female's belly to aid in the birth process. The ritual helped the mother relax and have a normal labor. It is possible that in a similar way, the Chinchorro could have carried these wooden figurines as a teaching tool, or a portable ancestor totem when traveling or visiting distant groups, or likewise they could have been used as a healing aid.

Mud-Coated Mummies

In preparing bodies to be mummified in this style, the morticians first smoked the corpses, as evidenced by slightly singed hair and skin. Later, the bodies were covered from head to toe with a thick layer of cementlike paste or mud substance. Today, it looks like a hard, thick layer of a grey sandy crust, about one to two centimeters thick (pl. 18). If the body was not immediately buried after placement in the grave pit, this paste helped prevent decomposition by encasing the body, thus eliminating external microbial attacks. It also could have prevented the foul smell of the partially rotting body. Sometimes the cement paste was mixed with bits of vegetal fibers. This also could have been the result of the cadaver resting on a mat while the mud coating was being applied. Chemical analyses by Figueroa reveal that the mud-coating was a mixture of sand and clay, plus a proteinaceous binder. Possible sources of protein could have been the blood of sea lions, birds, humans, or camelids; eggs; or glues made of boiled fish or animal remains. Two subtypes of mud-coated mummies can be discerned: one with evisceration and one without. In only one case found so far from Morro 1 (T25C6), evisceration was performed in the thoracic and abdominal cavities. The cavities were filled with ashes, and the body was later coated with the mud substance. Mud-coated mummies do not show evidence of the use of longitudinal sticks to reinforce the body.

Comments
The mud-coated type of treatment is of special interest because it greatly contrasts with the mobile nature of the black, red, and bandage styles. The mud mummies seem to have been glued to the floor of the grave pit, as if the mudlike cement had been spread onto the floor of the grave as well as on the mummy. This means that the mud-coated

mummies were prepared in the same place where they were buried and were not moved after the coating was applied. This stylistic change may reflect major innovations in ancestor worship and beliefs concerning the afterlife. It is unknown why these mummification changes took place, but they do not seem to represent abrupt changes. There is a slight overlap of radiocarbon dates of the first eviscerated mud-coated mummy (only one) and the last red mummies. This early mud-coated mummy had greater energy input than later mud-coated mummies because of its evisceration. The mud-coated mummies without evisceration are more recent, and they represent the simplest of all artificial mummification techniques. There seems to have been a gradual decline over hundreds of years in the sophistication of mortuary practices rather than a sudden switch caused by, for instance, external cultural influences. It is conceivable that during the mud-coated period the Chinchorro people felt they did not need to treat the cadaver to such an extreme degree in order to preserve the integrity of the soul of the deceased. Or they felt it was no longer necessary to maintain the deceased relatives within the household or community. Perhaps at this time the Chinchorro people began to perceive that they and their ancestors belonged firmly rooted to the land and symbolically fastened them to the earth. The gluing could have signaled territoriality. However, forces such as ecological constraints, new waves of immigrants, or reduction in the availability of time for the more elaborate mortuary treatments could also explain these changes.

The best evidence of mud-coated mummies comes from those described by Uhle (1922) and those studied from the Morro 1 site, totaling twenty-seven mummies (tables 1, 6). All these mummies come from Arica. This treatment was performed on adults and subadults of both sexes.

At the Huaca Prieta (ca. 3,000 B.C.) and La Paloma sites in Peru, various bodies in a flexed position were covered with solidified ashes (Bird, 1985, Quilter, 1989:76), which may resemble Chinchorro mud-coated mummies. The influence of these cultures upon Chinchorro, however, seems unlikely, as the Chinchorro were at the peak of their complex mummification practice at 3,000 B.C.

Implements Used for Mummification

Stone knives of quartz were used to butcher animals, and similar tools may have been used by the Chinchorro morticians to make incisions, remove the skin, or disarticulate human bodies during the process of artificial mummification. Pelican beaks were frequently found with the mummies too, and they could have been used as tools as they were sharp and hard. But they were often painted red, so they may have had a symbolic significance instead. Bone awls were used to make perforations. Incisions were sewn using needles made of cactus thorns, bone, or wood, and thread was made from either vegetal fibers or human hair and possibly native cotton. The sticks used to reinforce the mummies were about 150 centimeters long and two centimeters in diameter, and many had sharpened ends. Stone or wooden mortars and pestles were used to grind red ocher and black manganese, which were stored in leather bags. A pigment paste was applied to the mummies using small grass brushes. Wood, bone, or stone objects were used as polishers to smooth or retouch the external surfaces of the mummies (fig. 42).

Preparation of the Chinchorro mummies, especially the complex types, must have taken place over a period of weeks. The mortuary procedures for the mud-coated and natural mummies could have been finished in a day or two, but the ceremony for all the mummies might have lasted for months, or years if the mummies were revisited or housed within the community before final burial.

As artificial mummification practices declined, the preparers began putting thin cords around the fingers and toes of the cadaver, starting and finishing with the same finger, thus giving the appearance of a cord ring for each finger and toe (fig. 43). Anthropologist Olivia Harris (1983) comments that the culture of the Laymi of present-day Bolivia includes the tradition of tying the neck, feet, and hands of the deceased with a cord to prevent the soul from departing the body too soon after death. Perhaps the Chinchorro put cords around the fingers and toes for a similar purpose. This also may have been the reason for applying the mud coating that glued the mummies to the earth. There seems to be no association between sex, age, and type of artificial mummification, except in the case of the bandage mummies who were all infants. Otherwise, adults and subadults of both sexes received the same treatment.

Specialist and Apprentices

Handling a dead body, with the unpleasantries of its smell, decomposition, and the likely fear of unknown dangers (e.g., spirits), necessitated precautions. It was not a job for just anyone. Possible biological contaminants presented danger, as well. In Melanesia, dead bodies were often feared for the negative mana they possessed. People avoided excessive handling or physical contact with the dead; they thought death was contagious because the corpse contained evil spirits (Malinowski, 1948). Perhaps they were not far from the truth: some people have contracted kuru, a neurological disorder, through handling decomposed bodies (Steadman and Merbs, 1982). The Inuit from Greenland also highly fear the corpse (Hansen et al., 1991:56). The repulsion, or fear, of the dead body seems to be universal, but so is recognition that someone needs to do the unpleasant job. The elaborate mummification techniques—evisceration, cutting of bones, reassembly, maintenance of anatomical proportions, and eventual retouching—suggest preparation by specialists. The system used to reinforce the mummies with sticks created a mummy rigid enough to be transported in a mat and perhaps left standing inclined or upright in the camp for ritual ceremonies. This mortuary technology appears to have developed gradually, undergoing transformations with time. Several cultural considerations need to be evaluated to gain more insight into this practice.

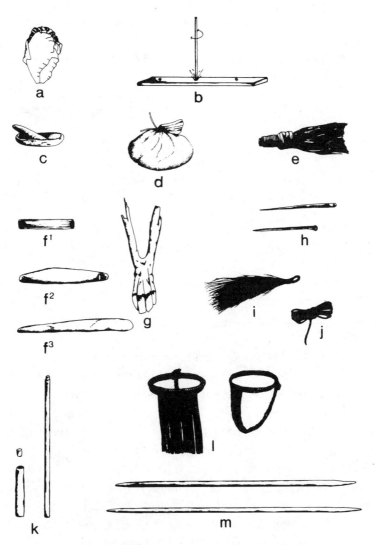

Fig. 42. Mummy-maker's tools: *a,* stone knife; *b,* fire drill; *c,* mortar and pestle; *d,* bag with pigment; *e,* twig brush; *f,* polishers; *g,* camelid mandible; *h,* cactus needle and pin; *i,* human hair tassels; *j,* cords; *k,* bird bone tubes (possibly part of a hallucinogenic kit); *l,* pubic covers; *m,* wooden poles for body reinforcement; (drawing: D. Kendrick-Murdock).

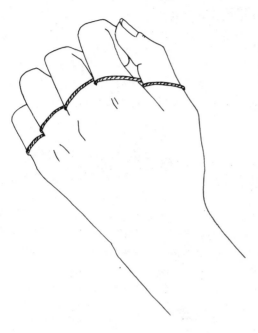

Fig. 43. Hand with yarn binding of fingers as seen in late Chinchorro mummies (drawing: B. Szuhay).

A well-organized division of labor must have guided the practice. Probably specially designated older individuals were the masters in mummy making, as manual and technical skills would develop with experience and time. Apprentices could have helped find the necessary raw organic materials such as reeds, feathers, camelid fibers, and sticks to reinforce and fill the body. Also, they could have assisted with the production of cords, strips of animal or bird skin, preparation of wigs, and the making of mats or grass skirts. Collecting inorganic substances such as ashes and clay for stuffing and modeling the body, plus ocher and manganese pigments for painting also could have been apprentice tasks. The apprentices could have cooperated in the collection or preparation of proteinaceous substances such as blood from dead animals or the deceased or from birds' eggs to be added as a binder to the manganese paste or to the mud-coating that covered some mummies.

The sources of their raw materials were mostly local. The river delta provided the plants and reeds and the nearby beaches and hills provided the manganese and ocher. In fact, even today in Arica there is a beach called Black Sands (Arenillas Negras). X-ray fluorescence of a sand sample taken from it, carried out by Janice Carlson, Winterthur Museum Analytical Laboratory, reveals a high concentration of manganese. This was the most likely source of manganese for the Chinchorro people of Arica. The local mountains are rich in red soils, which X-ray fluorescence analysis reveals have high levels of iron. Thus, the Chinchorro did not have to venture far away to obtain some of the raw materials to make artificial mummies; they used what nature provided them. The knowledge of mummy preparation would have been passed verbally from generation to generation, from parents to children, or from specialist to apprentice, to keep alive the Chinchorro tradition of mummifying their dead for nearly 4,000 years (fig. 44).

Fig. 44. Artistic representation of daily life in a Chinchorro settlement (drawing: R. Rocha and D. Kendrick-Murdock).

Similar techniques found in different cemeteries (e.g., red mummies from Morro 1 and Patillos, fig. 2) suggest that specialists were teaching by either traveling to neighboring groups to mummify their members, or different groups were learning from a specialist by coming together for mortuary ceremonies. Perhaps, among other uses, the wooden effigies or statuette mummies may have been very handy for showing what the mummies should look like when finished.

Sedentism created the necessity of a more organized life style to ensure harmony in the daily lives of the Chinchorro people. The mummification techniques reached levels so sophisticated that specialization would have been needed. Also someone likely took charge of social arrangements in each group. More charismatic people, the elder, or a highly respected person could have been in charge of making such decisions. A shaman must have presided over the final ceremony to bring the spirit(s) back to the mummy. Such leaders would not likely have gained any special accoutrements of rank, as no special status burials have been found.

Color Symbolism

The use of color to paint the Chinchorro mummies is intriguing. According to anthropologist Victor Turner (1970), colors are experiences of social relationships. The use of particular colors in prehistory, then, have meaning even if today we cannot comprehend these meanings. Turner said that white, red, and black are the earliest colors produced by humans and they "provide a kind of primordial classification of reality" (Turner, 1970:90). This color trilogy is associated with reproduction, life, and death. Obviously, in the case of the Chinchorros, black and red colors predominated. Black is equated with darkness, like the night, invisible yet present. Black is what is hidden, it is a mystical transition (Turner, 1970:109,89–73). Black represents death, but not the end of a cycle, not an annihilation, rather a change of status and existence (Turner, 1970:71–72). Red on the other hand is equal to membership, change, blood, and social place (Turner, 1970:90). Red can be associated with life, here and in the afterworld.

The use of colors as symbols is rather universal, but the meaning of each color varies from culture to culture. In Western societies black may be worn to symbolize mourning, but on other occasions it signifies elegance. The Yahgan Indians in South America used body painting with intricate patterns of black, white, and red to show their sadness and grief when someone died (Gusinde, 1937). Black was the color to symbolize mourning among the Incas (Montell, 1929:222; Zuidema, 1992:23).

The meaning of Chinchorro paint colors is unknown, yet it is interesting to speculate about the possibilities. For the Chinchorros, the duration of three millennia for the use of black manganese paint implies a demanding spiritual necessity to keep things the way they were. Black must have symbolized the unknown and the eternity of the hereafter. It is interesting that black-colored objects do not appear in post-Chinchorro cultures from the Arica region. Why the Chinchorros changed from black to red and then to brown is certainly intriguing. Possibly it reflects body painting practiced by the Chinchorros during their lives and thus changes in world view. However, most mummies have the same solid color, either black or red. The exceptions are two complex mummies described by Uhle (1922:64), who have vertical lines painted on their facial mask, and a unique black mummy from Maderas Enco who has red and yellowish bands on the trunk and arms. Within the natural Chinchorro mummies only one body was found to be decorated: the face had a dotted mustachelike tattoo (Allison et al, 1984; Arriaza, 1988).

The black mummy with a series of red stripes (pl. 19) may indicate experimentation and possibly the discovery of a rich ocher source that later became highly utilized. The red style lasted about 500 years, until 2,090 B.C., but in Arica naturally mummified bodies with evidence of red paint on the body are found until about 1,600 B.C. In late Chinchorro, grave goods were painted solid red. In the highlands of Arica (pl. 8) and at La Capilla cave (fig. 45) on the coast, many pictographs were drawn also using red pigment. However, grave goods and fishing objects were commonly painted with bands

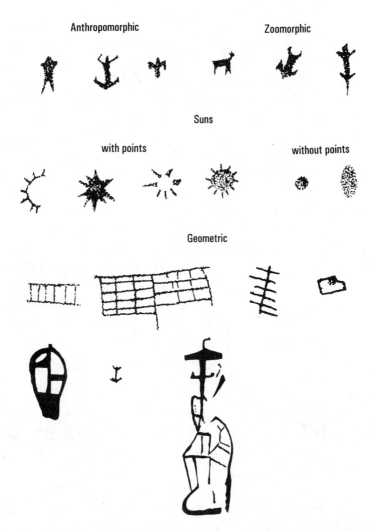

Fig. 45. Pictographs from La Capilla cave, Arica (after Muñoz and Chacama, 1982:35; drawing: D. Kendrick-Murdock).

of red (instead of solid) in the agropastoral societies of Arica, indicating a continuous use of red color, but with changes occurring in its pattern and symbolism.

The brown color of the mud-coated mummies also deserves some discussion. It possibly reflected the color of the earth, and therefore a concept of territoriality and belonging to the earth. This notion of belonging is given further credence by the mud-coated bodies seeming to be glued to the grave pit by the same coating.

In the case of the Yahgan, after they completely painted themselves, mortuary ceremonies followed. These ceremonies included invoking their gods for clemency, screaming, swearing, and accusing their deities of having too much rage. The Yahgan's gods were represented by forces of nature such as thunder and lightening. But the environment where the Chinchorros lived is stable; thus, these scary weather-related phenomena seen in southern Chile were absent in Arica. The Chinchorro's gods may likely have been related to the forces of the ocean or perhaps to the maritime fauna. The heavenly bodies like the stars, the sun, and the moon probably were also worshiped, as illustrated in the rock art from La Capilla (fig. 45). Using the Yahgan analogy, it is not far fetched then to speculate that Chinchorros also painted themselves black or red as a sign of mourning during their mortuary ceremonies.

Post-Chinchorro Burial Practices

Basic post-Chinchorro religious and mortuary practices for the Arica region until the arrival of the Spanish Conquistadors can be outlined as follows: In Quiani, the period following Chinchorro in Arica, the body was flexed and buried lying on one side with a variety of grave goods. The corpse was dressed with an elaborate turban. Subsequent to Quiani, in the Alto Ramirez phase (ca. 500 B.C. to A.D. 320), the body was buried lying on one side in a mound made of layers of earth, branches, vegetal mats, and bodies. Several individuals, some well attired and others unclothed, were buried in several layers within the mound. In the subsequent Regional Cultures or Chiefdoms, and Inca Empire, the body was buried in a sitting position in a more elaborate grave. The corpse was well dressed and ornamented according to gender and social class. A variety of grave goods was common. Lastly, with the arrival of the Spanish and Christianity, the body was buried again in an extended position, hands over chest holding a cross, facing the sunrise to the east. Grapes were often placed over the face.

Cross-cultural Comparison

A comparison of Chinchorro and Egyptian mummies can be made using three features common to both cultures. Both cultures lived in an arid environment during a similar period of history; both practiced complex mummification techniques. With these similarities in mind it is also necessary to remember that the Chinchorro, unlike the sophisticated Egyptians, were small groups of fishers, who had no written language or complex political organization.

Both the Egyptian and the Chinchorro cultures lived in arid environments, where natural mummification took place spontaneously. Artificial mummification practices may therefore represent another instance of the human desire to improve upon what nature provides. The similar ecological settings probably influenced both cultures in the development of artificial mummification.

Both Egyptian and Chinchorro techniques varied over time with increasing complexity and subsequent decline. The main objective was to avoid decomposition and preserve the cadaver as it was in life, and both cultures discovered the same solution: incision, evisceration, and external treatment of the body.

In Egypt, the first evidence of crude attempts at mummifying artificially or embalming date to 3,000 B.C. with the First Dynasty (David and Tapp, 1984). The Egyptian practices peaked about 1,000 B.C. under the rulers of the New Kingdom. The Egyptians eviscerated through incision or through the normal body apertures. All the organs were extracted except the heart, which was left intact because it was believed the soul resided there. The other organs were preserved in canopic jars especially designed to deposit and protect each type of organ. In Egypt they also mummified animals. After the body was eviscerated it was salted using natron, hydrated sodium carbonate. Then the body was wrapped with many linen bandages. The body was deposited in a series of elaborate sarcophagi.

The Egyptians believed that a person has several souls, such as the Ka and the Ba. The souls left the body after death, but in the hereafter the souls began a search for the body in an attempt to reunite for eternity. It was essential to preserve the features of the person as much as possible, so that the soul could recognize the body and, thus, more easily become reunited. The Egyptian rulers created large and complex pyramids, in many cases well in advance of their deaths, as their abode for the hereafter. In Egypt, artificial mummification was reserved for the upper class and royalty. Thus, the elaborateness of the mummification process and tomb depended upon how much the individual or the family could afford to pay.

The Chinchorro culture began to preserve their dead artificially about 5,050 B.C. and they reached the maximum complexity in their mummification techniques between 3,000 and 4,000 B.C. The Chinchorro, therefore, practiced the oldest form of artificial mummification. The Chinchorros preceded Egyptian mummification by nearly 2,000 years. Chinchorros also eviscerated the bodies, and if not disarticulated, the cavities were dried. In the case of the black mummies the treatment of the body was even more sophisticated, as discussed previously. No evidence of preserved eviscerated internal organs have been found for the Chinchorro culture. Manganese, ocher, or sand plus a protein binder, depending on the period, were used as elements to add external protection. Facial and sexual features were present, but stylized, not as exact representations of the individual. The Chinchorro deposited the artificial mummies in a mat shroud and buried them in the sand, probably after a period of keeping them above ground for ceremonial purposes. In Chinchorro culture, unlike that of the Egyptians, all members of the society were artificially mummified.

It is interesting that both cultures, at one point in time, altered the body to such an extent that few original biological materials were left. Egyptologists Rosalie David and Eddie Tapp (1984:37–40) described an Egyptian mummy made with mud and wooden sticks that greatly resembles a black Chinchorro mummy.

Chinchorro mummification techniques also parallel those of Melanesia where the bodies, once the soft tissue had decomposed, were exhumed and the facial features restored to some extent (see Bittmann and Munizaga, 1980). The Melanesian mummification practices seem to be a rather recent cultural practice. Artificial mummification and embalming treatments can also be found in many modern Western cultures. However, they appear to be more related to status and practical considerations, such as making the body presentable for display, as opposed to spiritual needs for preserving the body for eternity.

CHAPTER 10

CHINCHORRO CHRONOLOGY

The Chinchorro chronology proposed here is based on mummification styles and radiocarbon dates of the mummies and associated sites (table 3). This chronology is by no means definitive, but it is an effort to intentionally subdivide the Chinchorro culture in order to gain insight into cultural and technoeconomic changes. This chronology should be viewed as a starting point for understanding Chinchorro cultural evolution. Common to all the Chinchorro mummies in this chronology is the extended burial position, reflecting a common ideology. Their different mummification techniques set them apart as separate pieces of the puzzle.

Most Chinchorro studies have focused on the Arica and Camarones area, where artificial mummification originated. The chronology presented here is obviously also biased toward this geographic area, rather than its peripheries.

Chinchorro can be divided into five cultural epochs. A cultural epoch is defined here as a block of time in which sociocultural and technological changes were minimal. The term "epoch" is preferred over "phase" to highlight the need to identify and understand the smaller changes within a time of cultural continuity. These epochs also emphasize what is unique to Chinchorro—its artificial mummification. Unfortunately, the mummies have few grave goods, therefore a cross-correlation between technology and types of mummies is not currently possible. Moreover, the Chinchorro practice of cemetery reuse complicates such a study because individuals living in different millennia are buried next to one another and their grave goods could have easily been mixed. For now, the detailed study of the processes used to create the mummies provides the best tool for deriving a Chinchorro chronology.

Chinchorro chronology has changed drastically since the first studies by Uhle (1917), who placed the Arica Aborigines around the time of Christ (fig. 5). Núñez (1965:23) obtained the first dates for a Chinchorro mummy from Pisagua Viejo 4. Two radiocarbon dates from the same mummy (3,270 and 2,930 B.C.) placed the Chinchorros around 3,100 B.C. Later, Vera (1981) dated two more mummies from Arica (3,290 and 3,060 B.C.) confirming the antiquity of the Chinchorro mummies found by Núñez. And in 1984 the work of Schiappacasse and Niemeyer extended the chronology even farther back to 5,050 B.C. At the Morro 1 site a mummy was dated to 5,860 B.C. by Allison and co-workers (1984), but this date, as discussed in chapter 6, was found to be faulty by Standen (1991) who redated the same mummy, obtaining a date of 2,570 B.C. This early Morro 1 date, then, will not be considered here. Recently, the naturally mummified body from Acha 2 was dated to 7,020 B.C. by Muñoz and Chacama (1993). This date currently marks the beginning of Chinchorro. At the other extreme, the end of Chinchorro seems to be about 1,500 B.C. for Arica and 1,110 B.C. for Camarones. Thus, the Chinchorro culture lasted for at least 5,520 or 5,910 years.

A synthesis of the preceramic coastal dates for the Atacama region is presented in table 3. These dates show a continuous occupation of the Atacama coast for thousands of years. In Arica human occupation started about 7,000 B.C., or almost a millennium earlier if the calibrated date for the Acha 2 inhumation is used (table 3, fig. 46). For the Chinchorro decline, however, calibrated dates are only about two centuries older than the original dates (fig. 46). The following chronological sketch for Chinchorro is based on the uncalibrated dates since these are the dates familiar to most scholars.

In Arica the naturally mummified, extended bodies are first found from 7,020 B.C. to 5,050 B.C., lasting about 1,970 years. About 5,050 B.C., artificial mummification (black through to mud-coated styles) developed and declined about 1,720 B.C., lasting 3,330 years. Within this category, complex mummification techniques (black, red, and bandage mummies) were found between 5,050 to 2,090 years B.C., lasting 2,960 years. The duration of the mud-coated mummies is unclear, as only two mummies of this style have been dated. Natural mummies, or desiccated bodies, reappear around 1,880 B.C. to 1,500 B.C. If the date (2,250 B.C.) for the outlier (with natural mummification) (table 3) is ignored, then the late natural mummification stage lasted 380 years.

Chinchorro mummification practices follow a linear pattern, that is, natural, black, red, mud-coated, and natural epochs rather than a multiple overlapping of mummification styles. For simplicity, only the mean dates are used in the following chronology (fig. 47).

Chinchorro Founder (7,020 B.C. to 5,050 B.C.)

This epoch corresponds to the first highlander populations that arrived at the Arica-Camarones coast, who apparently did not practice artificial mummification. These people lived in villages, such as the one found at Acha 2. The bodies were not abandoned when someone died in the group, but were wrapped in a reed sleeping mat or shroud and buried in an extended position near to where they lived. Two natural mummies dated to 7,020 B.C. and 6,000 B.C. from the Acha gorge provide evidence of the antiquity of this epoch. Other sites that could be associated with this cultural stage are Villa del Mar in Peru (Wise, 1991) dating to 5,850 B.C., Aragon (6,710 B.C.), and Camarones 14 (5,470 B.C) in Chile (table 3). The Las Conchas (7,730 B.C) and Tiliviche 1b (7,180 B.C.) sites could perhaps be included as part of this early Chinchorro stage of coastal adaptation, but further confirmation is needed (see table 3).

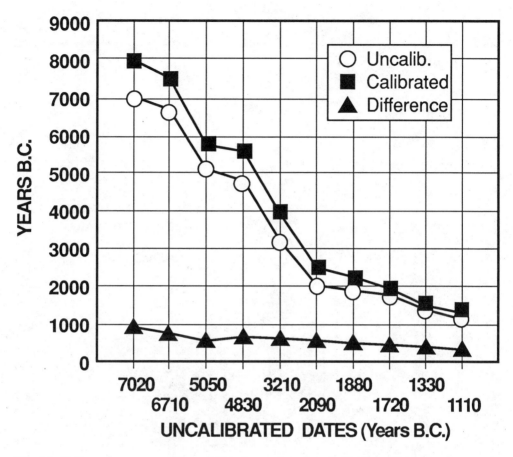

Fig. 46. Calibrated versus uncalibrated Chinchorro dates (graph: T. Cantrell).

The first evidence of artificial mummification appeared in Camarones 14 about 5,050 B.C., marking the end of the founder epoch. Thus, the first epoch lasted 1,970 years (7,020 B.C. to 5,050 B.C.). During this founder epoch twined reed mats and fishing technology, including both shell and cactus fishhooks and lines, were already in use. At this time the people had a mixed subsistence consisting of shellfish collecting and hunting marine and terrestrial animals; however, procuring resources from the sea was likely the main mode of subsistence.

Initial Chinchorro (5,050 B.C. to 4,980 B.C.)

This epoch marks the beginning of artificial mummification practices and their subsequent development. The oldest anthropogenic body came from the Camarones 14 site,

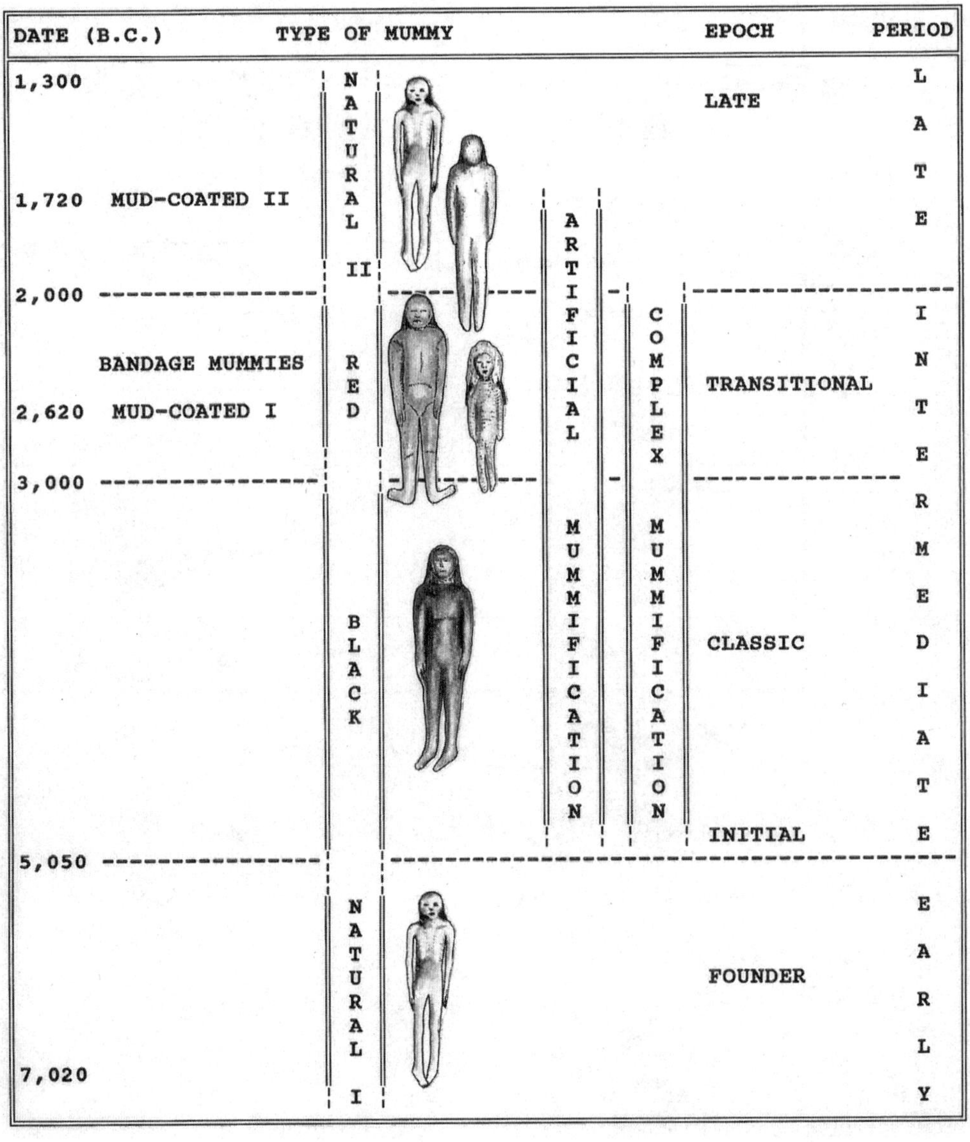

DATE (B.C.)	TYPE OF MUMMY		EPOCH	PERIOD

Fig. 47. Chinchorro chronology (drawing: D. Kendrick-Murdock).

where one of the five artificially prepared mummies described by Schiappacasse and Niemeyer (1984) was dated to 5,050 B.C. In these mummies the arms and legs did not receive much treatment; instead, concentration was more on the face and trunk. Apparently, at this time, only children were given the honor of artificial mummification. The Camarones 14 site also provides the earliest date for the existence of a formalized cemetery as well as indications of a sedentary population. Evidence of basketry technology and fully maritime subsistence practices developed significantly. Seventy years after the first artificially prepared mummies from Camarones 14, artificial mummification had become very elaborate with head to toe treatments, as demonstrated by the mummies from Camarones 17, which mark the beginning of the next epoch of classic black mummies.

Classic Chinchorro (4,980 B.C. to 2,800 B.C.)

This classic epoch represents the period when the cadaver was intensely manipulated, and in a technical sense, these bodies go beyond the definition of a mummy. The bodies were completely dismembered and then reassembled without most of their soft tissue, which was replaced with a white-ash paste, sticks, and twigs, and then painted black. A wig of short human hair was normally added to the head. The mummies were most likely kept in the settlement for religious ceremonies and later buried as a group. Possibly these black mummies were also subsequently revisited, exhumed, and reburied.

The mummies from Camarones 17 represent the earliest evidence of classic black mummies found so far, marking the beginning of this classic phase about 4,980 B.C. to 4,830 B.C. (Aufderheide, Muñoz, and Arriaza, 1993). These two dates from Camarones 17 were both from children. In Arica the earliest black mummy, also a child, has a date of 4,120 B.C., 860 years later than Camarones 17. Other black mummies found in Arica cluster around 3,000 B.C. and include adults of both sexes. The black mummies from Camarones 17 are slightly less complicated than those of Arica. For example, they lack the elaborate reed bindings on the arms and legs.

Classic black Chinchorro mummies have been found in Arica at Hipodromo, Chinchorro 1, Morro 1, and Maderas Enco sites, and perhaps at Pisagua Viejo 4. Adults and children were treated in much the same way for the black style. Recently, three spectacular, but extremely brittle, black mummies were found in Arica during expansion of a lumberyard. One has bands of dull yellow and red ocher on top of the outer black coat of the trunk and arms (pl. 19). A wooden stick used in the construction of this striped mummy gave a radiocarbon date of 2,800±155 B.C. (Krueger Enterprises, Cambridge Mass. USA, GX-17464). Because of the use of the color red and the late date, this mummy is considered the link to the next transitional epoch.

A total of eight classic black mummies have been dated with a range of 4,980 B.C to 2,800 B.C. (or nine if the one from Pisagua Viejo is included). This black style lasted 2,180 years. However, it could extend to a maximum of 2,250 years (5,050–2,800 B.C.) if the oldest mummy from Camarones 14 is included as the first evidence of a black mummy.

Dwelling sites dating to this black epoch have been found along the coast, and a population increase is evident judging by the various middens found along the coast (table 3). Sites without mummies can be assigned to this classic period by their proximity to the cemeteries and their corresponding dates: Quiani 9 (4,420 B.C), Camarones 14 (4,700–4,665 B.C.), Camarones Punta Norte (4,320–3,650 B.C), Quiani 1 and 2

(4,220–3,680 B.C.), Cobija (4,080–2,930 B.C.), and Caleta Huelén 42 (2,830 B.C.). Tiliviche 1b (4,955–4,110 B.C.) could also be included; it was at least influenced by Chinchorro (table 3).

During this black phase, cultural novelties include the first clear appearance of the atlatl and throwing sticks, along with refinements in the fishing tool kit, such as camelid fiber cords used for fishing lines or made into fringe skirts for females.

Transitional Chinchorro (2,620 B.C. to 1,720 B.C.)

A wide variety of mummies was produced at this time which can be characterized by red and mud-coated styles. Red mummies had distinct long black wigs and were buried in groups. Mud-coated mummies were buried separately, though still within a cemetery. This period of artificial mummification beginning with red and including mud-coated lasted approximately 900 years, starting about 2,620 B.C. and disappearing around 1,720 B.C.

In Arica the red stage started about 2,570 B.C. and declined about 2,090 B.C., enduring for 480 years. In Camarones the earliest red mummy dates to 2,685 B.C. The best evidence for the red mummies comes from the Morro 1 site (fig. 2). Subsequent excavations of areas adjacent to the main Morro 1 site by Focacci have revealed the presence of at least seventeen more Chinchorro mummies from Morro 1-5 and sixty-nine from Morro 1-6. The mummies of Morro 1-5 were painted red, and apparently they were eviscerated and treatment focused mainly on the abdominal area. They have incipient headbands, and were buried in an extended position. Morro 1-6 had naturally desiccated bodies found in an extended position. One of the Morro 1-5 mummies is dated to 2,170 B.C. (Guillen, in press). Focacci and Chacón (1989:46) reported seven dates for Morro 1-6 ranging from 2,360 to 1,610 B.C. The simpler treatment of the mummies from Morro 1-6 and their corresponding dates are consistent with an overall decline in artificial mummification practices (fig. 48). Other sites such as Aragon 1, dated to 2,530 B.C., and Patillos (no date) seem to be associated with this red period (see table 3).

Sites such as Conanoxa (ca. 2,070–1,790 B.C) in Camarones gorge could likewise be part of this period, but the evidence is not yet available to support this. In Arica the La Capilla site, with a date of 1,720 B.C., seems to be a ceremonial cave, where bundles of unused grass skirts were buried. This date corresponds to the mud-coated epoch.

Only two mud-coated mummies have been dated. The radiocarbon date for the mud-coated mummy with evisceration, whose abdominal cavities were filled with ashes, was 2,620 B.C. This is a very important mummy because it represents a transition in mortuary practices, marking the decline of the complex treatment and the appearance of the simpler mud-coated type. A radiocarbon date for a mud-coated mummy without evisceration was

Fig. 48. Late Chinchorro natural mummy from Arica (M1-6C53, adult female) (photo: B. Arriaza).

1,720 B.C. Duration of the mud-coated mummies is unknown because only two, with different techniques, have been dated.

During the transitional epoch, the use of clothing became more evident. The apparel worn by the red and mud-coated mummies indicates that Chinchorro males wore small leather breach cloths and females wore grass skirts. Use of narrow head bands became common in the red and mud-coated mummies of both sexes, but the hair was still unbraided. Copper ore apparently was being used as ornaments by some Chinchorros at this time, especially the red mummies from Patillos.

The end of the second millennium B.C. marks the disappearance of the red mummies, and thus all of the complex mummies. At this time (2,620 B.C. to 1,720 B.C.) the Chinchorro culture was disrupted, for some unknown reason; it seems that different Chinchorro groups were breaking away from traditions as seen in the adoption of new mortuary techniques and in a new cultural innovation—intentional cranial deformation (annular type), which first appeared with the red mummies (ca. 2,570 B.C. to 2,090 B.C.; fig. 4). This annular cranial deformation correlates well with the use of headbands. This transitional stage needs further study to understand why and how this breakup was taking place and what these synchronic differences in mummification styles represent.

Late Chinchorro (1,720 B.C. to 1,110 B.C.)

During this period the artificial mortuary practices observed in the Chinchorro culture, including the simple mud-coated mummies, were abandoned. This final or late epoch is typified by the return to simple burial of the bodies in extended positions that allowed nature to naturally mummify the bodies.

By 1,720 B.C. artificial mummification practices had almost completely disappeared in Arica, the last vestiges being the mud-coated mummies. In some cases, as found at the Camarones 15 site (Rivera et al., 1974), the mud coating was only applied to the face until 1,110 B.C. In Arica the naturally mummified bodies, buried in an extended position lying on their backs, began to become common starting at 1,880 B.C. and then declined about 1,500 B.C. This period of natural mummification lasted about 380 years. However, if the early natural mummy, an outlier, is considered, the time span increases to 750 years (table 3).

During this late Chinchorro epoch, the naturally mummified bodies still were buried wrapped in a reed mat shroud and lying on their backs. Annular skull deformation was further developed. At the end of this epoch, about 1,500 B.C., the bodies were placed lying to one side with legs and arms flexed. Another cultural innovation appeared—hair braiding and wrapping (fig. 48). Also, elaborate wrapping of the head with yarns resembling turbans started to become common. Socioeconomic developments included fine basketry and evidence of horticulture (tubers). These changes are part of the Quiani phase considered subsequent to Chinchorro (Dauelsberg, 1974).

Comments

The extended duration of 3,330 years of sustained Chinchorro artificial mummification practices (5,050 B.C. to 1,720 B.C.) has been viewed with suspicion by some scholars for two reasons. First, they believe the dates for the artificial mummies are too early. Second, the complex mummification practices do not fit well with the Chinchorros' simple sociopolitical organization. The evidence, however, is accumulating and confirms this long tradition of the Chinchorro culture, which apparently went through several ideological and mortuary transformations, as illustrated by the various epochs presented here. Chinchorro mortuary practices not only lasted many millennia, but also extended to a large geographic area along the Atacama coast (fig. 2).

In summary, of all Chinchorro artificial mummies, the black were the oldest and lasted the longest, about 2,180 years (4,980 B.C. to 2,800 B.C.). During this epoch Chinchorro mortuary practices spread outside the Arica-Camarones cultural core. The red stage followed the black, and was much shorter, lasting about 480 years (2,570 B.C. to 2,090 B.C.). It seems about 2,000 B.C. to 1,700 B.C. the Chinchorros were changing rapidly, as compared with the more stable black period. The late epoch of natural mummification was even shorter, lasting only about 380 years.

CHAPTER 11

THE DEAD AMONG THE LIVING

Origin of Huacas

To fully understand the power of preserving the dead in Andean rituals one must remember that *huacas* have been a cornerstone of Andean cosmology for hundreds, if not thousands, of years. *Huacas,* according to Garcilaso (1987:76–77), an Incan historian, are "a sacred thing." "*Huaca* is applied to any temple, large or small . . . [or] to all those things, which for their beauty or excellence stand above other things of the same kind . . . [or] everything that is out of the usual course of nature, as a woman who gives birth to twins . . . double-egged yokes are *huaca*." In Andean religions, mummies and ancestral burial places were often considered *huacas*. Mummy *huacas* were venerated because they had the power to generate life (see Allen, 1988:59; Salomon and Urioste, 1991:16–19). Mummy *huacas* also represented continuity of life, linking the present with the past, and the real world with the supernatural world. In their translation and commentary of the ancient Andean manuscript of Huarochiri, anthropologists Frank Salomon and George Urioste (1991:129#358) commented that the Huarochiri people believed that the soul left the body as a fly and that life was eternal: "Our dead will return in five days. Let's wait for him" (Salomon and Urioste, 1991:130#365). Thus, mummy *huacas* and other types of *huacas* generally were considered living entities with potentially eternal existence. As long as some part of the dead person such as clothes, bones, or an effigy was preserved, the *huaca* remained a real entity (Allen, 1988:59; Salomon and Urioste, 1991:130, footnote 693).

In Andean cosmology, people not only respected their mummy *huacas,* but they also even traced their lineage back to specific *huacas*. The mummy *huacas* were seen as providers of fertility and order; thus, their bodies were cared for and preserved (Allen, 1988:58–59; Salomon and Urioste, 1991:20). The *huacas* were periodically visited, fed, and consulted in important matters. The prosperity of a community was seen as the work of powerful mummy *huacas;* thus, sometimes living Inca kings would confiscate the *huaca* mummies of others and add these to his own shrine with the hope of enjoying good fortune and prosperity himself.

The Chinchorro also venerated their mummies, so perhaps the idea of mummy *huacas* was originated by the Chinchorros. Other Andean cultures could either have adopted the concept or have been influenced by it. With the arrival of the Spanish Conquistadors the millennial veneration of mummy *huacas* came to an abrupt end as Andean people were persecuted for worshiping their ancestors. The most famous, or infamous, hunter of mummy *huacas* was Padre Arriaga (1968) who published his work in 1621 under the title "Extirpación de las Idolatrías del Perú."

Possible Meaning of Artificial Mummification

What does Chinchorro artificial mummification represent? The meaning of artificial mummification and the diversity of mummy styles must be inferred from the mummies themselves and from the artifacts because there are no Chinchorro written records. At least five possibilities can be explored: (1) social stratification in which only certain people were mummified; (2) coexistence of different ethnic groups, clans or sodalities with different mortuary practices; (3) ancestor worship in which the artificial mummies represented images of ancestors; (4) beliefs in life after death; (5) needs or desires for perpetuity or continuity of life. It is argued here that Chinchorro artificial mummification does not represent sociobiological processes such as rank, ethnicity, or sodalities; instead, it illustrates religious beliefs such as ancestor worship, life after death, and continuity of life in this or in a parallel world.

Rank

Were artificial mummification practices reserved for higher ranking Chinchorros only? Chinchorro cemeteries contain both naturally and artificially mummified bodies. At the Morro 1 site, 62% (60/96) of the bodies were artificially mummified and 38% (36/96) were not (fig. 49). If ranking was present, then commoners would have burials of lower energy expenditure, such as natural mummification which requires minimal energy expenditure in terms of body preparation. These low-rank natural bodies should be in the majority and should be associated with fewer grave goods. However, there is a conspicuous absence of contemporaneous low-rank natural burials during the complex stages (black, red, and bandage) that would support a rank hypothesis. Also, most mummies had only a few artifacts. For example, throwing sticks, small harpoons, or lithic knives were put in the hands of the mummies or were found on top or alongside of them. And no significant sex and age differences in the kinds of grave goods were noted (see Standen, 1991). Also there is no evidence for monumental architecture, accumulation of material wealth, or exotic grave goods with the complex mummies that would support the argument that they represent an elite group in a ranked society.

One hypothesis that may favor the argument for ranking would be that lower ranking individuals, commoners, were disposed of in a manner that left no trace, such as being thrown to the ocean where decomposition and ocean scavengers would remove all

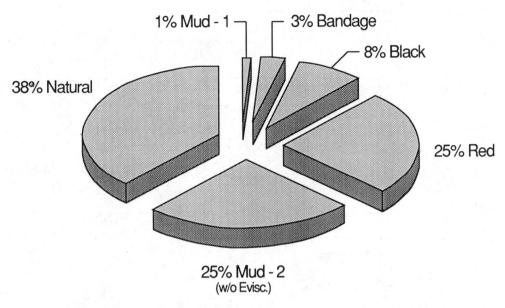

1% Mud - 1   3% Bandage

8% Black

38% Natural

25% Red

25% Mud - 2
(w/o Evisc.)

Fig. 49. Frequency distribution of mummy types found at the Morro 1 site (graph: T. Cantrell).

evidence. But this does not seem to be the case, as the limited settlement data that exists does not show status distinctions either. There do not appear to have been high and low status houses for instance.

For now, radiocarbon dates are the best evidence against the existence of rank. The radiocarbon dates for natural mummies found in Arica, pre- and postdate the complex artificial mummies. Only one natural mummy, however, does overlap at the tail end of the more than 3,000 years of complex mummies, but not if a two-sigma variation is used for all dates (table 3). Thus, equating a higher rank for people with artificial mummification is not supported, as no lower-ranking contemporary individuals have been identified.

Instead, it appears that everyone was entitled to such treatment. Both adults and subadults were artificially mummified (fig. 50); however, there is a predominance of the latter. At Morro 1, of the complex Chinchorro mummies (black, red, and bandage), 57% were subadult mummies (table 6). This does not indicate that children had a higher rank than adults; this difference was likely due to a high prevalence of infant mortality (fig. 14). Artificial mummification of infants and especially fetuses is highly unusual: cross-culturally, infants, and to a greater extent fetuses, often are not considered full members of a society. Only after a rite of passage has been successfully undertaken does the child become a social persona, a true member of the group, with rights and obligations. Death

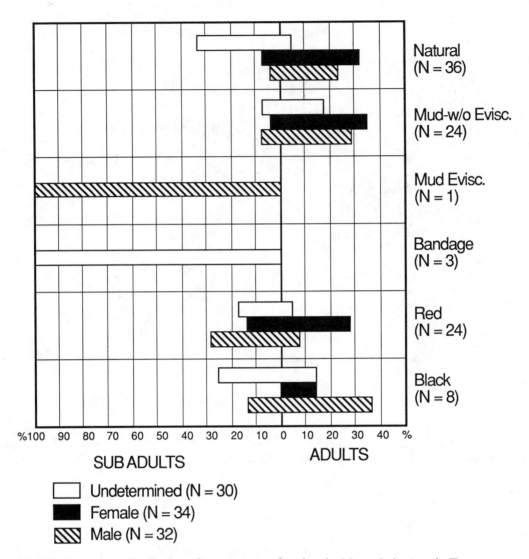

Fig. 50. Sex and age distribution of mummy types found at the Morro 1 site (graph: T. Cantrell).

Table 6. Types of Chinchorro mummies found at the Morro 1 site

Sex	Black N=8		Red N=24		Bandage N=3		Mud eviscerated N=1		Mud simple N=24		Natural N=36		
	A	sa	A	sa	A	sa	A	sa	A	sa	A	sa	TOTAL
Male	3	1	2	7	0	0	0	1	7	2	8	1	32
Female	1	0	7	3	0	0	0	0	8	1	11	3	34
Undet.	1	2	1	4	0	3	0	0	4	2	1	12	30
Total	5	3	10	14	0	3	0	1	19	5	20	16	96

Codes: A = adults (N = 54); sa = subadults less than 15 years of age (N = 42)

before the essential rites of passage that guarantee membership often results in minimal or no burial treatment at all. The mummification of fetuses in Chinchorro is then puzzling and does not support the rank hypothesis either. Cross-culturally, complex mortuary treatment of a child's body (or adult's) correlates well with inherited high social rank (Chapman, Kinnes, and Randsborg, 1981). Contrary to this notion, artificial mummification was most likely an egalitarian practice for the Chinchorros. Likewise, at the equally early Peruvian La Paloma site, children were treated identically to or even more elaborately than adults. They sometimes had greater numbers of exotic grave goods than adults (Quilter, 1989:62,66). In summary, although artificial mummification seems to have involved too much energy expenditure for a nonranked society, it seems that the Chinchorros did develop artificial mummification as part of their ideology or world view and everyone was treated more or less equally.

Ethnicity

The Chinchorro cemeteries were small, ranging from 100 to 200 square meters, and may contain one or several mummification styles. Sometimes over 100 individuals representing several styles occupied different sections of the same cemetery or were mixed together. Some were naturally mummified and others were prepared artificially. If the natural and artificially prepared mummies do not represent rank, they may represent two coexisting populations. Although not all the mummies have been dated, the coexistence of two groups, at least for the black period, seems unlikely. If two groups coexisted they most likely would have used different cemeteries or different sections within a cemetery. This is not the case in Chinchorro burials, as natural and artificially prepared bodies were buried in the same cemetery and the burial pattern appears most often to be random with one mummy on top of another. At Morro 1, despite the mixing, most mummies had their heads pointing northeast (fig. 9). The chaotic burial pattern can be explained as a consequence of the scarcity of places adequate for burials and the intensive use of the cemeteries over thousands of years. It appears as if the ancient remains were barely moved aside to bury the newcomers. New bodies and old ones were placed together intimately. As a matter of fact, in Arica, burial patterns have not changed much. The same random pattern can be seen today in the Azapa Valley, where Christians bury their dead either on top of or next to a 1,000-year-old body.

In summary, natural and artificial mummification represent variations through time rather than coexisting groups with different mortuary treatments. Natural mummification with extended bodies was found twice, at the beginning of the initial settlement of the coast (about 7,000 B.C) and at the end of the Chinchorro culture (1,500 B.C.). Artificial mummification was practiced between these dates.

Images of the Dead

Though there were shared styles of mummification, no two Chinchorro artificially prepared mummies are identical. Each body is unique. Although the facial features were not fully reconstructed, the mummies' faces have enough features to represent the individual. Apparently, the Chinchorro wanted to keep the image of the individual—something like a portrait in a modern analogy, except that the mummies were not meant to be an exact copy of the person. The complex mummies have human bones, hair, skin, and facial features—enough elements to symbolize the individual. The Chinchorro mummies, especially the black, red, and bandage types, were images of the dead.

It is not uncommon to find groups that have a cult to the dead in which body segments are kept as tokens to obtain the individual's vital power or as a memento. Such was the case of the 19th century Victorian European custom of keeping locks of hair from the deceased. It is not the exact replica that counts, but rather that some part of the individual remains preserved.

Historically, in the Andes desiccated mummies were kept and revered. The Incas periodically dressed up and fed the desiccated mummies of their rulers. These mummy *huacas* were also carried in processions because they were a central part of the Inca's religious ceremonies (Cobo, 1964:73; MacCormack, 1991:94). A similar cult to the ancestors was associated with the Muisca Indians from Colombia, who even carried their artificially mummified rulers to battle so the living could benefit from their strength and wisdom (Cárdenas, in press; Krickeberg et al., 1969:93–94). Likewise, the Chinchorro could have easily recognized mummified individual ancestors and possibly displayed them as part of their religious ideology.

The modeling of facial features and sexual organs in Chinchorro mummies points toward a need for individualization in the creation of the death image, but the consistency of the styles and materials for a given epoch reflect the group's identity and cohesion. The maintenance of this tradition for so long is also a manifestation of strong social integration or a sense of community. The practice of mummification not only immortalized the individual, it also probably symbolized survival of the group. It was sedentism, kinship, common ideology, stable subsistence, technoeconomic traditions, recognition of mummies, and their mortuary rites that kept the Chinchorro culture flourishing for thousands of years.

Artificial Mummification and Life after Death

Many cultures believe in the duality of the individual—a body and a spirit. For simplicity, here the spiritual part will be called the soul. Some cultures believe that temporary loss of the soul causes sickness, with prolonged losses of the soul presumably resulting in death. And after death, what happens to the soul? Where does it go?

After death it is the duality of human nature that makes it precarious for the living, because while the body can be seen to decompose, the soul is invisible (to most). Mortuary rites are viewed as a way to satisfy the necessities of the soul to assure its departure from the body and to reach its final destination. Otherwise, it could stay to haunt and spread sickness among the living (see Allen, 1988:60). The Runa people of Peru, for example, believe that the spirits of bad individuals continue to live in their rotting corpses. In bad people the dead are transformed into monsters called *Kukuchi* and they eat people. "Driven by their appetite for human flesh, they beguile unsuspecting individuals to their death" (Allen, 1988:62). Thus, perhaps the *Kukuchi* kill to inhabit a new body.

After the soul departs from the body, it needs a place to stay. The sophisticated mummification techniques used by the Chinchorro morticians demonstrated a great deal of caring and specific intentions for preserving the dead for an afterlife and ancestral worship. At the final burial, the mummies were furnished with food and a few fishing implements representing terrestrial existence and necessities needed in the hereafter. Their artificial mummification likely allowed the body to host its soul again. The preservation of individual features (e.g., facial characteristics and sexual organs) could have provided an identity so only the proper soul could enter the prepared body. Likewise, the Egyptians mummified the body artificially in order to ensure immortality of the deceased, and they painted the face of the deceased outside the sarcophagus so the soul could recognize its body.

Chinchorro artificial mummification practices were carried out to endure. Artificial mummification even of the fetuses is consistent with the Pan-Andean view that everything may become a *huaca* and that all matter is alive and must be respected (see Allen, 1988:62,63).

The Dead among the Living

Chinchorro burial practices and rituals belong to a remote past; any attempt to reconstruct their death-related ceremonies runs the risk of being condemned as pure speculation. Yet the risk is worth taking because the rituals and mummies reflect beliefs and ideology that are the essence of the Chinchorro people. If speculation is avoided, then ideas are not available for the future when these hypotheses might become testable. Despite the lack of direct evidence in the archaeological record, an attempt must be made to interpret the life of this ancient people as it was—alive.

Chinchorro artificial mummification seems to represent a belief system in which the dead continued to interact with the living. It produced a cultural and metaphysical coexistence in which the dead and living used the same physical space, but existed in different planes, as in the case of the Laymi or Runa from Bolivia and Peru, respectively (see Allen, 1988:56,63; Harris, 1982:62). According to Salomon and Urioste (1991:130, note 699): "Andean people considered Christian burial, which Spanish clerics forced upon them, an affliction because it precluded feeding and clothing one's departed kin. Ancestors buried in Christian graveyards were imagined as starving and suffering while they decayed" (see also Arriaga, 1968; Harris, 1982:46)

In Andean cosmology the preservation of ancestors allowed for continuity of life. As Donovan (1985:28) wrote: "The Waru Chiri Andean's foremost anxiety appears to be not so much the inevitability of death, but rather the fear of death without hope of regeneration." Similarly, Chinchorro artificial mummification practices lasted many millennia, demonstrating the tremendous power of their beliefs in the benefits of artificially mummifying relatives.

Symbolically, without artificial mummification their society would die. It would be a cataclysm of enormous proportions, resulting in a severing of relations between deities, ancestors, and the living community. Continuation of life, or the journey to the afterlife, was accomplished through "transformation of substances" using Donovan's (1985:35) words. The transformation of substances guarantees the continuity of life. Metaphorically, preserved ancestors can be equated with a dry fish in a marine society or a dry potato (*chuño*) in an agricultural group. Though the fish and the potato are dead, both have the power to give life through nourishing others. The mummies nourished the spiritual emotions of the worshipers. The resemblance of the complex Chinchorro mummies to their former selves must have helped the Chinchorros to believe the mummies were not dead, but only transformed into imperishable entities to be venerated and cared for.

Donovan noted that "within the context of continuity it is logical and appropriate that Andean ancestors in their mummy bundles be celebrated and offered food and drink" (Donovan, 1985:35). This Andean belief can be seen as a system of reciprocal altruism: the living protect the dead (e.g., prevent decomposition), and in return, the dead help the living with all their spiritual needs.

The Chinchorro people mummified their dead possibly as a means to reach immortality, but more likely to have the physical presence of their ancestors to guide and act as go-betweens with the supernatural world for protection of the living. Rather than a regeneration of life, a belief more appropriate for agricultural societies, Chinchorro mummies

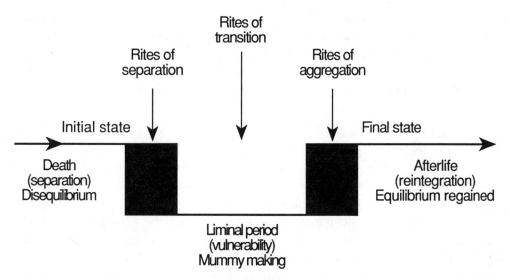

Fig. 51. Stages within mortuary rites (modified version of Leach, 1976:78; graph: T. Cantrell).

represented an extension of life. Artificial mummification can be seen as an act of denial of death and as a symbol of perpetuity of life because the corpses were still among the living. Therefore, artificially mummified bodies and the living were both active participants in Chinchorro society.

Social Significance of Artificial Mummification

Artificial mummification was central to Chinchorro culture for several thousand years. After a Chinchorro died, rites of separation, liminality, and reintegration obviously took place (fig. 51). Feasting with the dead and the possibility of cannibalism are others themes worth exploring.

Rites of Separation

When someone near and dear dies, the daily routine is destroyed and the community must join together to cope with the loss. The private act of dying suddenly is transformed into a public event (Malinowski, 1948:48). Caring for the corpse becomes an immediate need. However, treatments of cadavers are often considered dangerous and repugnant (Harris, 1982:49; Malinowski, 1948:48). But it must be done. If not treated, a cadaver left alone would undergo decay and its foul smell would affect all people living nearby. In the case of the Chinchorros, likely owing to their powerful beliefs already discussed, the preparation for artificially mummifying the body would have started right away. Selecting the place for body preparation, the mortician, the helpers, and mummification materials were all immediate needs. This implies community organization, experts, cooperation, and solidarity in mitigating the grief of mourners.

Rites of Liminality

According to anthropologist Edmund Leach (1976:77) liminality is a period of timelessness. In mortuary rites, liminality is a stage of uncertainty for the living and for the dead, it is a dangerous time (see Turner, 1970:94). The living are concerned with what happens to the body, the presence of bad spirits, observance of taboos, and proper mourning. In a modern study of Greek death rituals, anthropologist Loring Danforth (1982:55) wrote, "During this liminal period the mourners are isolated socially from the world of the living while they are linked symbolically to the world of the dead. They themselves are socially dead and remain so until the rite of exhumation, when they rejoin the world of the living." Ceremonies are, therefore, necessary to protect the living from the uncertainties brought on by death, and to assure that the souls of the departed properly travel to the hereafter or enter their new plane of existence and do not stay to traumatize the living.

In the case of the Chinchorros, liminality was the time when the mummy was being prepared. The mortician's worries must have centered around everything going smoothly, that the soul would like its new body, and that evil entities would stay away. It is possible that many rituals were carried out to protect the mourners, the morticians, and the mummies. Unwanted spirits could have materialized in the form of winds or dust storms common to Arica. Peruvian Runa Indians, for example, fear unexpected winds blowing from ancient chulpas (aboveground tombs) because they believe these are the bad spirits of the dead (Allen, 1988:56).

Although today only the mummies remain, they have embedded in their always crumbling surfaces the grief and beliefs of those who made them. The mechanical process of undertaking the creation of an artificial mummy and the ceremonial aspects of the mortuary ritual must have coaxed up powerful supernatural images for the Chinchorro people. The awareness and perception that one day he or she will be mummified in a similar manner would have created a personal sense of belonging and exploration of the self. As Turner (1970:105) noted, liminality is a period of reflection during which "neophytes are alternately forced and encouraged to think about their society, their cosmos, and the powers that generate and sustain them."

For a small group of Chinchorros this liminal period also would have been the right time to carry out initiations of youth or perhaps a new shaman. Such initiations cross-culturally are also associated with social isolation. What better location for isolation than inside the protective walls of a dark cave. There are many caves at the Morro 1 site next to where Chinchorro mummies have been found. Today these caves are closed for security reasons, but in 1825, British explorers, searching for ancient cemeteries and gold, entered the deep caves and reported anthropomorphic red figures painted on the rock walls (Canales, 1912:286). We do not know if the Chinchorros were responsible for the pictographs found there, but they may well have used these caves for ceremonial purposes owing to their central locations. In Arica south of the Morro 1 site, in a small coastal cave called La Capilla, Muñoz and Chacama (1982) reported finding a burial of many unused grass skirts, as well as geometric wall paintings (fig. 45). La Capilla cave dates to about 1,720 B.C (table 3), consistent with the mud-coated Chinchorro mummies. The grass skirts found there are typical female Chinchorro garments and their discovery provides a glimpse into ceremonies that might be associated with Chinchorro fertility or female initiation rites.

Rites of Reintegration

Artificial mummification allowed the body to be kept above ground without problems of decay. Distant relatives could have had the time to travel, to gather, and to mourn a beautiful mummy instead of decaying flesh. A mummy was more than just a body: it was a perpetuation of the individual in the present and in the hereafter. And as such, it could help the living. After the main funerary ceremonies, the mummy most likely was kept in the settlement for other ceremonial purposes, perhaps as a spiritual link to supernatural beings to help the living obtain good health, fertility, and successful fishing and hunting.

The ethnographic literature is rich in descriptions of elaborate reintegration rituals that go on in nonindustrialized societies today (see Habenstein and Lamers, 1960; Harris, 1983; Krickeberg et al., 1969; MacCormack, 1991). It is conceivable that the Chinchorro practiced many death-related rituals that we can only speculate about today. Mortuary ceremonies like dancing, body painting, sexual activities, food sharing, and exhumations could appear bizarre and out of context, but each mortuary activity had a social meaning beyond its obvious and immediate action. The social and cognitive processes necessary to carry out Chinchorro mummification and the likely associated ceremonies were something deeper than a simple cult to the dead. The complex preparation of the mummies, the existence of statuette mummies, and the burial goods imply an intricate doctrine or belief system about life, death, the afterworld, and the supernatural. It was a belief we can only envision by inference from the mummies, as the Chinchorro did not leave written records to guide us.

There must have been a sense of fulfillment and satisfaction when the mummification process was finished for a beloved member of the group. With so much investment, a finished mummy would hardly have been abandoned. It seems likely that during the reintegration stage religious ceremonial chants, crying, and dancing were performed. Uhle (1922) found a flute and rattles and also a mummified leg with a rattle attached to it. It is not hard to imagine a shaman chanting spells and invocations to the tutelary spirits at this time. Also, hallucinogenic kits have been found among the grave goods of late Chinchorro burials (Standen, 1991). This suggests that hallucinogenic drugs were consumed by the Chinchorro or by a religious leader in order to communicate with the other world during the ceremony of presenting the finished mummy to the ancestors and for reintegration of the mourners. Mythical legends of their ancestors, origin myths, and memories of the deceased's accomplishments might have been shared around a hearth after dark. A storyteller or a shaman possibly emphasized the need for proper ceremonial respect for ancestors and the spiritual and physical feeding of the mummies. The feeding of ancestors is still practiced today in rural areas of the Andes. To her surprise, Allen (1988:165) found Runa friends feeding themselves the food prepared for the dead, and when asked what happened they simply replied, "The souls didn't eat it." Despite this incongruity, it is irrelevant whether the dead ate or not—the importance is the act of pleasing the dead. Andean people believe that all matters are interconnected, as is life and death; the living, then, can eat on behalf of the dead (Allen, 1988:164). In a reciprocal fashion the dead may help the living with better crops or resources.

The final Chinchorro mortuary ceremony provided a time for special social events or an occasion for bringing different groups or families together to cement social ties. An event like this could have allowed access to resources through gift exchange and to renewal of spiritual connections to their common ancestors and tutelary spirits. Simultaneously, the gathering contributed to the spread of mummification technology or to its change. For those members of the Chinchorro community entering puberty, ceremonial gatherings could have been the propitious opportunity to find a mate from another group. Thus, this social bonding mechanism may have helped to avoid inbreeding and could have generated social and political ties between groups. On the basis of archaeological evidence of house foundations, a Chinchorro group can be hypothesized to have consisted of several families, made up of ten to fifty individuals. For the hypothesized mortuary rites, the gathering could have temporarily doubled the population size.

In summary, despite the existence of a division of labor among the living, artificial mummification was independent of age, sex, and social status, implying a collective concern for the individual and the community. Apparently, mummification treatments were not dependent on the social contribution of the individual during life, as fetuses were treated as adults. Instead, perhaps the deceased's potential future contributions in the spiritual world were given priority. At the individual level, the deceased received the proper respect and an adequate burial to ensure life in the hereafter. For the community the pain and the funerary rituals presumably renewed social unity (fig. 52). The funerary rites may also have contributed to perpetuate social roles and community traditions. Finally, mortuary rituals would have been necessary to avoid further deaths and to regain balance in daily life. The rituals reintegrated mummies, spirits, and mourners into the routines of their daily lives and into the cosmos of the supernatural.

Fig. 52. Artistic representation of a funerary rite in honor of a female and her fetus who were mummified (drawing: D. Kendrick-Murdock).

Feasting with the Dead

Rituals provide the opportunity to regain equilibrium with the world beyond. Describing her experiences among the Laymi people, at the time of a "Carnival for the Devils," Harris (1982:58) wrote, "I had been recording the *wayñu* melodies of the flutes, and later that evening began to play the music back. I was immediately stopped by a horrified audience: *wayñu* music belonged to the devils who were now safely dispatched on their way to the land of the dead, and would be drawn back if they heard the sound of the flutes. It thus emerged that the devils whose feast is Carnival are in some form the spirits of the dead."

On the basis of evidence of the energy used to create the Chinchorro mummies, evidence of retouching, and the rigidity which allowed for their movement, it is possible to assume that the mortuary ritual could have gone on for weeks and even years after the death of an individual member. Because mummies are found buried in groups, the artificial mummies could have been kept for years in the settlement until others had died and the people decided it was time to bury a group of mummies. The sophisticated treatments of the black and red mummies and the rejuvenation or subsequent layers of paint applied to the face, especially in some specimens, reflect long-term attention to the mummies. Bittmann and Munizaga (1977) postulated that the mummies were kept in the settlement and transported in vegetable mats when the population moved. But the Chinchorros were sedentary; thus, it is possible the artificially prepared bodies were moved only short distances. They may have been brought along to periodic gatherings to take part in fertility rites or spiritual renewal for the whole community. Allison and co-workers (1984; Allison, 1985b) suggested that the Chinchorro mummies were placed in an upright position, like statues used in cult rituals to the dead for ancestor worship. This certainly could have been true for the natural, red, and black mummies, but not for the mud-coated types, which were fixed to the grave bottoms. It is more likely that the complex mummies were placed in a reclining position rather than completely upright. Being upright for any period would have placed much weight on their relatively weak feet. A lack of feet is pronounced among adult Chinchorro mummies in museum collections today. Hands and feet are generally more vulnerable to damage and their absence may reflect their joint fragility rather than their usage and loss due to placement in an upright position.

Commemorating the dead provided an opportunity for the living to get together, but also "an uneasy truce" (Harris, 1982:69) with the spiritual entities. Well known is the case of the Huron Indians from Canada who gathered their dead relatives in a special pit and celebrated with them as a means of strengthening the social alliances among the living (Trigger, 1969:106–112). The Incas paraded their mummies at religious festivals. Also in South America the Yanomamos, about one year after the death of a relative, hold a feast to consume the deceased's ashes mixed with plantain. "Endocannibalism, to the Yanomamo, is the supreme form of displaying friendship and solidarity" (Chagnon, 1977:50–51). And in other parts of the world, postburial practices, as in the case of modern rural Greece described by Danforth (1982:55–56), included exhumation of the deceased's bones; the occasion was cause for rejoicing and the village was united through exchange of food. The clean bones indicated the soul had reached its final state and the mourners could regain their normal status.

The study of our own behavior is a mirror of the past, and the past is a mirror of the present. Today, the living still fear the dead, consciously or subconsciously; if they did not, movies about ghosts, near-death experiences, zombies, and vampires would never be as popular as they are. Feasting with the dead is also still practiced by many. In Chile a popular song by folklorist Nano Parra playfully describes the happiness surrounding feasting with the dead: "When I die I want a wake with people eating delicious meat turnovers and drinking good red and white wines. I want my family to sing and the guests to dance because the barbecue smells great . . . I will be laughing in my grave at the things that the priest will say." ("El día que yo me muera quiero un velorio / con mistela, empanadas, blanco, y tintolio / que mi familia cante / bailen los invitados / en la parrilla aumean ricos asados / . . . yo me estaré riendo bajo mi sepultura / por las cosas que diga el señor cura.")

In Latin America, All Saints' Day (November 1) and All Souls' Day (November 2) are holidays in which food is prepared in large quantities for the dead, as well as for the living. In the United States, the holiday has taken on new traditions and we know it as Halloween. On All Souls' Day (or Day of the Dead), a visit to the cemetery is mandatory to pay respect to the ancestors whose spirits may come back to join the living at the feast. Feasting with the dead certainly is not specifically the legacy of the Chinchorros, but rather the emotional thread that unites us all. The same search for answers to the question that haunted the Chinchorros thousands of years ago—the nature of life, death, and the supernatural—still haunts us today.

Cannibalism

Because the mummies were defleshed with removal of brain, heart, lungs, and intestines, Alvarez (1969) stated the Chinchorros practiced cannibalism. Cannibalism is often thought to be a manifestation of starvation. The Chinchorro were not starving. The coast was rich in fish, birds, and land and sea mammals. The ocean provided large amounts of shellfish as evidenced by large shell middens about five meters in height found along the coast. Also, the presence of mummies of stillborn and the long-lasting practice of artificial mummification would suggest that cannibalism as a biological necessity to prevent starvation is not supported. However, the concept of a ritualistic cannibalism to obtain the energy or some desired qualities of the deceased was more likely, if cannibalism was practiced at all. It would not have been so far removed from rituals such as those practiced by Melanesians of New Guinea (Malinowski, 1948:50) who ate a piece of flesh as a sacred act of unity with the dead, and then vomited the flesh. Or as the Yanomamos who consumed the ashes of the departed (Chagnon, 1977:50–51). Symbolic cannibalism is also practiced by some Christians every weekend when they ceremonially drink the blood of Jesus (symbolized by wine) and eat his body (symbolized by wafers) to be reborn with him. At this time there is no evidence to either support or refute the suggestion of ritualistic cannibalism among the Chinchorro people.

CHAPTER 12

EPITAPH

 Most Chinchorro research has been based on the study of particular cemeteries, often motivated by rescue operations necessitated by expansion of modern cities. A total of 282 bodies can be accounted for in the literature since Uhle's (1917) first publication. It is estimated that 53% (149/282) were artificially mummified and 47% (133/282) naturally mummified. The total number of mummies represents mostly the Arica area, but the Chinchorro populated about 900 kilometers of the Atacama coast; considering their 5,500-year chronology, this is hardly a representative sample. Where are the other bodies? In Arica most Chinchorro sites are found near the ocean. The paucity of sites could be explained by rising sea levels, storms, or tidal waves that destroyed the cemeteries and settlements where the Chinchorro once lived. Canales (1912:284) commented that after an earthquake the overflow of the ocean (*salidas de mar*) "cleaned" a large part of the city of Arica, moving remains inward toward the hills. Also, some Chinchorro sites could have been destroyed by the growing needs of ever-expanding coastal cities. But the most likely reason for the missing sites and bodies is a lack of systematic study of the Chinchorro that utilizes an all-encompassing archaeological research design. A survey of possible Chinchorro sites—many of which are likely in danger of destruction—along the Atacama coast and in nearby cities is the next step that urgently needs to be undertaken.

Yet, with the few excavations to date, it has been possible to piece together some important aspects of Chinchorro prehistory. For instance, Chinchorro beginnings have been pushed back dramatically from Uhle's first suggestion that the Chinchorro lived about the time of Christ. The oldest Chinchorro evidence dates from at least 7,020 B.C. Artificial mummification, often seen as a trademark of Chinchorro, did not develop until two millennia later. From a practical point of view Chinchorro mortuary changes and, thus, cultural development can be broken down into five main epochs which correlate with mortuary treatments: natural I, black, red, mud-coated, and natural II (fig. 47). The first, natural I, corresponds to the pioneer populations who settled and prospered along the coast and became fishers, but lacked artificial mummification. The second, when artificial mummification began (ca. 5,050 B.C), is characterized by the most complex style, the black mummies. The third, the red mummy epoch (ca. 2,600 B.C), also involved sophisticated treatment for the dead, but to a slightly lesser extent than that used during the black epoch. By the time of the red epoch, artificial mummification practices had expanded along the entire Atacama coast. The fourth epoch, characterized by the mud-coated mummies, marks the last evidence of artificial mummification and further simplification of mortuary treatment (ca. 1,700 B.C). And the fifth epoch, natural II, denotes the return of natural mummification and the disappearance of artificial mummification. Throughout these five epochs the bodies were buried in an extended position.

It is important that researchers begin to be more specific about the particular type of Chinchorro mummy being described, such as natural, black or red, rather than using more general terms such as artificial or complex mummies. The Chinchorro complex period (black and red) lasted about 3,000 years (5,050 to 2,090 B.C.). The classic black epoch was the longest, lasting about 2,000 years (4,980 to 2,800 B.C.), but the red lasted only about 500 to 600 years (2,685 to 2,090 B.C.). A clear categorization of future finds and discussions will facilitate the understanding of Chinchorro world view and its changes through time.

Various points still need further clarification. One of them is the origin of the Chinchorro. However, the biological origin of the Chinchorros and the social origin of their artificial mummification should not be treated as one category of analysis. For the moment, the bioarchaeological data suggest that the most likely geographic area for Chinchorro biological origin is the highland area of Arica. However, the scarcity of early skeletons to assess biological affinity for the region has inhibited such studies. Therefore, neither a coastal, highland, nor Amazon origin can be statistically and biologically substantiated at this point. On the other hand, the question of where artificial mummification practices developed appears to have a solid answer. Although many cemeteries have been found in central Peru that are contemporary to those of the Chinchorros, none show evidence of artificial mummification. During the Atacama preceramic period (ca. 7,000 to 1,500 B.C.) artificial mummification appears to have been a cultural practice unique to the Chinchorro. It originated and sustained itself on the Arica-Camarones coast. And within this core area, Camarones gorge hosted the cultural genesis for Chinchorro artificial mummification, about 5,050 B.C. From the Arica-Camarones area artificial mummification spread north and south. This is the oldest known system of artificial mummification in the world. This mortuary sophistication is remarkable inasmuch as the Chinchorros were otherwise technologically a simple society, unfamiliar with ceramic technology, metallurgy, or the manufacture of woven textiles.

Caring for the dead is an ancient social custom, but if conditions of the Atacama Desert naturally created a mummy, why did the Chinchorro need to go to the extreme of artificially mummifying their dead? The hypotheses discussed in the text attempting to answer this question can be summarized as follows:

1. An ideological hypothesis of a Chinchorro belief that the dead cooperated with the living, whereby it was essential to preserve the body and its image to ensure sur-

vival of the living as well as the spirits of the dead. This mortuary system provided insurance of continuity of life for everyone.

2. An environmental hypothesis which suggests the Chinchorro people improved upon nature and natural mummification, as they must have observed the natural process of mummification of animal and human bodies going on around them.

3. A natural disaster hypothesis that survivors of catastrophes in a search for answers sought help from the supernatural through the bodies of their newly departed family members.

Most likely a combination of these three main hypotheses triggered and helped maintain the artificial mummification practices. But sedentism permitted the Chinchorros to elaborate upon their rituals. However, not all sedentary coastal peoples developed artificial mummification. It was the Chinchorro faith in an afterlife, devotion to their ancestors, and the functional benefits of death-related rituals that enabled Chinchorro artificial mummification practices, black to mud-coated styles, to flourish for about three and half millennia.

This work, attempting to synthesize our present knowledge about the Chinchorros, shows that there is still much to be learned. It also shows the need for further scholarly discussions and debates, which should engender the possibility of some speculation in order to understand the complex burial practices and world view of these ancient fishing peoples. The meanings behind Chinchorro behavior are not always straightforward and often must be inferred. Although it is most certainly true that their mummification techniques paralleled an equally complex world view, it is not an easily testable hypothesis. Death rituals and the notions of the supernatural often go unnoticed in the archaeology of many ancient societies. Rituals become buried behind more testable research questions of economic or sociopolitical significance that have more "solid data." But the Chinchorro death rituals were likely a central focus of their social lives, and thus warrant our efforts to rescue as much of them as we can.

Human nature involves much experimentation in the ongoing search for answers to life and death. This leads to a rich variety of explanations, mythology, and rituals. Archaeologically, such beliefs and practices can be reflected in mortuary practices and grave goods. The power behind Chinchorro death rituals in their everyday life was materialized in artificial mummification. The Chinchorro as a cultural group reveal a complex tradition of practical and esoteric knowledge concerning death, the supernatural, and the afterlife. The variations in mortuary practices of the Chinchorro were cultural transformations that must have denoted a shift in their social and spiritual perceptions, as exemplified by the changes in body treatment and color symbolism of black and red mummies or red and mud-coated mummies. The shift from transportable mummies that were likely displayed above ground in a semiupright position to mummies that were mud-coated and glued to the grave pit shows an even greater shift in beliefs.

It seems obvious the Chinchorros did not fear corpses as modern Andean people do, yet Chinchorros must have feared unwanted spirits. The mummies were "living corpses" housing the souls of the dead. Not only did their maintenance perpetuate the memories of the deceased, like a statue or a picture, but the living could seek advice from the dead as "living entities." The mummies linked this world with the world beyond. Probably, these mummies were imbued with accumulated ancestral knowledge and wisdom. In other words, it is likely the Chinchorros believed in a coexistence and cooperation between dead ancestors and their living descendants. Therefore, Chinchorro mummies became functional religious objects that served the purpose of acting as a social buffer, providing answers to their metaphysical questions and satisfying the social needs of daily life.

The finished Chinchorro mummies were most likely displayed. This cultural practice of displaying mummies to participate or interact in the affairs of the living seems to have been a long-standing Andean tradition, as it is found in Inca times, as described by the Spanish chroniclers during the conquest of the Incas (see Guaman Poma, 1980).

In many cultures the maintenance of mummies of dead relatives in temples or special areas and the participation of the mummies in religious festivals are essential to gain prosperity or advantage (see Krickeberg et al., 1969; MacCormack, 1991). Obviously, we cannot see the Chinchorro rites in the archaeological record, but the complex mortuary practices and the retouching of the mummies suggest that the Chinchorros held special ceremonies years after the artificial mummification took place.

Chinchorro mummification became a fundamental rite of passage for the Chinchorro people, assuring not only eternity for the individual (body and soul), but also continuity of the group. Artificial mummification was likely at the root of group cohesion in the Chinchorro culture. Wishing to receive the proper mortuary treatment and burial ceremony must have been the last desire in the social persona of a Chinchorro individual when feeling close to death. For the young members of the Chinchorro community, the mortuary ceremony must have been a significant opportunity to learn traditional values, social rules, and how to revere and serve their ancestors and the spiritual entities. The long duration of artificial mummification practices can be partially explained by the centrality of its purpose and meaning. Uncertainty about life, death, and the afterlife is still with us and consolation is sought when dealing with the loss of a loved one. These archaic uncertainties which are brought to mind by the anguish of death also seem to have been a natural social bonding mechanism that kept the Chinchorro tradition alive and strong for hundreds of generations. But after thousands of years of successful ancestral worship, as most things in life, artificial mummification also declined and then disappeared.

It is interesting that the complex mortuary rites of the Inca civilization parallel the sophisticated mortuary practices of the Chinchorro fishing people, although the Chinchorro were technologically and politically a simpler society. During Inca times sophisticated mortuary rituals related to ancestral cult worship were pivotal to Inca sociopolitical organization. Mummified Incas literally were present for the important affairs of the living during religious festivals. Therefore, Chinchorro mortuary practices demonstrated that complex ideology and mortuary rituals involving dead ancestors is by no means an exclusive characteristic of complex and ranked societies. The realms of the spiritual world and the notion of the hereafter play an essential role in mortuary behavior that can be independent of the rank of the individuals involved and the degree of political complexity of the society.

Though ancestor worship through mummification was likely a common theme among the Inca and Chinchorro, apparently artificial mummification was a unique mortuary phenomenon that did not repeat itself in post-Chinchorro Andean coastal societies. Archaeologist Julio Tello (1929:131–135, in Cockburn and Cockburn, 1980:140) stated that Paracas mummies (ca. A.D. 200) were artificially mummified; however, later studies of Paracas mummies have failed to confirm Tello's claim (Allison and Pezzia, 1973). Despite the assertion by Spanish chroniclers (e.g., Garcilaso, 1987:306–308) that artificial mummification was practiced by the Inca, this claim has never been proven and remains dubious.

Garcilaso (1987) thought the Inca mummies were artificially preserved. In 1560, before going to Spain, he had the opportunity to see several royal mummies confiscated by the Spaniards, and his description may indicate that the mummies were not artificially mummified after all. "I remember having touched one of the fingers of Huaina Cápac, which seemed like that of a wooden statue, it was so hard and stiff. The bodies weighed so little that any Indian could carry them in his arms or on his back from house to house, wherever gentlemen asked to see them" (Garcilaso de La Vega, 1987:308, Bk. V, Chap. XXIX). If the Royal Incas were artificially mummified, herbs, earth, pieces of cloth, or cotton would have been used for packing, thus increasing the body weight. The body weight would not increase much if only cotton balls were used, but, most likely, the light weight implies that stuffing was not added to the bodies and that evisceration had not likely taken place. Naturally desiccated bodies are normally extremely light weight, therefore, Garcilaso's statement indicates that these mummies were likely desiccated rather than artificially mummified. However, not all natural mummies are light weight: the naturally preserved "greasy mummies" in Arica, with all their organs and a significant amount of fluids remaining, are quite heavy. Recently, anthropologist Sabine MacCormack (1991:129) stated that the body of Inca Huaina Cápac was made into a mummy by having its internal organs removed and by air drying the body. The mummification of a Royal Inca was probably achieved by wrapping the corpse with vast amounts of cloth to absorb body fluids, and perhaps temporarily placing the mummy in a warm, dry place. Smoke and heat also may have been used to dry the body. Subsequently the dried body was exhumed, if buried, and stripped of its stained clothes, redressed, ornamented, and displayed. The way the Royal Inca mummies were preserved has never been confirmed because they were never studied and, unfortunately, no longer exist. They were either burned by the Conquistadors, buried during Colonial times, or simply lost.

During Inca times, Salomon (1991) and archaeologist John Rowe (1991) noted, the Inca lord was not buried; the mummy continued to live in the palace. New Inca kings were required to build their own palaces which later became their mausoleums. This parallels Egypt where the pharaohs built their tombs during their lifetimes. Andean Inca and Egyptian kings both strove to build larger and more ostentatious tombs. The size of their temples likely mirrors their egocentric views that they were the sons of god. It can be argued that in these two complex societies, the elaborate mortuary rites for the disposal of the dead evolved to economically benefit the living king and his family, but were not meant to simply honor the dead. The Chinchorro case was very different because economic gains were unlikely goals, and therefore ancestor worship and devotion to the deceased were likely primary motives. Social cohesion was probably a secondary effect.

The study of the Chinchorros provides new understandings of cultural adaptation and the complexity of world view that were possible in early societies. Just as Moseley (1975, 1992) and Benfer (1984) have argued for early sedentary populations along the coast of central Peru, so, too, the evidence for Chinchorro also indicates early fully sedentary lifestyles based entirely on maritime subsistence. For instance, the study of Chinchorro middens revealed a high level of maritime products. Tools and artifacts showed specialized maritime harvesting techniques (e.g., nets and fishhooks), and the chemistry and pathology of human bones indicated consumption of their maritime harvests. The zoonosis acquired from sea mammals and fish indicated the variety of marine resources consumed and the health consequences of improper food processing. Also, the extensive reoccupations of cemeteries, as well as the development of various complex mummification techniques, all indicate that the Chinchorro were sedentary, with specialization and division of labor, but without manifestations of rank or persons of greatly elevated status. Every society needs an organizer; thus, it is likely that the most charismatic and gifted persons, through respect or achievement, gained social prestige and became the natural Chinchorro leaders. But their status was not accorded personal wealth, a special type of mummification, or any other markers that would set them apart archaeologically.

The removal of inner organs with subsequent internal and external treatment of the cadaver to achieve artificial mummification and the high energy expenditure and skill required for these practices reveal planned strategies and the mastery of specialized morticians. There could have been a few specialists who traveled to help prepare dead bodies, but more likely there was a specialist in each group. This would explain the slight variations in mummification techniques within a style, such as seen in the black mummies found at Morro 1 and Chinchorro 1. Regional variations were also found in facial masks, which were sometimes reddish, greenish, yellowish, or black (Bittmann, 1982; Latcham, 1938:70; Olmos and Sanhueza, 1984; Uhle, 1922:66), probably reflecting local soil and pigment availability or perhaps signifying kinship identity.

The Chinchorro were not only a society that had clever morticians, but they were also clever fishers. Chinchorros were a continuum of coastal people, with a long tradition of efficient maritime adaptation, who maximized the exploitation of the coasts and river drainages to survive and multiply along the fringes of the Atacama Desert. Although the Chinchorro lived in relatively pleasant ecological zones, their sedentism, maritime subsistence, and mortuary practices had some drawbacks on their overall health. Chinchorro males suffered from several kinds of subsistence-induced pathologies such as ear inflammations, traumas (spondylolysis) and degenerative diseases (arthritis).

Without food or territorial constraints they did not have pressures to regulate their fertility culturally. A high fertility rate, however, did not permit females to recuperate normal bone chemistry between pregnancies. Therefore, by middle age, females suffered the consequences of their great fertility: their osteoporotic bones were prone to vertebral fractures. Mortuary practices likely also created a great potential for the transmission of infectious diseases. If females were in charge of both food preparation and cleaning infected decomposing cadavers they could have contaminated their children and others with many germs. Treponematosis-like infections noted in the tibias of younger and older people could have been easily and unwittingly spread.

Resistance to Change

Chinchorro mummification practices did not undergo abrupt drastic changes. Reluctance or resistance to change is not unique to the Chinchorro. It was also present in other contemporary Andean cultures. Quilter (1989:53), for example, was impressed by the fact that burial practices at La Paloma site did not change very much in 3,000 years of human occupation. Paucity of mortuary changes was also reported for the Las Vegas site by Stothert (1988). It seems the resistance to change involved both ideological and technological realms. The rich coastal environment and strong ideological convictions may have been stabilizing factors that allowed these ancient coastal peoples to maintain their mortuary traditions for millennia. In Peru, by about 3,000 B.C. some coastal populations grew large enough to undertake construction of monumental buildings. In the Arica-Camarones area, population density must have remained low, despite evidence of high female fertility, thus making conflict less likely and fortification and elaboration of villages unnecessary.

Many early sites, such as Las Vegas and La Paloma, share several other cultural features with Chinchorro. Each had the following: continuous occupations of a site for thousands of years, coastal and riverain subsistence practices, early evidence for formal burial treatments of the dead, few grave goods accompanying the dead, often group or collective burials, intermingling of cemeteries and habitation sites, and disturbance of burial sites. This disturbance was likely a consequence of long human occupation in the same place and residences being built close to cemeteries rather than contemporaneous desecration. Also common to all these sites was the fact that infants were treated as full members of the society, rather than being buried with fewer artifacts or less mortuary preparation.

This equality shows the grief that ancient people felt when losing a group member and the potential contribution to their society that all members made in the afterlife. It does not seem to reflect the existence of special children with inherited rank deserving proper burial.

Fate of the Chinchorros

The Chinchorro people did not disappear or vanish. They continued to live along the coast. But what did change was their belief system as reflected in their mortuary practices. Changes eventually led to the disappearance of artificial mummification practices (ca. 1,700 B.C.) and the return to natural mummification. Thus, the use of "Chinchorro" to denote only complex artificial mummification would be erroneous, because that would exclude the simpler mud-coated and natural mummies.

  Biologically the Chinchorro and later inhabitants of Arica were related, but to avoid confusion the term Chinchorro or Chinchorro culture should be used as a general term to be applied to the early people of the south-central Andes who were characterized by a simple fishing technology, burial of their dead in an extended position, and the use of both natural and artificial mummification. Mortuary practices had become markedly different about 1,500 to 1,300 years B.C. denoting the beginning of the Quiani phase, directly following Chinchorro. In Quiani, the body was only naturally mummified, lying on one side with legs flexed, and wearing a turban. Various other technological changes were taking place. At this time fishing technology and subsistence practices were changing and diversifying. There is evidence of incipient horticulture. Subsequent post-Quiani cultural development continued to increase in complexity leading to the formation of regional chiefdoms in Arica, about 1,400 A.D. (fig. 53). These chiefdoms were eventually conquered by the Incas and later by the Spanish

Future Research

Future research must look at specific periods within the Chinchorro culture to understand better the cultural changes reflected by variations in mummy styles through time. Research on the Chinchorro culture is becoming more intense, and future work should address both specific and general topics. The specific topics include: (1) what is Chinchorro and what does it represent? (2) who were the morticians? and were they males or females? (3) why and how did stylistic changes take place? (4) what were the geographic boundaries of the Chinchorro? (5) do the individuals buried together with artificial mummification, normally five to six individuals of different ages and sex, represent a family or a particular clan? (6) where were the locations of all freshwater resources in the Arica area? and (7) what are the genetic relationships between different

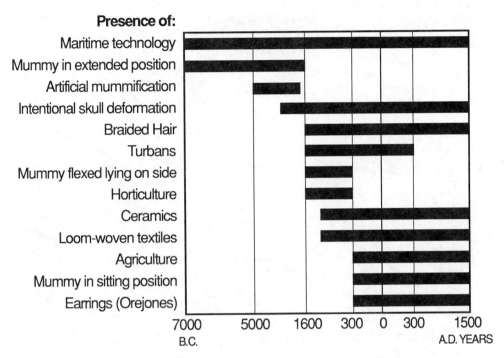

Presence of:
Maritime technology
Mummy in extended position
Artificial mummification
Intentional skull deformation
Braided Hair
Turbans
Mummy flexed lying on side
Horticulture
Ceramics
Loom-woven textiles
Agriculture
Mummy in sitting position
Earrings (Orejones)

7000   5000   1600   300   0   300   1500
B.C.   A.D. YEARS

Fig. 53. Basic cultural traits through time in Arica (graph: T. Cantrell).

Chinchorro groups found at different sites? Are the artificially prepared mummies of the periphery a consequence of cultural diffusion or are they genetically closely related to those of the core (Arica-Camarones)?

More general Chinchorro problems are: (1) what were the mechanisms of interaction between preceramic highland, lowland, valley, and coastal populations of the Atacama? (2) what would demographic reconstructions look like if detailed settlement pattern, cemetery, and midden data were included? (3) what were regional settlement patterns and how do they relate to population movements along the coast? (4) have there been ecological changes? and (5) what is the best way to insure the continued existence of the Chinchorro mummies and their research potential in museum collections? After surviving thousands of years, today they are fragile and subject to deterioration.

Conservation

It is ironic that we must worry and actively seek new solutions for the preservation of the Chinchorro mummies and cultural materials, after they have survived many thousands of

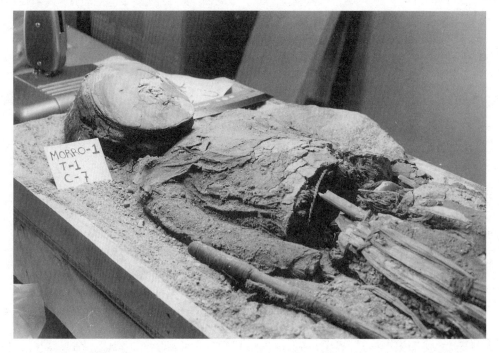

Fig. 54. A fragile black mummy from the Morro 1 site (M1T1C7, young adult) (photo: V. Cassman and S. Schnepp).

years without our interference. However, they survived exactly for that reason: they were enshrined for thousands of years by a sandy, stable environment, without light, human handling, insects, or microorganisms (Cassman, 1991). Now that they have been excavated, the mummies are paying a heavy price for the rich knowledge they provide about their culture and past lives (pls. 20, 21, fig. 54).

The Chinchorro mummies and most of their accompanying material remains are now a fragile complex assortment of composite materials (unbaked clay, ashes, bones, skins, resins, human hair, reeds, fibers, and miscellaneous items). These materials have different rates and causes of deterioration. The greatest damage, however, is caused by excessive vibrations during handling and transportation. There are no miracles, sprays, or preservative agents to conserve the mummies, and anything we add to them detracts from their integrity and future studies. Therefore, the best course to pursue is preventive conservation.

Concluding Remarks

Cross-culturally, the practice of preserving the body seems related to the belief of a spiritual and eternal life for the body and soul. Artificial mummification practices arouse the imagination and question human powers and desires to influence destiny. Even with modern medical advances, our vulnerability to disease, and finally death, has changed little since humans first inhabited the Earth. Thus, studying Chinchorro mortuary practices gives us a depth of perspective for comparison to our own existential, subsistence, economic, and even environmental problems.

The past is not only encoded in our genes, but also in the cultural material left behind by ancient cultures. It is human plasticity or adaptation to environmental changes and subsequent cultural, economic, and political accomplishments that make the study of ancient humans a fascinating mystery to unravel. Chinchorro preoccupation with the dead was not in vain; their artificially prepared mummies are still with us. It is now our responsibility to preserve these unique mummies as testimonies of life and desires thousands of years old. It is their complex artificial mummification practices, small population sizes, simple sociopolitical organization, and their antiquity and persistence through time that make the Chinchorro culture a wonder of world prehistory.

BIBLIOGRAPHY

Allen, C.
1988   *The Hold Life Has: Coca and Cultural Identity in an Andean Community*. Washington: Smithsonian Institution Press.

Allen, E.
1993   Death of a matriarch. *California Anthropologist* 20(2):31–36.

Allison, M.
1985a   Pre-Columbian American disease, 1977–1982. *National Geographic Society, Research Reports* 18:109–130.
1985b   Chile's ancient mummies. *Natural History* 94(10):74–81.

Allison, M., and A. Pezzia
1973   Preparation of the dead in pre-Columbian coastal Peru. Part 1. *Paleopathology Newsletter* 4:10–12.

Allison, M., G. Focacci, E. Gersztein, C. Santoro, M. Rivera, and J. Munizaga
1982a   Estudio radiográfico y demográfico de morbilidad y mortalidad de pueblos precolombinos del Perú y Chile. *Chungará* 8:265–274.

Allison, M., G. Focacci, E. Gersztein, M. Fouant, and M. Cebelin
1982b   La sífilis, una enfermedad americana? *Chungará* 9:275–283.

Allison, M., B. Arriaza, G. Focacci, and I. Muñoz
1983   Los orejones de Arica. *Chungará* 11:167–172.

Allison, M., G. Focacci, B. Arriaza, V. Standen, M. Rivera, and J. Lowenstein
1984   Chinchorro momias de preparación complicada: Métodos de momificación. *Chungará* 13:155–173.

Alvarez, L.
1961   Culturas precerámicas en la arqueología de Arica. *Boletín del Museo Regional de Arica* 5:1–4.
1969   Un cementerio precerámico con momias de preparación complicada. *Rehue* 2:181–190.

Arriaga, P.J.
1968   *The Extirpation of Idolatry in Peru*. C. Keating, trans. and ed. Lexington: University of Kentucky Press. [Original published 1621.]

Arriaza, B.
1988   Modelo bioarqueológico para la búsqueda y acercamiento al individuo social. *Chungará* 21:9–32.
1993a   A synthesis of Chinchorro culture. Paper presented at the symposium, Centrality of Bioarchaeology: Andean Instances. Organizer: R. Benfer. Discussant:

R. Burger. 58th Annual Meeting of the Society for American Archaeology, St. Louis, Missouri.

1993b   Seronegative spondyloarthropathies and diffuse idiopathic skeletal hyperostosis in ancient northern Chile. *American Journal of Physical Anthropology* 91:263–278.

1993c   Preparation of the dead in coastal Andean Preceramic populations. Paper presented at the International Mummy Symposium, Forschunginstitut für Alpine Vorzeit der Leopold-Franzens-Universität Innsbruck, Innsbruck, Austria.

In press   Spondylolysis in paleopathology. *Bioantropología*.

Arriaza, B., M. Allison, and E. Gerszten

1988   Maternal mortality in pre-Columbian Indians of Arica. *American Journal of Physical Anthropology* 77:35–41.

Arriaza, B., M. Allison, and V. Standen

1984a   Momificación artificial en el extremo Norte de Chile. Sitio Morro 1 (5,860–2,090 A.C.). Informe Técnico de Laboratorio de Paleobiología. Report on file at the Archaeology Department of the University of Tarapacá.

1984b   Líneas de Harris en una población arcaica tardía del extremo Norte de Chile: Morro-1. *Chungará* 13:187–191.

Arriaza, B., I. Muñoz, and A. Aufderheide

1993   Análisis antropológico físico de la inhumación de Acha-2. In *Acha-2 y los Orígenes del Poblamiento Humano en Arica*, I. Muñoz, B. Arriaza, and A. Aufderheide, eds., 47–62. Arica: Universidad de Tarapacá.

Arriaza, B., W. Salo, and A. Aufderheide

1994   Mycobacterium tuberculosis DNA extracted from a pre-Columbian mummy from northern Chile. Paper presented at the symposium: Examining Ancient Mummified Remains. Organizer: R. Pickering. Annual Meeting of the Paleopathology Association and the American Association of Physical Anthropology. Denver, Colorado.

Arriaza, B., M. Allison, V. Standen, and G. Focacci

1986a   The practice of artificial mummification in the Chinchorro culture from the Morro-1 site, Arica, Chile. Paper presented at the Annual Meeting of the Paleopathology Association and the American Association of Physical Anthropology. Albuquerque, New Mexico.

Arriaza, B., M. Allison, V. Standen, G. Focacci, and J. Chacama

1986b   Peinados precolombinos en momias de Arica. *Chungará* 16–17:353–375.

Aufderheide, A.

1989   Chemical analysis of skeletal remains. In *Reconstruction of Life from the Skeleton*, M.Y. Iscan and K.A.R. Kennedy, eds., 237–260. New York: Alan R. Liss.

Aufderheide, A., and M. Allison

1992   Chemical dietary reconstruction of north Chile prehistoric populations by trace mineral analysis. Manuscript on file, Department of Pathology, University of Minnesota, Duluth.

1994   Bioanthropological studies of spontaneously mummified bodies of a late phase Chinchorro site (Morro 1–6) in northern Chile. Paper presented at the symposium: Bioarchaeology of the Chinchorro People. Organizers: B. Arriaza and Vicki Cassman. Discussant: J. Verano. 59th Annual Meeting of the Society for American Archaeology, Anaheim, California.

Aufderheide, A., I. Muñoz, and B. Arriaza
   1993   Seven Chinchorro mummies and the prehistory of northern Chile. *American Journal of Physical Anthropology* 91:189–201.

Belmonte, E., T. Torres, and Y. Molina
   1993   Análisis de fragmentos vegetales del asentamiento de Acha-2. In *Acha-2 y los Orígenes del Poblamiento Humano en Arica*, I. Muñoz, B. Arriaza, and A. Aufderheide, eds., 91–106. Arica: Universidad de Tarapacá.

Benfer, R.A.
   1977   Post Pleistocene biological/cultural evolution in coastal Peru. Paper presented at the 76th Annual Meeting of the American Anthropological Association, Houston, Texas.
   1984   The challenges and rewards of sedentism: The preceramic village of Paloma, Peru. In *Paleopathology at the Origins of Agriculture*, M.N. Cohen and G.J. Armelagos, eds., 531–558. Orlando, Fla.: Academic Press.

Binford, L.R.
   1971   Mortuary practices: Their study and their potential. In *Approaches to the Social Dimensions of Mortuary Practices*, J.A. Brown, ed., 6–29. Society for American Archaeology Memoir 25.

Bird, J.
   1943   *Excavations in Northern Chile.* Anthropological Papers of the American Museum of Natural History, vol. 38, pt. 4. New York.
   1946   The cultural sequence of the north Chilean coast. In *Handbook of South American Indians,* vol. 2, 587–594. Bureau of American Ethnology Bulletin 143. Washington: Smithsonian Institution Press.
   1985   *The Preceramic Excavations at the Huaca Prieta, Chicama Valley, Peru,* J. Hyslop, ed. Anthropological Papers of the American Museum of Natural History, vol. 62, pt. 1. New York.

Bittmann, B.
   1982   Revisión del problema Chinchorro. *Chungará* 9:46–79.
   1984   El Proyecto Cobija: Investigaciones antropológicas en la costa del desierto de Atacama (Chile). Paper presented at the 44th International Congress of Americanists, Manchester, New Hampshire.

Bittmann, B., and J. Munizaga
   1976   The earliest artificial mummification in the world? A study of the Chinchorro Complex in northern Chile. *Folk* 18:61–92.
   1977   Algunas consideraciones en torno al "Complejo Chinchorro" (Chile). In *Actas del VII Congreso Nacional de Arqueología Chilena*, vol. 1, 119–130. Ediciones Kultrun. Santiago.
   1979   El arco en América: Evidencia temprana y directa de la Cultura Chinchorro (Norte de Chile). *Indiana* 5:229–251.
   1980   Momificación artificial en el Pacífico Sur? Paralelismo o difusión? *Indiana* 6:381–397.

Bloch, M., and J. Parry
   1982   Introduction. In *Death and the Regeneration of Life*, M. Bloch and J. Parry, eds., 1–44. Cambridge: Cambridge University Press.

Boissett, G., A. Llagostera, and E. Salas
   1969   Excavaciones arqueológicas en Caleta Abtao, Antofagasta. In *Actas del V Congreso Nacional de Arqueología Chilena*, 75–112. La Serena.

Bonavia, D.
    1988   Exostosis el conducto auditivo externo. Notas adicionales. *Chungará* 20:63–68.
Brothwell, D.
    1987   *The Bog Man and the Archaeology of People*. Cambridge: Harvard University
                Press.
Brown, J.A.
    1981   The search for rank in prehistoric burials. In *The Archaeology of Death*, R. Chap-
                man, I. Kinnes, and K. Randsborg, eds., 25–37. Cambridge: Cambridge Uni-
                versity Press.
Buikstra, J.E., ed.
    1981   *Prehistoric Tuberculosis in the Americas*. Northwestern University Archeological
                Program. Scientific Papers, no. 5. Evanston, Ill.
Byrner, K., and D. Parris
    1987   Reconstruction of the diet of the Middle Woodland Amerindian population at
                Abbott Farm by bone trace- element analysis. *American Journal of Physical An-
                thropology* 74:373–384.
Canales, P.
    1912   Los cementerios indígenas en la costa del Pacífico. In *Actas del XVII Congreso
                Internacional de Americanistas*, 273–297. Buenos Aires.
Cárdenas, F.
    In press   Momias, santuarios y ofrendas: El contexto ritual de la momificación en el altiplano
                central de los Andes Colombianos. In *Memorias del I Congreso Internacional de
                Estudios Sobre Momias*. [Meeting held in 1992, Santa Cruz, Tenerife.]
Cassman, V.
    1991   Las momias Chinchorro tratamiento de conservación. Proyecto Conservación
                Momias Chinchorro. Universidad de Tarapacá. Manuscript on file, Department
                of Archaeology, Universidad de Tarapacá.
Chagnon, N.
    1977   *Yanomamo: The Fierce People*. New York: Holt, Rinehart and Winston.
Chapman, R., I. Kinnes, and K. Randsborg, editors
    1981   *The Archaeology of Death*. Cambridge: Cambridge University Press.
Chauchat, C.
    1988   Early hunter-gatherers on the Peruvian coast. In *Peruvian Prehistory*, W. Keating,
                ed., 41–66. Cambridge: Cambridge University Press.
Cieza de León, Pedro de
    1959   *The Incas*, H. de Onis, trans., V.W. von Hagen, ed. Norman: University of
                Oklahoma Press. [Original published 1553.]
Cobo, B.
    1964   *Historia del Nuevo Mundo*. In Obras del P. Bernabe Cobo. Vol. 2. Biblioteca de Auto-
                res Españoles. F. Mateos, ed. Madrid: Ediciones Atlas. [Original published 1653.]
Cockburn, A., and E. Cockburn, eds.
    1980   *Mummies, Diseases and Ancient Cultures*. Cambridge: Cambridge University
                Press.
Cohen, M., and G. Armelagos (eds.)
    1984   *Paleopathology at the Origins of Agriculture*. Orlando, Fla.: Academic Press.
Comas, J.
    1974   Orígenes de la momificación prehispánica en América. *Anales de Antropología*
                11:357–382.

Craig, A.
1982   Ambiente costero del Norte de Chile. *Chungará* 9:4–20.
Crom, W.
1993   Medio ambiente del sitio Acha-2. In *Acha-2 y los Orígenes del Poblamiento Humano en Arica*, I. Muñoz, B. Arriaza, and A. Aufderheide, eds., 15–19. Arica: Universidad de Tarapacá.
Danforth, L.
1982   *The Death Rituals of Rural Greece*. Princeton: Princeton University Press.
Dauelsberg, P.
1963   Complejo arqueológico del Morro de Arica [summary]. Congreso Internacional de Arqueología de San Pedro de Atacama. *Anales de la Universidad del Norte*, No. 2, 200–201.
1974   Excavaciones arqueológicas en Quiani. Provincia de Tarapacá, Depto. de Arica, Chile. *Chungará* 4:7–38.
1983   Tojo-Tojone: un paradero de cazadores arcaicos (características y secuencias). *Chungará* 11:11–30.
David, R., and E. Tapp
1984   *Evidence Embalmed: Modern Medicine and the Mummies of Ancient Egypt*. New Hampshire: Manchester University Press.
Donnan, C.B.
1964   An early house from Chilca, Peru. *American Antiquity* 30(2):137–144.
Donovan, M.
1985   Nacieron del fruto del arbol: Transformations toward continuity. In *Weaving and Symbolism in the Andes*, J. Sherbondy, ed., 27–42. Andean Studies Occasional Papers, vol. 2 (Spring). Bloomington: Indiana University.
Durkheim, E.
1965   *The Elementary Forms of the Religious Life*, J.W. Swain, trans. New York: Free Press. [Original published 1912.]
Engel, F.A.
1963   A preceramic settlement on the central coast of Peru: Asia, Unit 1. *Transactions of the American Philosophical Society* 53(3).
1981   *Prehistoric Andean Ecology, Man, Settlement, and Environment in the Andes, the Deep South*. New York: Humanities Press.
1984   *Chilca*. Prehistoric Andean Ecology Series, 4. New York: Humanities Press.
Ferreira, L.F., A.J.G. Araújo, U.E.C. Confalonieri, and L. Núñez
1984   The finding of eggs of *Diphyllobothrium* in human coprolites (4,100–1,950 B.C.) from northern Chile. *Memórias do Instituto Oswaldo Cruz* 79:175–180.
Figueroa, L., B. Razmilic, M. Allison, and M. González
1988   Evidencia de arsenicismo crónico en momias del Valle de Camarones. Región Tarapacá, Chile. *Chungará* 21:33–42.
Focacci, G.
1974   Excavaciones en el cementerio Playa Miller-7, Arica. *Chungará* 3:23–74.
Focacci, G., and S. Chacón
1989   Excavaciones arqueológicas en los faldeos del Morro de Arica, sitios Morro 1/6 y 2/2. *Chungará* 22:15–62.
Fouant, M.
1984   The skeletal biology and pathology of pre-Columbian Indians from northern Chile. Ph.D. dissertation, Virginia Commonwealth University, Richmond.

Garcilaso de la Vega, El Inca
   1987   *Royal Commentaries of the Incas, and General History of Peru*. Part 1. H. Liver-
             more, trans. Austin: University of Texas Press. [Original published 1609.]
Geertz, C.
   1973   *The Interpretation of Cultures*. New York: Basic Books, Inc.
Goldstein, L.G.
   1980   *Mississippian Mortuary Practices: A Case Study of Two Cemeteries in the Lower Illi-
             nois Valley*. Northwestern University Archeological Program. Scientific Papers
             no. 4. Evanston, Ill.
Gowlett, J.
   1993   *Ascent to Civilization: The Archaeology of Early Humans*. 2d ed. New York:
             McGraw-Hill, Inc.
Guaman Poma de Ayala, F.
   1980   *Nueva Coronica y Buen Gobierno*. V. Murra and R. Adorno, eds., J. Urioste,
             trans. Mexico City: Siglo XXI. [Original published 1615.]
Guillen, E.S.
   In press Sinostosis craneana prematura en momias Chinchorro de Morro 1–5, Chile. In
             Memorias del I Congreso Internacional de Estudios Sobre Momias. [Meeting held in
             1992, Santa Cruz, Tenerife.]
Gusinde, M.
   1937   *Die Yamana: Vom Leben und Denken der Wassernomaden am Kap Hoorn*. Modling
             bei Wien: Anthropos-Bibliothek.
Habenstein, R.W., and W.M. Lamers
   1960   *Funeral Customs the World Over*. Milwaukee, Wisc.: Bulfin Printers, Inc.
Hansen, J.P.H., J. Meldgaard, and J. Nordqvist, eds.
   1991   *The Greenland Mummies*. Washington: Smithsonian Institution Press.
Harris, O.
   1982   The dead and the devils among the Bolivian Laymi. In *Death and the Regenera-
             tion of Life*, M. Bloch and J. Parry, eds., 45–73. Cambridge: Cambridge Univer-
             sity Press.
   1983   Los muertos y los diablos entre los Laymi de Bolivia. *Chungará* 11:135–152.
Hempel, C.G.
   1966   *Philosophy of Natural Science*. Englewood Cliffs, N.J.: Prentice-Hall, Inc.
Hertz, R.
   1960   A contribution to the study of the collective representation of death. In *Death
             and the Right Hand*, 27–86. Glencoe, Ill.: Free Press. [Original published
             1907.]
Höpfel, F., W. Platzer, and K. Spindler, eds.
   1992   *Der Mann im Eis: Band 1: Bericht über das Internationale Symposium 1992 in
             Innsbruck*. Innsbruck: Universität Innsbruck.
Huntington, R., and P. Metcalf
   1985   *Celebrations of Death*. New York: Cambridge University Press.
Kamps, J.
   1984   Paleodemografía del cementerio de Camarones 14. In *Descripción y Análisis Inter-
             pretativo de un Sitio Arcaico Temprano en la Quebrada de Camarones*, V.
             Schiappacasse and H. Niemeyer, eds., 163–187. Publicación ocasional, no. 41.
             Santiago: Museo Historia Nacional de Historia Natural.

Kelley, M., D. Levesque, and E. Weidl
    1991   Contrasting patterns of dental disease in five early northern Chilean groups. In
            Advances in Dental Anthropology, M. Kelley and K. Spencer, eds., 203–213.
            New York: Wiley-Liss.
Krickeberg, W., H. Trimborn, W. Muller, and O. Zerries
    1969   *Pre-Columbian American Religions*. History of Religion Series. New York: Holt,
            Rinehart, and Winston.
Lanning, E.P.
    1967   *Peru before the Incas*. Englewood Cliffs, N.J.: Prentice-Hall.
Lastres, J.
    1951   *Historia de la Medicina Peruana*. Vol. 1. Lima: Universidad Nacional Mayor de
            San Marcos.
Latcham, R.E.
    1928   *La Prehistoria Chilena*. Santiago: n.p.
    1938   *Arqueología de la Región Atacameña*. Santiago: Universidad de Chile.
Leach, E.
    1976   *Culture and Communication*. New York: Cambridge University Press.
Llagostera, A.
    1979   9,700 years of maritime subsistence on the Pacific: An analysis by means of
            bioindicators in the north of Chile. *American Antiquity* 4(2):309–324.
    1989   Caza y pesca marítima (9.000 a 1.000 A.C.). In *Prehistoria*, J. Hidalgo, V.
            Schiappacasse, H. Niemeyer, C. Aldunate, and I. Solimano, eds., 57–79. Chile:
            Andres Bello.
    1992   Early occupations and the emergence of fishermen on the Pacific Coast of South
            America. *Andean Past* 3:87–109.
MacCormack, S.
    1991   *Religion in the Andes: Vision and Imagination in Early Colonial Peru*. Princeton:
            Princeton University Press.
Malinowski, B.
    1948   *Magic, Science and Religion*. Garden City, New York: Doubleday Anchor Books.
Martínez, S., and C. Munizaga
    1961   La colección arqueológica A. Nielsen, de Iquique. *Revista Chilena de Historia y
            Geografía* 129:232–246. Santiago, Chile
Merbs, C.F.
    1989   Spondylolysis: Its nature and anthropological significance. *International Journal
            of Anthropology* 4(3):163–169.
Montell, G.
    1929   *Dress and Ornaments in Ancient Peru; Archaeological and Historical Studies*.
            Göteborg: Elanders Boktryckeri Aktiebolag.
Moseley, M.E.
    1975   *The Maritime Foundations of Andean Civilization*. Menlo Park, Calif.: Cummings
            Publishing Co.
    1992   Maritime foundations and multilinear evolution: Retrospect and prospect.
            Andean Past 3:5–42.
Mostny, G.
    1964   Anzuelo de Concha 6170±220 años. *Noticiero Mensual Museo Nacional Historia
            Natural Santiago*, Año 9, 98:7–8.

Munizaga, J.
  1980   Esquema de la antropología física del Norte de Chile. *Chungará* 6:124–136
Muñoz, I.
  1985   Introducción al estudio de las poblaciones costeras durante la etapa arcaica en el
              Norte de Chile. *Revista Antropológica* 3:262–286.
Muñoz, I., B. Arriaza and A. Aufderheide
  1993   El poblamiento Chinchorro: nuevos indicadores bioantropológicos y discusión
              en torno a su organización social. In *Acha-2 y los Orígenes del Poblamiento Hu-
              mano en Arica*, I. Muñoz, B. Arriaza, and A. Aufderheide, eds., 107–132.
              Arica: Universidad de Tarapacá.
Muñoz, I., and J. Chacama
  1982   Investigaciones arqueológicas en las poblaciones precerámicas de la costa de
              Arica. In *Documento de Trabajo* 2:3–97. Arica: Universidad de Tarapacá.
  1993   Patrón de asentamiento y cronología de Acha-2. In *Acha-2 y los Orígenes del
              Poblamiento Humano en Arica*, I. Muñoz, B. Arriaza, and A. Aufderheide, eds.,
              21–46. Arica: Universidad de Tarapacá.
Núñez, L.
  1965   Desarrollo cultural prehispánico del Norte de Chile. *Estudios Arqueológicos* 1:37–
              106. Antofagasta: Universidad de Chile.
  1969   Sobre los Complejos Culturales Chinchorro y Faldas del Morro del Norte de
              Chile. *Rehue* 2:111–142.
  1976   Registro regional de fechas radiocarbónicas del Norte de Chile. *Estudios
              Atacameños* 4:74–123.
  1989   Hacia la producción de alimentos y la vida sedentaria (5.000 a.C. a 900 d.C.)
              In *Prehistoria*, J. Hidalgo, V. Schiappacasse, H. Niemeyer, C. Aldunate, and I.
              Solimano, eds., 81–106. Chile: Andres Bello.
Núñez, L., and C. Moragas
  1978   Ocupación arcaica temprana en Tiliviche, Norte de Chile. *Boletín del Museo
              Arqueológico de la Serena* 16:52–76.
Núñez, L., and V. Zlatar
  1976   Radiometría de Aragón-1 y sus implicancias en el precerámico costero del Norte
              de Chile. In *Actas y Memorias IV Congreso Arqueología Argentina*, vol. 1, 105–
              118. Mendoza.
Núñez, L., V. Zlatar, and P. Núñez
  1975   Caleta Huelén-42: Una aldea temprana en el Norte de Chile. *Hombre y Cultura*
              2(5):67–103.
Olmos, O., and J. Sanhueza
  1984   El precerámico en la costa sur de Iquique. *Chungará* 13:143–154.
Ortner, D.J., and W.G.J. Putschar
  1985   *Identification of Pathological Conditions in Human Skeletal Remains*. Washington:
              Smithsonian Institution Press.
Painter, T.J.
  1991   Preservation in peat. *Chemistry and Industry*. June 17:421–424.
Quevedo, S.
  1984   Análisis de los restos óseos humanos del sitio Cam-14. In *Descripción y Análisis
              Interpretativo de un Sitio Arcaico Temprano en la Quebrada de Camarones*, V.
              Schiappacasse and H. Niemeyer, eds., 103–139. Publicación ocasional, no. 41.
              Santiago: Museo Historia Nacional de Historia Natural.

Quilter, J.
    1989   *Life and Death at Paloma Society and Mortuary Practices in a Preceramic Peruvian Village*. Iowa City: University of Iowa Press.

Reinhard, K.
    1992   Parasitology as an interpretative tool in archaeology. *American Antiquity* 57(2):231–245.

Reinhard, K.J., and A.C. Aufderheide
    1990   Diphyllobothriasis in Precolumbian Chile and Perú: Adaptive radiation of a helminth species to Native American populations. Paper presented at the European Paleopathology Conferences, Cambridge.

Reitz, E.J.
    1986   Maritime resource use at Paloma, Peru. Paper presented at the 51st Annual Meeting of the Society for American Archaeology, New Orleans.

Resnick, D., and G. Niwayama
    1988   *Diagnosis of Bone and Joint Disorders*. Vol. 5, 2786–2792. Philadelphia: W.B. Saunders Company.

Rivera, M.
    1975   Una hipótesis sobre movimientos poblacionales altiplánicos y transaltiplánicos a las costas del Norte de Chile. *Chungará* 5:7–31.
    1976   Cronología absoluta y periodificación en la arqueología Chilena. *Boletín del Museo Arqueológico de la Serena* 16:13–41.
    1977   Prehistoric chronology of northern Chile. Ph.D. dissertation, University of Wisconsin, Madison.
    1980   *Temas Antropológicos del Norte de Chile*. Antofagasta: Ediciones Universidad de Chile.
    1984   Cuatro fechados radiocarbónicos para sitios arqueológicos del litoral Norte de Chile. *Nuestro Norte* 2:5–11, Iquique.
    1985   Alto Ramirez y Tiwanaku, un caso de interpretación simbólica a traves de datos arqueológicos en el área de los Valles Occidentales, Sur del Perú y Norte de Chile. *Dialogo Andino* 4:39–58.
    1988   The Chinchorro people of northern Chile 5000 B.C.–500 B.C.: A review of their culture and relationships. Paper presented at the XII International Congress of Anthropological and Ethnological Sciences, Zagreb.
    1991   The prehistory of northern Chile: A synthesis. *Journal of World Prehistory* 5: 1–47

Rivera, M., and F. Rothhammer
    1986   Evaluación biológica y cultural de poblaciones Chinchorro: Nuevos elementos para la hipótesis de contactos trasaltiplanicos, cuenca Amazonas-Costa Pacífico. *Chungará* 16–17:295–306.

Rivera, M., P. Soto, L. Ulloa, and D. Kushner
    1974   Aspectos sobre el desarrollo tecnológico en el proceso de agriculturización en el norte prehispano, especialmente Arica (Chile). *Chungará* 3:79–107.

Rogan, P., and S. Lentz
    1994   Molecular genetic evidence suggesting treponematosis in pre-Columbian, Chilean mummies [abstract]. *American Journal of Physical Anthropology* Supplement 18, 171–172.

Rothhammer, F., J. Cocilovo, S. Quevedo, and E. Llop
    1983   Afinidad biológica de las poblaciones prehistóricas del litoral ariqueño con

grupos poblacionales costeros peruanos y altiplánicos. *Chungará* 11: 161–165.

Rothschild, B.M., and R.J. Woods
1989   Spondyloarthropathies in gorillas. *Seminars in Arthritis and Rheumatism* 18:265–276.

Rowe, J.H.
1991   Behavior and belief in ancient Peruvian mortuary practice. Paper presented at the conference: Tombs for the Living: Andean Mortuary Practices, Dumbarton Oaks, Washington, D.C.

Salomon, F.
1991   "The beautiful grandparents": Andean ancestor shrines and mortuary ritual as seen through colonial records. Paper presented at the conference: Tombs for the Living: Andean Mortuary Practices, Dumbarton Oaks, Washington, D.C.

Salomon, F., and G. Urioste, trans.
1991   *The Huarochirí Manuscript: A Testament of Ancient and Colonial Andean Religion.* Austin: University of Texas Press.

Sandweiss, D.M., J.B. Richardson, E.J. Reitz, J. T. Hsu, and R.A. Feldman.
1989   Early maritime adaptations in the Andes: Preliminary studies at the Ring site, Peru. In *Ecology, Settlement and History in the Osmore Drainage, Peru,* D.S. Rice, C. Stanish, and P.R. Scarr, eds., pt. 1, 35–84. Oxford: BAR International Series.

Sanhueza, J.
n.d.   Caramucho 3: Un sitio precerámico en el litoral sur de Iquique. I región Norte de Chile. Manuscript on file at the Archaeology Department, University of Tarapacá.

Santoro, C.
1989   Antiguos cazadores de la puna (9.000 a 6.000 a.C.). In *Prehistoria,* J. Hidalgo, V. Schiappacasse, H. Niemeyer, C. Aldunate, and I. Solimano, eds., 33–56. Chile: Andres Bello.
1993   Complementariedad ecológica en sociedades arcaicas del Area Centro Sur Andina. In *Acha-2 y los Orígenes del Poblamiento Humano en Arica,* I. Muñoz, B. Arriaza, and A. Aufderheide, eds., 133–150. Arica: Universidad de Tarapacá.

Santoro, C., and J. Chacama
1982   Secuencia cultural de las tierras altas del Area Centro Sur Andina. *Chungará* 9:22–45.

Santoro, C., and L. Núñez
1987   Hunters of the Dry Puna and the Salt Puna in northern Chile. *Andean Past* 1:57–109.

Santoro, C., and L. Ulloa, eds.
1985   *Culturas de Arica.* Arica: Universidad de Tarapacá.

Saxe, A.A.
1970   Social dimensions of mortuary practices. Ph.D. dissertation, University of Michigan.

Schaedel, R., ed.
1957   *Arqueología Chilena: Contribuciones al Estudio de la Región Comprendida Entre Arica y la Serena.* Santiago: Universidad de Chile.

Schiappacasse, V., and H. Niemeyer
1969   Comentario a tres fechas radiocarbónicas de sitios arqueológicos de Conanoxa

(valle de Camarones, Prov. de Tarapacá). *Noticiero Mensual del Museo Nacional de Historia Natural,* no. 151.

1984   (editors) *Descripción y Análisis Interpretativo de un Sitio Arcaico Temprano en la Quebrada de Camarones.* Publicación ocasional, no. 41. Santiago: Museo Historia Nacional de Historia Natural.

Skottsberg, C.
1924   Notes on the old Indian necropolis of Arica. *Meddelanden fran Geografiska Föreningen i Gotebörg* 3:27–78.

Sledzik, P.S., and N. Bellantoni
1994   Bioarchaeological and biocultural evidence for the New England vampire folk belief. *American Journal of Physical Anthropology* 94:269–274.

Sowers, M., C. Genie, B. Shapiro, M. Jannausch, M. Crutchfield, M. Smith, J. Randolph, and B. Hollis
1993   Changes in bone density with lactation. *JAMA* 269(24):3130.

Spencer, R.F.
1977   Reproduction, childbirth and population limitation in preindustrial societies. In *Culture, Disease, and Healing,* D. Landy, ed., 287–299. New York: Macmillan Co.

Standen, V.
1991   El Cementerio Morro 1: Nuevas Evidencias de la Tradición Funeraria Chinchorro (período arcaico, Norte de Chile). Thesis. Universidad Católica de Lima, Peru.

Standen, V., and L. Núñez
1984   Indicadores antropológico-físico y culturales del cementerio precerámico Tiliviche-2 (Norte de Chile). *Chungará* 12:135–153.

Standen, V., M. Allison, and B. Arriaza
1984   Patologías óseas de la población Morro-1, asociada al complejo Chinchorro: Norte de Chile. *Chungará* 13:175–185.

1985   Osteoma del conducto auditivo externo: Hipótesis en torno a una posible patología laboral prehispánica. *Chungará* 15:197–209.

Steadman, L.B., and C.F. Merbs
1982   Kuru and cannibalism? *American Anthropologist* 84:611– 627.

Stothert, K.
1985   The preceramic Las Vegas culture of coastal Ecuador. *American Antiquity* 50(3):613–637.

1988   *La Prehistoria Temprana de la Península de Santa Elena, Ecuador: Cultura Las Vegas.* Miscelánea Antropológica Ecuatoriana Serie Monográfica 10. Guayaquil: Museos del Banco Central del Ecuador.

Stuiver, M., and P.J. Reimer
1993   Radiocarbon calibration program rev. 3.0. *Radiocarbon* 35:215–230.

Tainter, J.A.
1978   Mortuary practices and the study of prehistoric social systems. In *Advances in Archaeological Method and Theory,* no.1, M.B. Schiffer, ed., 106–137. New York: Academic Press.

Tattersall, I.
1985   The human skeletons from Huaca Prieta, with a note on exostoses of the external auditory meatus. In *The Preceramic Excavations at the Huaca Prieta, Chicama*

        Valley, Peru, J. Hyslop, ed., 60–64. Anthropological Papers of the American
        Museum of Natural History, vol. 62, pt. 1. New York.

Trigger, B.
    1969   *The Huron Farmers of the North,* 106–112. New York: Holt, Rinehart, and Win-
                ston.

True, D.L., and H. Crew
    1980   Archaeological investigations in northern Chile: Tarapacá 2A. In *Prehistoric
                Trails of Atacama: Archaeology of Northern Chile,* C.W. Meighan and D.L. True,
                eds., 59–90. Monumenta Archaeologica 7. Los Angeles: Institute of Archaeol-
                ogy, University of California, Los Angeles.

True, D.L., and L. Núñez
    1971   Modeled anthropomorphic figurines from northern Chile. *Ñawa Pacha* 9:65–
                85.

Turner, V.
    1970   *The Forest of Symbols: Aspects of Ndembu Ritual.* Ithaca, N.Y.: Cornell University
                Press.

Tylor, E.B.
    1920   *Primitive Culture.* 6th ed. New York: G.P. Putnam's Sons.

Uhle, M.
    1917   Los aborígenes de Arica. *Publicaciones del Museo de Etnología y Antropología de
                Chile* 1(4–5):151–176. Santiago, Chile.
    1919   La arqueología de Arica y Tacna. *Boletín de la Sociedad Ecuatoriana de Estudios
                Históricos Americanos* 3(7–8):1–48.
    1922   *Fundamentos étnicos y arqueología de Arica y Tacna.* 2d ed. Quito, Ecuador:
                Sociedad Ecuatoriana de Estudios Históricos.

Urioste, G.
    1981   Sickness and death in preconquest Andean cosmology: The Huarochirí oral tra-
                dition. In *Health in the Andes,* J. Bastien and J. Donahue, eds., 9–18. Washing-
                ton: American Anthropological Association.

Van Gennep, A.
    1960   *The Rites of Passage.* Chicago: University of Chicago Press. [Original published
                1909.]

Vera, J.
    1981   Momias Chinchorro de preparación complicada del Museo de Historia Natural
                de Valparaíso: 3,290 y 3,060 A.C. *Anales del Museo de Historia Natural de Valpa-
                raíso* 14:5–17.

Vik, R.
    1971   Diphyllobothriasis. In *Pathology of Protozoal and Helminthic Diseases,* R. Marcial-
                Rojas, ed., 572–584. Baltimore: The Williams and Wilkins Company.

Vilaxa, A., and J. Corrales
    1993   Descripción y comentario de la fauna malacológica del sitio Acha-2. In *Acha-2 y
                los Orígenes del Poblamiento Humano en Arica,* I. Muñoz, B. Arriaza, and A.
                Aufderheide, eds., 81–90. Arica: Universidad de Tarapacá.

Wise, K.
    1991   Complexity and variation in mortuary practices during the preceramic period in
                the south central Andes. Paper presented at the Annual Meeting of the Ameri-
                can Anthropological Association, Chicago.

In press   Chinchorro in Ilo: Early coastal mortuary practices at Villa del Mar. In *Osmore Mortuary Studies*, J. Buikstra, ed.

Woodburn, J.
1982   Social dimensions of death in four African hunting and gathering societies. In *Death and the Regeneration of Life*, M. Bloch and J. Parry, eds., 187–210. Cambridge: Cambridge University Press.

Zuidema, R.
1992   Inca cosmos in Andean context: From the perspective of the Capac Raymi Camay Quilla feast celebrating the December solstice in Cuzco. In *Andean Cosmologies through Time,* R. Dover, K. Seibold, and J. McDowell, eds., 17–45. Bloomington: Indiana University Press.

INDEX